Other Books and Series by Jeff Bowen

Applications for Enrollment of Chickasaw Newborn Act of 1905
Volumes I, II, III, IV, V & VI

Visit our website at **www.nativestudy.com** to learn more about these
and other books and series by Jeff Bowen

I0222749

APPLICATIONS FOR ENROLLMENT OF CHICKASAW NEWBORN ACT OF 1905 VOLUME VII

TRANSCRIBED BY
JEFF BOWEN

NATIVE STUDY
Gallipolis, Ohio
USA

Other Books and Series by Jeff Bowen

1901-1907 Native American Census Seneca, Eastern Shawnee, Miami, Modoc, Ottawa, Peoria, Quapaw, and Wyandotte Indians (Under Seneca School, Indian Territory)

1932 Census of The Standing Rock Sioux Reservation with Births And Deaths 1924-1932

Census of The Blackfeet, Montana, 1897- 1901 Expanded Edition

Eastern Cherokee by Blood, 1906-1910, Volumes I thru XIII

Choctaw of Mississippi Indian Census 1929-1932 with Births and Deaths 1924-1931   Volume I
Choctaw of Mississippi Indian Census 1933, 1934 & 1937, Supplemental Rolls to 1934 & 1935 with Births and Deaths 1932-1938, and Marriages 1936-1938 Volume II

Eastern Cherokee Census Cherokee, North Carolina 1930-1939
Census 1930-1931 with Births And Deaths 1924-1931 Taken By Agent L. W. Page Volume I
Eastern Cherokee Census Cherokee, North Carolina 1930-1939
Census 1932-1933 with Births And Deaths 1930-1932 Taken By Agent R. L. Spalsbury   Volume II
Eastern Cherokee Census Cherokee, North Carolina 1930-1939
Census 1934-1937 with Births and Deaths 1925-1938 and Marriages 1936 & 1938 Taken by Agents R. L. Spalsbury And Harold W. Foght Volume III

Seminole of Florida Indian Census, 1930-1940 with Birth and Death Records, 1930-1938

Texas Cherokees 1820-1839 A Document For Litigation 1921

Choctaw By Blood Enrollment Cards 1898-1914 Volumes I thru XVII

Starr Roll 1894 (Cherokee Payment Rolls) Districts: Canadian, Cooweescoowee, and Delaware Volume One
Starr Roll 1894 (Cherokee Payment Rolls) Districts: Flint, Going Snake, and Illinois   Volume Two
Starr Roll 1894 (Cherokee Payment Rolls) Districts: Saline, Sequoyah, and Tahlequah; Including Orphan Roll   Volume Three

Cherokee Intruder Cases Dockets of Hearings 1901-1909 Volumes I & II

Indian Wills, 1911-1921 Records of the Bureau of Indian Affairs Books One thru Seven;
Native American Wills & Probate Records 1911-1921

Other Books and Series by Jeff Bowen

Turtle Mountain Reservation Chippewa Indians 1932 Census with Births & Deaths, 1924-1932

Chickasaw By Blood Enrollment Cards 1898-1914 Volume I thru V

Cherokee Descendants East An Index to the Guion Miller Applications Volume I
Cherokee Descendants West An Index to the Guion Miller Applications Volume II (A-M)
Cherokee Descendants West An Index to the Guion Miller Applications Volume III (N-Z)

Applications for Enrollment of Seminole Newborn Freedmen, Act of 1905

Eastern Cherokee Census, Cherokee, North Carolina, 1915-1922, Taken by Agent James E. Henderson   *Volume I (1915-1916)*
            Volume II (1917-1918)
            Volume III (1919-1920)
            Volume IV (1921-1922)

Complete Delaware Roll of 1898

Eastern Cherokee Census, Cherokee, North Carolina, 1923-1929, Taken by Agent James E. Henderson   *Volume I (1923-1924)*
            Volume II (1925-1926)
            Volume III (1927-1929)

Applications for Enrollment of Seminole Newborn Act of 1905 Volumes I & II

North Carolina Eastern Cherokee Indian Census 1898-1899, 1904, 1906, 1909-1912, 1914 Revised and Expanded Edition

1932 Hopi and Navajo Native American Census with Birth & Death Rolls (1925-1931) Volume 1 - Hopi
1932 Hopi and Navajo Native American Census with Birth & Death Rolls (1930-1932) Volume 2 - Navajo

Western Navajo Reservation Navajo, Hopi and Paiute 1933 Census with Birth & Death Rolls 1925-1933

Cherokee Citizenship Commission Dockets 1880-1884 and 1887-1889 Volumes I thru V

Originally published:
Baltimore, Maryland
2013

Reprinted by:

Native Study LLC
Gallipolis, OH
www.nativestudy.com
2020

Library of Congress Control Number: 2020917160

ISBN: 978-1-64968-069-3

Made in the United States of America.

This series is dedicated to the descendants of the Chickasaw newborn listed in these applications.

This map of Indian Territory shows how large the Choctaw and Chickasaw Nations' land base was that contained huge deposits of asphalt and coal. Just the size and territory involved was flooded with the "Grafters".

Rules and Regulations Governing the Selection of Allotments and the Designation of Homesteads in the Choctaw and Chickasaw Nations.

1. Selections of allotments and designations of homesteads for adult citizens and selections of allotments for adult freedmen must be made in person except as herein otherwise provided.

2. Applications to have land set apart and homesteads designated for duly identified Mississippi Choctaws must be made personally before the Commission to the Five Civilized Tribes. Fathers may apply for their minor children and if the father be dead the mother may apply. Husbands may apply for wives. Applications for orphans, insane persons and persons of unsound mind may be made by duly appointed guardian or curator, and for aged and infirm persons and prisoners by agents duly authorized thereunto by power of attorney, in the discretion of said Commission.

3. At the time of the selection of allotment each citizen and duly identified Mississippi Choctaw shall designate as a homestead out of said selection land equal in value to one hundred and sixty acres of the average allottable land of the Choctaw and Chickasaw Nations, as nearly as may be.

4. Each Choctaw and Chickasaw freedman, at the time of selection shall designate as his or her allotment of the lands of the Choctaw and Chickasaw Nations, land equal in value to forty acres of the average allottable land of the Choctaw and Chickasaw Nations.

5. Citizens, freedmen and identified Mississippi Choctaws who are married, whether they have attained their majority or not, will be regarded as of age for the purpose of making selections.

6. Selections may be made by citizen and freedman parents for unmarried male children under twenty-one years of age and for unmarried female children under eighteen years of age, and a male citizen or freedman may make selection for his wife, if she is entitled to make selection, unless she shall, at the time or previously thereto, protest in writing.

7. Where the father of an unmarried minor citizen, freedman or identified Mississippi Choctaw is a non-citizen, the citizen, freedman or identified Mississippi Choctaw mother of such children must make selection in person in behalf of said children.

8. Selections of allotments and designations of homesteads for minor citizens and selections of allotments for minor freedmen may be made by the citizen father or mother or freedman father or mother, as the case may be, or by a guardian, curator, or an administrator having charge of their estate, in the order named.

9. Selections of allotments and designations of homesteads for citizen, and selections of allotment for freedmen, prisoners, convicts, aged and infirm persons and soldiers and sailors of the United States on duty outside of Indian Territory, may be made by duly appointed agents under power of attorney, and for incompetents by guardians, curators, or other suitable person akin to them.

10. Selections may be made and homesteads designated by duly identified Mississippi Choctaws, who have, within one year after the date of their identification as such, made satisfactory proof of bona fide settlement within the Choctaw-Chickasaw country, at any time within six months after the date of their said identification.

11. Persons authorized to make selections by power of attorney, as provided in rules 2 and 9 hereof, must be the husband or wife, or a relative not further removed than a cousin of the first degree of the person for whom such selection is made.

12. It shall be the duty of the Commission to the Five Civilized Tribes to see that selections of allotments and designations of homesteads for the classes of persons mentioned in rules 2, 6, 7, 8 and 9 hereof, are made for the best interests of such persons.

13. Selections of allotments for citizens, freedmen and identified Mississippi Choctaws who have died subsequent to September 25, 1902, and before making a selection of allotment, shall be made by a duly appointed administrator or executor. If, however, such administrator or executor be not duly and expeditiously appointed, or fails to act promptly when appointed, or for any other cause such selections be not so made within a reasonable and practicable time, the Commission to the Five Civilized Tribes shall designate the lands thus to be allotted.

14. In determining the value of a selection the appraised value of the land selected shall be increased by the appraised value of such pine timber on such land as has heretofore been estimated by the Commission to the Five Civilized Tribes.

15. Selections of allotments may be made only by citizens and freedmen whose enrollment has been approved by the Secretary of the Interior, and by persons duly identified by the Commission to the Five Civilized Tribes as Mississippi Choctaws, and by none others.

16. When a selection of land has been made by a citizen, freedman or identified Mississippi Choctaw, and the land so selected is claimed by a person whose rights as a citizen or freedman have not been finally determined, contest for the land so selected may be instituted by the person claiming the land, formal application for the land being first made as is required by the Rules of Practice in Choctaw and Chickasaw allotment contest cases.

THE COMMISSION TO THE FIVE CIVILIZED TRIBES.

TAMS BIXBY, Chairman.

Muskogee, Indian Territory, March 24, 1903.

The above statement published prior to 1905, was established for what was supposed to be a set of guidelines when it came to allotments. But with supplemental agreements and Congressional legislation, time frames as well as rules and regulations often changed and were not the same for every tribe.

INTRODUCTION

The *Applications for Enrollment of Chickasaw Newborn Act of 1905*, National Archive film M-1301, Rolls 455-458, are found under the heading of Applications for Enrollment of the Commission to the Five Civilized Tribes. For this series, I have transcribed the application forms filled out by individuals applying for enrollment in the Five Civilized Tribes under the Dawes Commission. These applications contain considerably more information than stated on the census cards found in series M-1186. M-1301 possesses its own numerical sequence, separate from M-1186. To find each party's roll number you would have to reference M-1186.

The Chickasaw as well as the Choctaw allotments were likely some of the most sought after properties in Indian Territory. There was supposed to be a 25-year restriction on the sale or lease of any Indian lands so as to insure that the owners wouldn't be swindled, but that isn't what happened. This fact is borne out in the Dawes Commission General Allotment Act, of February 8, 1887, Section 5, which "Provides that after an Indian person is allotted land, the United States will hold the land 'in trust [1] for the sole use and benefit of the Indian' (or his heirs if the Indian landowner dies) for a period of 25 years. (Land held in trust by the United States government cannot be sold or in anyway alienated by the Indian landowner, since the United States government considers the underlying ownership of the land held by itself and not the tribe. After the period of trust ends, the Indian landowner is free to sell the land and is free from any encumbrance from the United States.)"[1] Instead, Native Americans were exploited by the devious. The Chickasaw and Choctaw Districts both had huge asphalt and coal deposits, so there was pressure from outsiders to acquire them from the minute they were discovered. After repeated attacks throughout the years and many legislative changes, President "Roosevelt finally signed the Five Tribes Bill at noon on April 26, 1906, the forces seeking to end all restrictions were disappointed. Section 19 removed restrictions from the sale of all inherited land but directed that no full-bloods could sell their land for twenty-five years. The Act also prohibited leases for more than one year without the approval of the Secretary of the Interior."[2]

Angie Debo described the opportunists that wanted these Native American allotments as, "Grafters". The parents of the newborns enumerated within this series would no sooner receive the approval for their child's allotment than there would be someone there with cash in hand holding a new deed or lease for the parents to sign their child's birthright away. Angie Debo said it best, "As the business incapacity of the allottees became apparent, a horde of despoilers fastened themselves upon their property." According to Debo, "The term 'grafter' was applied as a matter of course to dealers in Indian land, and was frankly accepted by them. The speculative fever also affected Government employees so that it was almost impossible to prevent them from making personal investments."[3]

---

[1] General Allotment Act, Act of Feb. 8, 1887 (24 Stat. 388, ch. 119, 25 USCA 331)
[2] The Dawes Commission and the Allotment of the Five Civilized Tribes, 1893-1914 by Kent Carter, pg. 173
[3] And Still the Waters Run, Angie Debo, p. 92.

INTRODUCTION

According to the Department of Interior in 1905, "It is estimated that there will be added to the final rolls of the citizens and freedmen of the Choctaw and Chickasaw nations the names of 2,000 persons, including 1,500 new-born children to be enrolled under the provisions of the act of Congress approved March 3, 1905."[4]

The quote below explains, in detail, the requirements for qualifying as a newborn Chickasaw, "By the act of Congress approved March 3, 1905 (H.R. 17474), entitled 'An act making appropriations for the current and contingent expenses of the Indian Department and for fulfilling treaty stipulations with various Indian tribes for the fiscal year ending June 30, 1906, and for other purposes,' it was provided as follows:

'That the Commission to the Five Civilized Tribes is hereby authorized for sixty days after the date of the approval of this act to receive and consider applications for enrollment of infant children born prior to September twenty-fifth, nineteen hundred and two, and who were living on said date, to citizens by blood of the Choctaw and Chickasaw tribes of Indians whose enrollment has been approved by the Secretary of the Interior prior to the date of the approval of this act; and to enroll and make allotments to such children.'

'That the Commission to the Five Civilized Tribes is authorized for sixty days after the date of the approval of this act to receive and consider applications for enrollment of children born subsequent to September twenty-fifth, nineteen hundred and two, and prior to March fourth, nineteen hundred and five, and who were living on said latter date, to citizens by blood of the Choctaw and Chickasaw tribes of Indians whose enrollment has been approved by the Secretary of the Interior prior to the date of the approval of this act; and to enroll and make allotments to such children.'

"Notice is hereby given that the Commission to the Five Civilized Tribes will, up to and inclusive of midnight, May 2, 1905, receive applications for the enrollment of infant children born prior to September 25, 1902, and who were living on said date, to citizens by blood of the Choctaw and Chickasaw tribes of Indians whose enrollment has been approved by the Secretary of the Interior prior to March 3, 1905."[5]

Following is the scope of these transcriptions: Besides the applications themselves, researchers will find the identities of other individuals within these applications -- doctors, lawyers, mid-wives, and other relatives -- that may help with you genealogical research.

Jeff Bowen
Gallipolis, Ohio
NativeStudy.com

---

[4] Annual Reports of the Department of the Interior For the Fiscal Year Ended June 30, 1905, p. 609.
[5] Annual Reports of the Department of the Interior For the Fiscal Year Ended June 30, 1905, p. 593.

Applications for Enrollment of Chickasaw Newborn
Act of 1905   Volume VII

Chic. N.B - 509
>   *(Nora Greenwood*
>   *Born August 14, 1903)*

DEPARTMENT OF THE INTERIOR.
COMMISSION TO THE FIVE CIVILIZED TRIBES.

IN RE APPLICATION FOR ENROLLMENT, as a citizen of the   Chickasaw   Nation, of   Nora Greenwood   , born on the   14   day of Aug   , 1903

Name of Father: Sim Greenwood   a citizen of the   Chickasaw Nation.
Name of Mother: Francis Greenwood   a citizen of the   Chickasaw Nation.

                                            Postoffice   Reagan I.T.

AFFIDAVIT OF MOTHER.

UNITED STATES OF AMERICA, Indian Territory, ⎫
     Southern   **DISTRICT.** ⎭

I,   Francis Greenwood   , on oath state that I am   20   years of age and a citizen by   Blood   , of the   Chickasaw   Nation; that I am the lawful wife of Sim Greenwood   , who is a citizen, by Blood   of the   Chickasaw Nation; that a   Female   child was born to me on 14th   day of   August   , 1903; that said child has been named   Nora Greenwood   , and was living March 4, 1905.

                                            Francis Greenwood
Witnesses To Mark:
     ⎰
     ⎱
     Subscribed and sworn to before me this 10th day of   April   , 1905

                              J.R. Vinyard
                              Notary Public.

AFFIDAVIT OF ATTENDING PHYSICIAN OR MID-WIFE.

UNITED STATES OF AMERICA, Indian Territory, ⎫
     Southern   **DISTRICT.** ⎭

I,   Malsey Keel   , a   Midwife   , on oath state that I attended on Mrs.   Francis Greenwood   , wife of   Sim Greenwood   on the 14   day of

1

August   , 1903; that there was born to her on said date a   Female   child; that said child was living March 4, 1905, and is said to have been named Nora Greenwood

her
Malsey x Keel

Witnesses To Mark: mark

    { C H Wade
    { J.R. Vinyard

        Subscribed and sworn to before me this 10 day of   April   , 1905

J.R. Vinyard
Notary Public.

Muskogee, Indian Territory, April 20, 1905.

Sim Greenwood,
        Reagan, Indian Territory.

Dear Sir:

        Receipt is hereby acknowledged of the affidavits of Francis Greenwood and Malsey Keel to the birth of Nora Greenwood, daughter of Sim and Francis Greenwood, August 14, 1903.

        It is stated in the affidavit of the mother that she is a citizen by blood of the Chickasaw Nation. If this is correct you are requested to state the name under which she was enrolled, the names of her parents, and if she has selected an allotment of the lands of the Choctaw or Chickasaw Nation please give her roll number as it appears upon her allotment certificate.

Respectfully,

Chairman.

(The letter below typed as given.)

(COPY)

Reagan, Ind. Ter.
May 1, 1905.

Commission to the Five Civilized Tribes,
        Muskogee, Ind. Ter.

Dear Sir:

    Your favor of the 20th ultimo came duly to hand. Stated in your letter that you requested me to state the name under which <u>Francis Greenwood</u> was enrolled. She was enolled under name of <u>Francis Brown</u>, and his <u>Roll number 2601, Chickasaw by blood</u>.

    that is what appears on upon her allotment Certificate when she selected his allotment of the land of the Chickasaw Land Office in July 9, 1904

    and her parents enrolled by the name under <u>Mary Colbert</u> and his <u>Roll No. 2599</u> Chickasaw by blood on his allotment certificate..

Yours Very Truly
Sim Greenwood.

9-NB-509

Muskogee, Indian Territory, July 6, 1905.

Sim Greenwood,
        Reagan, Indian Territory.

Dear Sir:

    Referring to the application for the enrollment of your infant child, Nora Greenwood born August 14, 1903, it is noted that in the affidavit of the mother, Francis Greenwood, executed April 10, 1905, she states that you are a citizen by blood of the Chickasaw Nation. If this is correct you are requested to state the name under which you were enrolled, the names of your parents, and if you have selected an allotment of the lands of the Choctaw or Chickasaw Nation, give your roll number as it appears upon your allotment certificate.

    Please give this matter your immediate attention as no further action can be taken relative to the enrollment of said child until the evidence requested is supplied.

7/11/1905 Sir in Reply   Respectfully,

to the above my alotment[sic] No on my certificate is #2280
my mothers[sic] name is Amanda Fisher.   Hoping this is Commissioner.
satisfactory, I am
                    Yours as ever
                              Simeon Greenwood.

———————

9-NB-509

Muskogee, Indian Territory, July 14, 1905.

Simeon Greenwood,
        Regean[sic], Indian Territory.

Dear Sir:

        Receipt is hereby acknowledged of your letter of July 11, 1905, stating that your roll number is 2280 and that your mother's name is Amanda Fisher.

        This information has been made a part of the record in the matter of the enrollment of your child Nora Greenwood for enrollment as a citizen by blood of the Chickasaw Nation.

                    Respectfully,

                              Commissioner.

———————

(The letter above given again except with date of July 15, 1905.)

═══

Chic. N.B - 510
        (Eliza Russell
        Born February 20, 1903)
        (Evison Russell
        Born February 9, 1905)

———————

Applications for Enrollment of Chickasaw Newborn
Act of 1905   Volume VII

BIRTH AFFIDAVIT.

IN RE-APPLICATION FOR ENROLLMENT, as a citizen of the   Chickasaw   Nation, of   Eliza Russell   , born on the   20   day of   Feb.   , 190 3

Name of Father: Silas Russell   a citizen of the   Chickasaw Nation.
Name of Mother: Elsie Russell   a citizen of the   Chickasaw Nation.

Postoffice   Mannsville

AFFIDAVIT OF MOTHER.

UNITED STATES OF AMERICA, INDIAN TERRITORY,
      Southern   District.

I,   Elsie Russell   , on oath state that I am   Thirty   years of age and a citizen by Blood   , of the   Chickasaw   Nation; that I am the lawful wife of   Silas Russell   , who is a citizen, by   Blood   of the   Chickasaw   Nation; that a   female   child was born to me on   20th day of   Feb   , 1903 , that said child has been named   Eliza Russell   , and is now living.

Elsie Russell

Witnesses To Mark:
      HM Hollingsworth
      HB Corey

Subscribed and sworn to before me this   30th day of   March   , 1905.

W.F. Noble
Notary Public.

AFFIDAVIT OF ATTENDING PHYSICIAN OR MID-WIFE.

UNITED STATES OF AMERICA, INDIAN TERRITORY,
      Southern   District.

I,   Francis Tyubby   , a   midwife   , on oath state that I attended on Mrs. – Elsie Russell–   , wife of   Silas Russell   on the   20th day of Feb , 190 3; that there was born to her on said date a   female   child; that said child is now living and is said to have been named   Eliza   her

Francis x Tyubby
mark

Witnesses To Mark:
      Noel Tyubby
      HB Corey

Subscribed and sworn to before me this   31   day of   March   , 1905.

W.F. Noble
Notary Public.

5

Applications for Enrollment of Chickasaw Newborn
Act of 1905   Volume VII

BIRTH AFFIDAVIT.

IN RE-APPLICATION FOR ENROLLMENT, as a citizen of the   Chickasaw   Nation,
of   Evison Russell   , born on the   9th   day of   Feb.   , 190 5

Name of Father: Silas Russell   a citizen of the   Chickasaw Nation.
Name of Mother: Elsie Russell   a citizen of the   Chickasaw Nation.

                                        Postoffice   Mannsville

---

AFFIDAVIT OF MOTHER.

UNITED STATES OF AMERICA, INDIAN TERRITORY,
     Southern   District.

I,   Elsie Russell   , on oath state that I am   Thirty   years of age and a citizen by
Blood   , of the   Chickasaw   Nation; that I am the lawful wife of   Silas Russell   , who
is a citizen, by   Blood   of the   Chickasaw   Nation; that a   male   child was born to
me on   9th   day of   Feb   , 1905 , that said child has been named   Evison Russell   , and is
now living.

                                        Elsie Russell

Witnesses To Mark:
     HM Hollingsworth
     HB Corey

Subscribed and sworn to before me this   30th   day of   March   , 1905.

                              W.F. Noble
                                   Notary Public.

AFFIDAVIT OF ATTENDING PHYSICIAN OR MID-WIFE.

UNITED STATES OF AMERICA, INDIAN TERRITORY,
     Southern   District.

I,   Francis Tyubby   , a   midwife   , on oath state that I
attended on Mrs. — Elsie Russell-   , wife of   Silas Russell   on the   9th   day of Feb
, 190 5; that there was born to her on said date a   male   child; that said child is now living and is
said to have been named   Evison   her
                                        Francis x Tyubby
Witnesses To Mark: mark
     Noel Tyubby
     HB Corey

6

Subscribed and sworn to before me this   31   day of   March   , 1905.

W.F. Noble
Notary Public.

Muskogee, Indian Territory, April 24, 1905,

Silas Russell,
Mannsville, Indian Territory.

Dear Sir:

Receipt is hereby acknowledged of the affidavits of Elsie Russell and Francis Tyubby to the birth of Evison Russell and Eliza Russell, children of Silas and Elsie Russell, February 20, 1903, and February 9, 1905.

It is stated in the affidavit of the mother that she is a citizen by blood of the Chickasaw Nation. If this is correct you are requested to state the name under which she was enrolled, the names of her parents, and if she has selected an allotment of the lands of the Choctaw or Chickasaw Nation please give her roll number as it appears upon her allotment certificate.

Respectfully,

Chairman.

---

9 NB 510

Muskogee, Indian Territory, May 13, 1905.

Silas Russell,
Mannsville, Indian Territory,

Dear Sir:

Referring to the application for the enrollment of your infant child, Eliza Russell, born February 20, 1903, it appears that you are a Chickasaw by blood.

If this is correct you are requested to state when, where and under what name you were listed for enrollment, the names of your parents and other members of your family for whom application was made at the same time, and if you have selected an allotment, give your roll number as the same appears on your allotment certificate.

Please give this matter your immediate attention.

Applications for Enrollment of Chickasaw Newborn
Act of 1905 Volume VII

Respectfully,

Chairman.

———————

Mannsville, I. T. 5/29/05.

Com. To The Five Civilized Tribes,
Muskogee, I. T.

Gentlemen:-

Replying to the enclosed enquiry, beg to say that my wife was enrolled under the name of Elsie McGuire, her father and mother's name was Sam and Nancey Tyubby, the Number of her allotment is 25.

Respectfully,

Silas Russell.

———————

(The letter below typed as given.)

Mannsville, Ind Ter June 1st 1905
Commission To the Five civilized Tribes
Muskogee

Gentlemen:

Referring to yours of the 13th ult. (9-NB-510) will state that I dont know when I was first listed for enrollment. I was listed at Tishomingo.
I was listed uner the name of Silas Russell.
My parents are dead and were never listed for enrollment There are no other members of my family except my wife and children.
My first wife was listed under the name of Maggie or Margarette Russell
My present wife was listed under the name of Elsie McGuire.
The number on my allotment certificate is 2529
My wifes is No 2251.
My daughter by my first wife was listed under name of Kate Russell and her number is 4594
Hoping this will be sufficient to answer your purpose.

I am yours Most Respectfully
Silas Russell

———————

8

(The letter below typed as given.)

Mannsville, Ind Ter June 1st 1905
Commission To the Five civilized Tribes
Muskogee

Gentlemen:

Referring to yours of the 18th ult (9-NB-510) will state that I dont know when I was first listed for enrollment. I was listed at Tishomingo.

I was listed under the name of Silas Russell.

My parents are dead and were never listed for enrollment.

There are no other members of my family except my wife and children.

My first wife was listed under the name of Maggie or Margarette Russell. My present wife was listed under the name of Elsie McGuire. The numbers on my allotment certificate is 2529. My wifes is No. 2251.

My daughter by my first wife was listed under name of Kate Russell and her number is 4594.

Hoping this will be sufficient to answer your purpose.

I am Yours most respectfully,
Silas Russell.

---

9 NB 510

Muskogee, Indian Territory, June 6, 1905.

Silas Russell,
Mansville[sic], Indian Territory.

Dear Sir:

Receipt is hereby acknowledged of your letter of June 1, 1905, giving information relative to your enrollment and the Commission has identified you upon its records as an enrolled citizen by blood of the Chickasaw Nation.

Respectfully,

Chairman.

9-NB-510

Muskogee, Indian Territory, July 31, 1905.

Silas Russell,
      Mansville[sic], Indian Territory.

Dear Sir:

Receipt is hereby acknowledged of your letter of July 26, 1905, asking if the application for the enrollment of your children Eliza and Evison Russell have been approved and if not if you can have their allotments set aside pending their enrollment.

In reply to your letter you are advised that the names of your children Eliza and Evison Russell have been placed upon a schedule of citizens by blood of the Chickasaw Nation which has been forwarded the Secretary of the Interior and you will be notified when their enrollment has been approved by the Department.

You are further advised that no reservation of land or selection of allotment can be made for children for whom application was made under the act of Congress approved March 3, 1905, until their enrollment has been approved by the Secretary of the Interior.

The matter of the land referred to in your letter has been made the subject of a separate communication.

           Respectfully,

              Commissioner.

(The letter above given again.)

Chic. N.B - 511
      (Joseph Jefflow
      Born December 11, 1902)

BIRTH AFFIDAVIT.   *#119*

DEPARTMENT OF THE INTERIOR.
COMMISSION TO THE FIVE CIVILIZED TRIBES.

IN RE APPLICATION FOR ENROLLMENT, as a citizen of the   Chickasaw   Nation, of   Joeph[sic] Jefalow[sic]   , born on the   11   day of   December   , 1902

Name of Father: Joe Jefalow   a citizen of the   Chickasaw   Nation.
Name of Mother: Molsy Jefalow   a citizen of the   Chickasaw   Nation.

Postoffice   Mead

AFFIDAVIT OF MOTHER.

UNITED STATES OF AMERICA, Indian Territory, }
     Central   **DISTRICT.** }

I,   Molsy Jefalow   , on oath state that I am   21   years of age and a citizen by blood   , of the   Chickasaw   Nation; that I am the lawful wife of   Joe Jefalow   , who is a citizen, by   blood   of the   Chickasaw   Nation; that a   mal[sic] child was born to me on   11   day of   December   , 1902, that said child has been named   Joeph Jefalow   , and is now living.

Molsy Jefalow

Witnesses To Mark:
{ Joe Jefalow
{ L T Jones

Subscribed and sworn to before me this   24 day of   February   , 1905.

S M Mead
Notary Public.

AFFIDAVIT OF ATTENDING PHYSICIAN OR MID-WIFE.

UNITED STATES OF AMERICA, Indian Territory, }
     Central   **DISTRICT.** }

I,   L.T. Joens[sic]   , a   midwife   , on oath state that I attended on Mrs.   Molsy Jefalow   , wife of   Joe Jefalow   on the   11   day of December , 1902; that there was born to her on said date a   mal   child; that said child is now living and is said to have been named Joeph

L T Jones

11

Witnesses To Mark:
- Joe Jefalow
- L T Jones

Subscribed and sworn to before me this 11 day of   February   , 1905.

S M Mead
Notary Public.

BIRTH AFFIDAVIT.

DEPARTMENT OF THE INTERIOR.
COMMISSION TO THE FIVE CIVILIZED TRIBES.

IN RE APPLICATION FOR ENROLLMENT, as a citizen of the   Chickasaw   Nation,
of   Joseph Jefflow   , born on the 11 day of December , 1902

Name of Father: Joe Jefflow   a citizen of the   Chickasaw   Nation.
Name of Mother: Malsie Jefflow   a citizen of the   Chickasaw   Nation.

Postoffice   Mead, Ind Ter

AFFIDAVIT OF MOTHER.

UNITED STATES OF AMERICA, Indian Territory,
Central   DISTRICT.

I, Malsie Jefflow   , on oath state that I am   about 25   years of age and a
citizen by   Blood   , of the   Chickasaw   Nation; that I am the lawful wife of
Joe Jefflow   , who is a citizen, by Blood   of the   Chickasaw   Nation; that
a   male   child was born to me on   11th   day of   December   , 1902; that said
child has been named   Joseph Jefflow   , and was living March 4, 1905.

her
Malsie x Jefflow
Witnesses To Mark: mark
- Amie Jones
- Jack *(Illegible)*

Subscribed and sworn to before me this 3 day of   April   , 1905

EQ Franklin
Notary Public.

12

AFFIDAVIT OF ATTENDING PHYSICIAN OR MID-WIFE.

UNITED STATES OF AMERICA, Indian Territory, ⎫
Central   DISTRICT. ⎰

I,   Mrs L.T. Jones   , a   Midwife   , on oath state that I attended on Mrs. Malsie[sic] Jefflow   , wife of   Joe Jefflow   on the 11ᵗʰ   day of December   , 1902; that there was born to her on said date a   male   child; that said child was living March 4, 1905, and is said to have been named Joseph Jefflow

Mrs L T Jones midwife

Witnesses To Mark:

⎰

Subscribed and sworn to before me this 3 day of   April   , 1905

EQ Franklin
Notary Public.

_____

Central District
Ind. Territory

Now comes Joe Jefflow and his wife Malsie Jefflow and being duly sworn state that they hereby authorize and request that their baby Joseph Jefflow be placed on tribal Roll of Chickasaw Indians. That it may take allotment and receive annuities as a Chickasaw

Witness our hands this May 9 1905   his
                                                    Joe x Jefflow
                                                      mark
Witness to mark   her
EQ Franklin   Malsie x Jefflow
(Name Illegible)   mark

Subscribed and sworn to before me this sworn to before me this May the 9ᵗʰ day 1905.

EQ Franklin
Notary Public.

_____

13

7--5483
9--1218
N B

Muskogee, Indian Territory, April 15, 1905.

Joe Jefflow,
Mead, Indian Territory,

Dear Sir:

Referring to the application for the enrollment of your infant child, Joseph Jefflow, it appears that you are a citizen by blood of the Chickasaw Nation, while your wife is a citizen by blood of the Choctaw Nation.

Your attention is called to the provision of the Act of Congress approved June 28, 1898, as follows:

"The several tribes may, by agreement, determine the right of persons who for any reason may claim citizenship in two or more tribes, and to allotment of lands and distribution of moneys belonging to each tribe; but if no such agreement be made, then such claimant shall be entitled to such rights in one tribe only, and may elect in which tribe he will take such right; but if he fail or refuse to make such selection in due time, he shall be enrolled in the tribe with whom he has resided, and there be given such allotment and distributions, and not elsewhere."

It will, therefore, be necessary for you and your wife to appear before a Notary Public or other officer authorized to administer oaths, and by affidavit elect in which nation you desire to have said child enrolled, forwarding same, when properly executed, to the Commission.

Respectfully,

Chairman.

9-NB-511
~~7 NB 680~~

Muskogee, Indian Territory, May 12, 1905.

Joe Jeflow[sic],
Mead, Indian Territory.

Dear Sir:

Receipt is hereby acknowledged of the joint affidavit of yourself and your wife Malsie Jeflow electing to have your child Joseph Jeflow enrolled as a Chickasaw and the same have been filed with the record in the matter of the enrollment of said child.

14

Respectfully,

Chairman.

Chic. N.B - 512
> *(Moss Ned*
> *Born February 5, 1905)*

BIRTH AFFIDAVIT.

DEPARTMENT OF THE INTERIOR.
COMMISSION TO THE FIVE CIVILIZED TRIBES.

IN RE APPLICATION FOR ENROLLMENT, as a citizen of the   Chickasaw   Nation,
of   Moss Ned   , born on the 5th   day of February , 1905

Name of Father: Hillis Ned   a citizen of the   Chickasaw Nation.
Name of Mother: Lela Ned   a citizen of the   Chickasaw Nation.

Postoffice   Randolph I.T.

AFFIDAVIT OF MOTHER.

UNITED STATES OF AMERICA, Indian Territory,
    Southern   DISTRICT.

I,   Lela Ned   , on oath state that I am   20   years of age and a citizen by
blood   , of the   Chickasaw   Nation; that I am the lawful wife of   Hillis Ned   ,
who is a citizen, by blood   of the   Chickasaw   Nation; that a   boy   child
was born to me on 5th   day of   February   , 1905; that said child has been named
Moss Ned   , and was living March 4, 1905.

                          her
                   Lela x Ned
Witnesses To Mark: mark
    JE Williams
    J R Colbert

Subscribed and sworn to before me this 19th   day of   April   , 1905

               JE Williams
                Notary Public.

Applications for Enrollment of Chickasaw Newborn
Act of 1905 Volume VII

AFFIDAVIT OF ATTENDING PHYSICIAN OR MID-WIFE.

UNITED STATES OF AMERICA, Indian Territory, ⎫
    Southern   DISTRICT. ⎭

    I,   Ella Smith   , a midwife   , on oath state that I attended on Mrs. Lela Ned   , wife of Hillis Ned   on the 5th day of February   , 1905; that there was born to her on said date a   male   child; that said child was living March 4, 1905, and is said to have been named Moss Ned

her
Ella x Smith
mark

Witnesses To Mark:
⎧ JE Williams
⎩ J R Colbert

    Subscribed and sworn to before me this 19th day of   April   , 1905

JE Williams
Notary Public.

BIRTH AFFIDAVIT.

DEPARTMENT OF THE INTERIOR.
COMMISSION TO THE FIVE CIVILIZED TRIBES.

IN RE APPLICATION FOR ENROLLMENT, as a citizen of the   Chickasaw   Nation, of Moss Ned   , born on the 5th day of Feby , 1905

Name of Father: Ellis[sic] Ned   a citizen of the Chickasaw Nation.
Name of Mother: Lela Fulsom   a citizen of the Chickasaw Nation.

          Postoffice   Randolph Ind Ter

AFFIDAVIT OF MOTHER.

UNITED STATES OF AMERICA, Indian Territory, ⎫
    Southern   DISTRICT. ⎭

    I,   Lela Fulsom   , on oath state that I am about 20 not years of age and a citizen by   blood   , of the   Chickasaw   Nation; that I am the lawful wife of Ellis Ned   , who is a citizen, by blood   of the   Chickasaw   Nation; that a male   child was born to me on 5th day of   Feby   , 1905; that said child has been named   Moss Ned   , and was living March 4, 1905.

her
Lela x Fulsom
mark

Witnesses To Mark:
   { J.B. Chastaine
   { Joe Mule

     Subscribed and sworn to before me this   17   day of   July   , 1905

                        C.F. Alexander
                           Notary Public.

AFFIDAVIT OF ATTENDING PHYSICIAN OR MID-WIFE.

UNITED STATES OF AMERICA, Indian Territory, }
    Southern   **DISTRICT.** }

    I,   Ella Smith   , a   midwife   , on oath state that I attended on
Mrs. Lela Fulsom   , ~~wife of~~ ———————— on the 5th   day of   Feby   , 1905; that
there was born to her on said date a   male   child; that said child was living March 4,
1905, and is said to have been named   Moss Ned

                       her
                 Ella x Smith
Witnesses To Mark: mark
   { J.B. Chastaine
   { Joe Mule

     Subscribed and sworn to before me this   17   day of   July   , 1905

                        C.F. Alexander
                         Notary Public.

                    Muskogee, Indian Territory, April 24, 1905.

Hillis Ned,
     Randolph, Indian Territory.

Dear Sir:

    Receipt is hereby acknowledged of the affidavits of Lela Ned and Ella Smith to
the birth of Moss Ned, son of Hillis and Lela Ned, February 5, 1905.

    It is stated in the affidavit of the mother that she is a citizen by blood of the
Chickasaw Nation. If this is correct you are requested to state the name under which she
was enrolled, the names of her parents, and if she has selected an allotment of the lands
of the Choctaw or Chickasaw Nation please give her roll number as it appears upon her
allotment certificate.

Respectfully,

Chairman.

———————

(COPY).

Randolph, I. Ty.,
May 6, 1905.

Hon. Tams Bixby,
Muskogee, I. Ty.

Dear Sir: I was shown a letter from you to Hillis Ned Concerning the enrollment of Mose[sic] Ned, a Chickasaw infant born on or about February 15[sic], 1905.

The mother of this child is named Lelia[sic] Folsom[sic]; her father was Dixon Folsom, and she states that she was allotted a an allotment but has lost the certificate of allotment; so does not know her roll No.

This child was born out of wedlock, the father being Hillis Ned, who is a Chickasaw by blood and has been allotted. He is married to another woman, but this woman states that he is the father of her child, and in making the application and affidavit at Tishomingo, they failed to understand the exact situation as to the father and mother. The child is a Chickasaw by blood on both sides. The woman is a full blood, very young, and has not been treated exactly right, and anything I can do to said her in this is purely gratis. So if there is any changes in the application, or in straightening out these affidavits, I will undertake to do so, if you will advise me accordingly how to proceed further in the matter, also as to what she must do about the loss of her certificate of allotment that is lost.

Very truly
J. B. Chastaine.

———————

9-NB-512.

Muskogee, Indian Territory, May 17, 1905.

Hillis Ned,
Randolph, Indian Territory.

Dear Sir:

Referring to the application for the enrollment of your infant child, Moss Ned, born February 5, 1905, it is noted that you claim to be a Chickasaw by blood.

18

Applications for Enrollment of Chickasaw Newborn
Act of 1905   Volume VII

If this is the case you are requested to state when, where and under what name you were listed for enrollment, the names of your parents and other members of your family for whom application was made at the same time, and if you have selected an allotment, give your roll number as the same appear on your allotment certificate.

Respectfully,

Chairman.

(COPY)

Randolph, I. T.

5--25--/ 05.

Hon. Daws[sic] Commission,

Gentlemen,

I am enrolled as Ellis Ned, and my roll no. on allotment certificate is 2039. I do not know my parents[sic] names as they died when I was very small-- I was enrolled by John Smith, I think, and they got my name on the roll as Ellis Ned, but the real name is Elas Ned; but nearly everyone calls me Helas Ned and I sign my name Helas Ned most of the time.

I think my father's name was Bondlan Ned. There is a certificate on file with the land office at Tishomingo setting forth these facts.

Yours truly

Ellis Ned

otherwise

Hillis Ned

I know these facts to be true

J. B. Chastaines[sic], P. M.

9-N.B. 512 &
514.

Muskogee, Indian Territory, June 2, 1905.

Ellis Ned,
      Randolph, Indian Territory.

Dear Sir:

Receipt is hereby acknowledged of your letter of May 25, stating that you are sometimes known as Ellis Ned and sometimes as Hillis Ned, but that your name appears upon the rolls as Ellis Ned.

This information has been made a matter of record.

Respectfully,

Commissioner in Charge.

(The letter below typed as given.)

9-NB-512.

(COPY)

Randolph, I. T.
June 26,   --05

Hon . Dawes Commission,

Dear Sir, replying to yours, as to who I was living with at the time of my enrollment, I think I was living with my Uncle John Smith, in 1896 & 1898. But I have lived part of the time with Hunta Pickens. My Uncle John Smith sayd that he had me enrolled at Tishomingo when the first enrollment was made. My father was Dixon Folsom, my Mother's name was Mahe Folsom so I am told. She died when I was very small.

Yours truly

lilier Folsom

Lela Folsom.

Signed for her by J. B. Chastaine

P. M.

---

9 NB 512

Muskogee, Indian Territory, July 1, 1905.

Lela Folsom,
    Randolph, Indian Territory.

Dear Madam:

Receipt is hereby acknowledged of your letter of June 22, 1905, giving information relative to your residence at the time of your enrollment and the names of your parents.

In reply to your letter you are advised that this information has been made a matter of record in the application for the enrollment of your child Moss Ned.

Respectfully,

Commissioner.

9-NB-512

Muskogee, Indian Territory, July 10, 1905.

J. B. Chastaine,
    Randolph, Indian Territory,

Dear Sir:

Referring to your letter of May 6, 1905, relative to the enrollment of Moss Ned, infant child of Ellis Ned and Lela Fulsom, in which you state that the said Moss Ned was born out of wedlock, that the said Ellis Ned is married to another woman, that at the time of the appearance of the mother at Tishomingo, Indian Territory, she failed to understand the exact situation "as to the father and mother" and that if any further information is necessary for the enrollment of this child you will undertake to furnish same.

In the affidavit of Lela Fulsom heretofore filed with the Commission to the Five Civilized Tribes she alleges that she is the lawful wife of Hillis (or Ellis) Ned, which from the statement in your letter appears to be incorrect.

There is inclosed you herewith application for the enrollment of said child made in conformity with the facts as stated in your said letter. Please have properly executed and return to this office.

This matter should receive your immediate attention as no further action can be taken relative to the enrollment of the applicant until the evidence requested is supplied.

Respectfully,

LM 10-2

Commissioner.

9-NB-512

Muskogee, Indian Territory, July 21, 1905.

J. B. Chastaine,
  Randolph, Indian Territory,

Dear Sir:

Receipt is hereby acknowledged of your letter of July 17, 1905, transmitting the affidavits of Lela Fulsom amd[sic] Ella Smith to the birth of Moss Ned, son of Ellis Ned and Lela Fulsom, February 5, 1905, and the same have been filed with the record in this case.

Respectfully,

Commissioner.

Chic. N.B - 513
  (Henley Harvy Hale
  Born June 10, 1904)

BIRTH AFFIDAVIT.

DEPARTMENT OF THE INTERIOR.
COMMISSION TO THE FIVE CIVILIZED TRIBES.

IN RE APPLICATION FOR ENROLLMENT, as a citizen of the   Chickasaw   Nation, of   Henley Harvy Hale   , born on the   10   day of   June   , 1904

Name of Father: William Hale   a citizen of the ....Nation.
Name of Mother: Josephine Hale   a citizen of the   Chickasaw   Nation.

Postoffice   Milo I T

Applications for Enrollment of Chickasaw Newborn
Act of 1905   Volume VII

AFFIDAVIT OF MOTHER.

UNITED STATES OF AMERICA, Indian Territory, ⎫
    Southern   **DISTRICT.** ⎰

    I,   Josiphine[sic] Hale   , on oath state that I am 20 years of age and a citizen by   Blood   , of the   Chickasaw   Nation; that I am the lawful wife of William Hale   , who is a citizen, by ⸺⸺⸺ of the ⸺⸺⸺ Nation; that a   male   child was born to me on 10 day of June   , 1904; that said child has been named Henley Harvy Hale   , and was living March 4, 1905.

                                            Josiephine[sic] Hale

Witnesses To Mark:
  ⎰ JC Bulla
  ⎱ J C Triphill

    Subscribed and sworn to before me this 19 day of   Apr   , 1905

                Com Ex   JL Wiggins
                Mar 1908   Notary Public.

AFFIDAVIT OF ATTENDING PHYSICIAN OR MID-WIFE.

UNITED STATES OF AMERICA, Indian Territory, ⎫
    Southern   **DISTRICT.** ⎰

    I, A B Davis M.D.   , a   Phy.   , on oath state that I attended on Mrs. Josiphine Hale   , wife of William Hale   on the 10 day of June   , 1904; that there was born to her on said date a   male   child; that said child was living March 4, 1905, and is said to have been named Henley Harvy Hale

                                            AB Davis M.D.

Witnesses To Mark:
  ⎰ JC Bulla
  ⎱ J C Triphill

    Subscribed and sworn to before me this 19 day of   Apr   , 1905

                Com Ex   JL Wiggins
                Mar 1908   Notary Public.

Applications for Enrollment of Chickasaw Newborn
Act of 1905   Volume VII

Muskogee, Indian Territory, April 24, 1905.

William Hale,
  Milo, Indian Territory.

Dear Sir:

Receipt is hereby acknowledged of the affidavits of Josephine Hale and A. B. Davis to the birth of Henley Harvy Hale son of William and Josephine Hale, June 10, 1904.

It is stated in the affidavit of the mother that she is a citizen by blood of the Chickasaw Nation. If this is correct you are requested to state the name under which she was enrolled, the names of her parents, and if she has selected an allotment of the lands of the Choctaw or Chickasaw Nation please give her roll number as it appears upon her allotment certificate.

Respectfully,

Chairman.

Sneed, Ind. Ty. May 7, 1905.

To the Commission of the five Civilized [sic]

I received your letter asking me to send my parent. My mother name is Susan McDonald father George Sealy Chickasaw by Blood my roll No. 1812 allotment certificate -8241.

Josie Hale

Chickasaw by blood.

9-596

Muskogee, Indian Territory, May 16, 1905.

Josie Hale,
  Sneed, Indian Territory.

Dear Madam:

Receipt is hereby acknowledged of your letter of May 7, giving the names of your parents and your roll number and the information has enabled us to identify you upon our records as an enrolled citizen by blood of the Chickasaw Nation and the affidavits heretofore forwarded to the birth of your child Henley Harvey[sic] Hale have been filed with our records as an application for the enrollment of said child.

Respectfully,

Chairman.

Chic. N.B - 514
  (Emily Ned
  Born July 14, 1904)

BIRTH AFFIDAVIT.

DEPARTMENT OF THE INTERIOR.
COMMISSION TO THE FIVE CIVILIZED TRIBES.

IN RE APPLICATION FOR ENROLLMENT, as a citizen of the   Chickasaw   Nation,
of   Emily Ned   , born on the   14   day of   July   , 1904

Name of Father: Ellis Ned   a citizen of the   Chickasaw   Nation.
Name of Mother: Susan Ned   a citizen of the   Chickasaw   Nation.

Postoffice   Randolph, I.T.

AFFIDAVIT OF MOTHER.

UNITED STATES OF AMERICA, Indian Territory,
   Southern   **DISTRICT.**

I,   Susan Ned   , on oath state that I am   20   years of age and a citizen by
blood   , of the   Chickasaw   Nation; that I am the lawful wife of Ellis Ned   ,
who is a citizen, by blood   of the   Chickasaw   Nation; that a   female
child was born to me on   14 day of   July   , 1904; that said child has been named
Emily Ned   , and was living March 4, 1905.

                                          her
                                Susan x Ned
Witnesses To Mark: mark
   Ellis Ned
   Henry Holder

Subscribed and sworn to before me this 18th   day of   April   , 1905

                                JE Williams
                                Notary Public.

25

Applications for Enrollment of Chickasaw Newborn
Act of 1905   Volume VII

UNITED STATES OF AMERICA, Indian Territory, ⎱
    Southern   DISTRICT. ⎰

     I,   Siney Sealy   , a midwife   , on oath state that I attended on
Mrs. Susan Ned   , wife of Ellis Ned   on the 14th day of July   , 1904;
that there was born to her on said date a   female   child; that said child was living
March 4, 1905, and is said to have been named Emily Ned

                                     her
                         Siney x Sealy
Witnesses To Mark: mark
    ⎰ Ellis Ned
    ⎱ Henry Holder

     Subscribed and sworn to before me this 18th day of April   , 1905

                         JE Williams
                         Notary Public.

                Muskogee, Indian Territory, April 24, 1905.

Ellis Ned,
     Randolph, Indian Territory.

Dear Sir:

     Receipt is hereby acknowledged of the affidavits of Susan Ned and Siney Sealy to
the birth of Emily Ned, daughter of Ellis and Susan Ned, July 14, 1904.

     It is stated in the affidavit of the mother that she is a citizen by blood of the
Chickasaw Nation. If this is correct you are requested to state the name under which she
was enrolled, the names of her parents, and if she has selected an allotment of the lands
of the Choctaw or Chickasaw Nation please give her roll number as it appears upon her
allotment certificate.
                Respectfully,

                       Chairman.

Randolph I Ty

5 - 16 - 05

Commission to the five tribes

Gentlemen,

Referring to your letter to Ellis Ned, of 4 - 24 - 05, will state that Susan Ned, was formerly named Susane[sic] Tyson, she has been alloted[sic], and her mothers[sic] name is Sina Seely; I do not know her roll No.

yours truly

(signed) J. B. Chastaine

for Ellis Ned,

in application for the enrollment of Emily Ned.

(COPY)

Randolph, I. T.

5--25--/ 05.

Hon. Daws[sic] Commission,

Gentlemen,

I am enrolled as Ellis Ned, and my roll no. on allotment certificate is 2039. I do not know my parents[sic] names as they died when I was very small-- I was enrolled by John Smith, I think, and they got my name on the roll as Ellis Ned, but the real name is Elas Ned; but nearly everyone calls me Helas Ned and I sign my name Helas Ned most of the time.

I think my father's name was Bondlan Ned. There is a certificate on file with the land office at Tishomingo setting forth these facts.

Yours truly

Ellis Ned

otherwise

Hillis Ned

I know these facts to be true

J. B. Chastaines[sic], P. M.

Applications for Enrollment of Chickasaw Newborn
Act of 1905   Volume VII

9-N.B. 512 &
514.

Muskogee, Indian Territory, June 2, 1905.

Ellis Ned,
     Randolph, Indian Territory.

Dear Sir:

    Receipt is hereby acknowledged of your letter of May 25, stating that you are sometimes known as Ellis Ned and sometimes as Hillis Ned, but that your name appears upon the rolls as Ellis Ned.

    This information has been made a matter of record.

                 Respectfully,

                         Commissioner in Charge.

Chic. N.B - 515
(George Washington Owens
Born July 19, 1903)

BIRTH AFFIDAVIT. *No 68*

DEPARTMENT OF THE INTERIOR.
COMMISSION TO THE FIVE CIVILIZED TRIBES.

IN RE APPLICATION FOR ENROLLMENT, as a citizen of the   Chickasaw   Nation, of   George Washington Owens   , born on the 19 day of July , 1903

Name of Father: Nealy A Owens   a citizen of the Chickasaw Nation.
Name of Mother: Mollie Owens   a citizen of the Chickasaw Nation.

                    Postoffice   Franks

Applications for Enrollment of Chickasaw Newborn
Act of 1905   Volume VII

AFFIDAVIT OF MOTHER.

UNITED STATES OF AMERICA, Indian Territory, }
   Southern   DISTRICT. }

     I, Mollie Owens   , on oath state that I am 29   years of age and a citizen by blood   , of the   Chickasaw   Nation; that I am the lawful wife of   Nealy A Owens   , who is a citizen, by   intermarriage   of the   Chickasaw   Nation; that a   male   child was born to me on 19   day of July   , 1903, that said child has been named   George Washington Owens   , and is now living.

                             Mollie Owens

Witnesses To Mark:

     Subscribed and sworn to before me this 16 day of January   , 1905.

                           W.H. Burdeshaw
                           Notary Public.

AFFIDAVIT OF ATTENDING PHYSICIAN OR MID-WIFE.

UNITED STATES OF AMERICA, Indian Territory, }
   Southern   DISTRICT. }

     I, Adline Owens   , a midwife   , on oath state that I attended on Mrs. Mollie Owens , wife of Nealy A. Owens on the 19   day of July , 1903; that there was born to her on said date a   male   child; that said child is now living and is said to have been named George Washington

                             Adline Owens

Witnesses To Mark:

     Subscribed and sworn to before me this 16 day of   January   , 1905.

                           W. H. Burdeshaw
                           Notary Public.

Applications for Enrollment of Chickasaw Newborn
Act of 1905 Volume VII

BIRTH AFFIDAVIT.

DEPARTMENT OF THE INTERIOR.
COMMISSION TO THE FIVE CIVILIZED TRIBES.

IN RE APPLICATION FOR ENROLLMENT, as a citizen of the   Chickasaw   Nation,
of   George Washington Owens   , born on the   19 day of   July   , 1903

Name of Father: N. A. Owens   a citizen of the   Chickasaw   Nation.
Name of Mother: Mollie Owens   a citizen of the   Chickasaw   Nation.

Postoffice   Franks

AFFIDAVIT OF MOTHER.

UNITED STATES OF AMERICA, Indian Territory,
　　Sou　　　　　　　　　**DISTRICT.**

I,   Mollie Owens   , on oath state that I am   29   years of age and a citizen
by   blood   , of the   Chickasaw   Nation; that I am the lawful wife of   Neely A
Owens   , who is a citizen, by   intermarriage   of the   Chickasaw   Nation;
that a   male   child was born to me on   19   day of   July   , 1903; that said child
has been named   Geo. Washington   , and was living March 4, 1905.

Mollie Owens

Witnesses To Mark:

Subscribed and sworn to before me this   5 day of   April   , 1905

W.H. Burdeshaw
Notary Public.

AFFIDAVIT OF ATTENDING PHYSICIAN OR MID-WIFE.

UNITED STATES OF AMERICA, Indian Territory,
　　Sou　　　　　　　　　**DISTRICT.**

I,   Adeline[sic] Owens   , a   midwife   , on oath state that I attended on
Mrs. Mollie Owens   , wife of Neely A Owens   on the 19 day of   July   ,
1903; that there was born to her on said date a   male   child; that said child was living
March 4, 1905, and is said to have been named   Geo Washington

Adline Owens

Witnesses To Mark:

30

Subscribed and sworn to before me this 5 day of   April   , 1905

W.H. Burdeshaw
Notary Public.

Muskogee, Indian Territory, April 12, 1905.

N. A. Owens,
Franks, Indian Territory.

Dear Sir:

Receipt is hereby acknowledged of the affidavits of Mollie Owens and Adeline Owens to the birth of George Washington Owens, son of N. A. and Mollie Owens, July 19, 1903.

It appears from the affidavit of the mother that she is a citizen by blood of the Chickasaw Nation and if this is correct you are requested to state the name under which she was enrolled, the names of her parents, and if she has selected an allotment of the lands of the Choctaw or Chickasaw Nation please give her roll number as it appears upon her allotment certificate.

Respectfully,

Commissioner in Charge.

Muskogee, Indian Territory, May 11, 1905.

Nealy A. Owens,
Franks, Indian Territory.

Dear Sir:

Receipt is hereby acknowledged of the affidavits of Mollie Owens and Adaline[sic] Owens to the birth of George Washington Owens, son of Nealy A. and Mollie Owens, July 19, 1903.

A letter was addressed to you a few days ago asking information in regard to the mother of the child, as it is stated in her affidavit that she is a citizen by blood of the Chickasaw Nation, and requesting you to give the name under which she was enrolled, the names of her parents, and if she has selected an allotment of the lands of the Choctaw or Chickasaw Nation please give her roll number as it appears upon her allotment certificate. No reply has as yet been received and until further information is received no action can be taken on the application for the enrollment of your child George Washington Owens.

31

You are requested to give this matter immediate attention so that proper disposition may be made of the application for the enrollment of said child.

Respectfully,

Chairman.

Chic. N.B - 516
(Mack Ott
Born March 8, 1904)

DEPARTMENT OF THE INTERIOR,
COMMISSION TO THE FIVE CIVILIZED TRIBES.
SOUTH McALESTER, I.T.   APRIL 29, 1905.

In the matter of the application for the enrollment of Mack Ott as a citizen by blood of the Chickasaw Nation.

Carney Ott being first duly sworn testifies as follows:

EXAMINATION BY THE COMMISSION:

Q What is your name? A Mack Ott.
Q How old are you? A Twenty-nine.
Q What is your post office address? A Stewart.
Q You have this day made application for the enrollment of your child Mack Ott; when was Mack Ott born? A 8th day March 1904.
Q Was Mack Ott living on March 4, 1905? A Yes, sir.
Q Living today? A Yes, sir.
Q Who is the mother of Mack Ott? A Eliza Ott.
Q Of what nation is she a citizen? A Chickasaw.
Q Of what nation are you a citizen? A Choctaw.
Q Do you desire to elect in which nation your child is to be enrolled? A Yes, sir - Chickasaw.
Witness excused.

Chas. T. Difendafer being first duly sworn states that the above and foregoing is a full, true and correct transcript of his stenographic notes taken in said cause on said date.

Chas. T. Difendafer

Subscribed and sworn to before me this 29th day of April 1905.

OL Johnson
Notary Public.

BIRTH AFFIDAVIT.

DEPARTMENT OF THE INTERIOR.
COMMISSION TO THE FIVE CIVILIZED TRIBES.

IN RE APPLICATION FOR ENROLLMENT, as a citizen of the   Chickasaw   Nation, of   Mack Ott   , born on the 8" day of   March , 1904

Name of Father: Carney Ott   a citizen of the   Choctaw Nation.
                                              Chickasaw
Name of Mother: Eliza Ott   a citizen of the   ~~Choctaw~~ Nation.

Postoffice   Stuart

AFFIDAVIT OF MOTHER.

UNITED STATES OF AMERICA, Indian Territory,
     Central   DISTRICT.

I,   Eliza Ott   , on oath state that I am   29   years of age and a citizen by Blood   , of the   ~~Choctaw~~ ~~Choctaw~~ Chickasaw   Nation; that I am the lawful wife of   Carney Ott   , who is a citizen, by blood   of the   ~~Choctaw~~ ~~Chickasaw~~ Choctaw Nation; that a   male   child was born to me on 8" day of   March   , 1904; that said child has been named   Mack Ott   , and was living March 4, 1905.

Eliza Ott

Witnesses To Mark:
   Clara Wooley
   JH Elliott

Subscribed and sworn to before me this 28" day of   April   , 1905

JH Elliott
Notary Public.
Comp Exp July 8 1908

33

AFFIDAVIT OF ATTENDING PHYSICIAN OR MID-WIFE.

UNITED STATES OF AMERICA, Indian Territory, ⎫
　　Central　　　　　　　DISTRICT. ⎰

I,　Siley Wesley　　　, a　midwife　　　, on oath state that I attended on Mrs. Eliza Ott　　　, wife of　Carney Ott　on the　8 day of　March　, 1904; that there was born to her on said date a　male　child; that said child was living March 4, 1905, and is said to have been named Mack Ott

Siley Wesley

Witnesses To Mark:
　⎧ Clara Wooley
　⎩ JH Elliott

Subscribed and sworn to before me this 28 day of　April　, 1905

JH Elliott
Notary Public.
Comp Exp July 8 1908

NEW-BORN AFFIDAVIT.

Number..............

...CHOCTAW ENROLLING COMMISSION...

IN THE MATTER OF THE APPLICATION FOR ENROLLMENT, as a citizen of the Chickasaw　　　　　　Nation, of　　　　Mack Ott

born on the　8th　day of ___March___ 190 4

Name of father　Carney Ott　　　　　a citizen of　　Choctaw
Nation final enrollment No.　123
Name of mother　Eliza Ott　　　　　a citizen of　　Chickasaw
Nation final enrollment No.　1033

Postoffice　　Stuart IT

Applications for Enrollment of Chickasaw Newborn
Act of 1905   Volume VII

AFFIDAVIT OF MOTHER.

UNITED STATES OF AMERICA
INDIAN TERRITORY
Central   DISTRICT

I   Eliza Ott   , on oath state that I am
28   years of age and a citizen by   blood   of the   Chickasaw   Nation,
and as such have been placed upon the final roll of the   Chickasaw   Nation, by the
Honorable Secretary of the Interior my final enrollment number being   1033   ; that I am the
lawful wife of   Carney Ott   , who is a citizen of the   Choctaw   Nation, and as
such has been placed upon the final roll of said Nation by the Honorable Secretary of the
Interior, his final enrollment number being   123   and that a   Male   child was born to
me on the   8th   day of   March   190 4; that said child has been named   Mack Ott   ,
and is now living.

                                          Eliza Ott

Witnesseth.

Must be two   ⎫   Ellis Noletubby
Witnesses who   ⎬
are Citizens.   ⎭   Elias Wesley

Subscribed and sworn to before me this   12th   day of   Jan   190 5

                                          W A Shoney
                                          Notary Public.

My commission expires:
Jan 11th 1909

Affidavit of Attending Physician or Midwife.

UNITED STATES OF AMERICA ⎫
INDIAN TERRITORY   ⎬
Central   DISTRICT ⎭

I,   Mollie Anderson   a   midwife
on oath state that I attended on Mrs.   Eliza Wade now Ott
wife of   Carney Ott   on the   8th   day of   March   ,
190 4 , that there was born to her on said date a   Male   child, that said child is now living,
and is said to have been named   Mack Ott

                                          Mollie Anderson   M.D.

Subscribed and sworn to before me this, the   4th   day of   March   190 5

                                          JH Elliott
                                          Notary Public.

Applications for Enrollment of Chickasaw Newborn
Act of 1905   Volume VII

WITNESSETH: his
Must be two witnesses   { Morris x Lender
who are citizens and   his mark
know the child.   { Alex x Leflore
                                mark

We hereby certify that we are well acquainted with   Mollie Anderson
a   midwife   and know   her   to be reputable and of good standing in the
community.   his
                                         Morris x Lender
                                    {   his mark
                                         Alex x Leflore
                                                mark

(The affidavit below typed as given.)

Stuart I.T.

MAY 18 1905

Commission to the five Civilized
Tribes Muskogee I.T.

Dear Sir   Rec yous of the 8"/05 in and will say that we want to enroll our baby
boy Mack Ott in the Chicksaw Nation as his mother is a Chicksaw by Blood
This is our desire and there fore set our Hand & Seal.

Witness   Carney Ott
    Clara Wooley   Eliza Ott

United States of America
    Indian Terry Central dist

be it Remembered that on this day 18 of May 1905 before me J H Elliott a Notary Public
within & for the said Territory and District duly commissioned and acting as sutch
Personaly[sic] appeared the above named Carry[sic] Ott and Eliza Ott his wife to me well
known as the Persons whoes names are subscribed to the above foregoing instrument as
parties *(illegible)* stated and acknowledged to me that they had voluntarily executed the
same as their desire herein mentioned. In testimony whereof I have hereunto set my hand
and seal as Notary Public aforesaid in the said Territory and District on that day and date
last aforesaid
                        JH Elliott Notary Public
My Com Exp July 8" 1908.

7-N.B. 1366.

Muskogee, Indian Territory, May 8, 1905.

Carney Ott,
    Stuart, Indian Territory.

Dear Sir:

Referring to the application for the enrollment of your infant child, Mack Ott, it appears that you are a citizen by blood of the Choctaw Nation, while your wife is a citizen by blood of the Chickasaw Nation.

Your attention is called to the provision of the Act of Congress approved June 28, 1898, as follows:

The several Tribes may, by agreement, determine the right of persons who for any reason may claim citizenship in two or more tribes, and to allotment of lands and distribution of moneys belonging to each tribe; but if no such agreement be made, then such claimant shall be entitled to such rights in one tribe only, and may elect in which tribe he will take such right; but if he fail or refuse to make such selection in due time, he shall be enrolled in the tribe with whom he has resided, and there be given such allotment and distributions, and not elsewhere.

It will therefore be necessary for you and your wife to appear before a Notary Public or other officer authorized to administer oaths and by affidavit elect in which nation you desire to have said child enrolled, forwarding same, when properly executed, to the Commission.

Respectfully,

Commissioner in Charge.

7-N.B. 1366.

Muskogee, Indian Territory, May 24, 1905.

Carney Ott,
    Stuart, Indian Territory.

Dear Sir:

Receipt is hereby acknowledged of the joint affidavit of yourself and Eliza Ott electing to have your child, Mack Ott, enrolled as a citizen by blood of the Chickasaw Nation and the same has been filed with our records in the matter of the enrollment of said child.

Respectfully

Chairman.

<u>Chic. N.B - 517</u>
(Charley Robeson
Born June 18, 1904)

BIRTH AFFIDAVIT.

DEPARTMENT OF THE INTERIOR.
COMMISSION TO THE FIVE CIVILIZED TRIBES.

IN RE APPLICATION FOR ENROLLMENT, as a citizen of the   Chickasaw   Nation, of   Charley Robson   , born on the 18   day of   June   , 1904

Name of Father: Joe Robson   a citizen of the   Choctaw   Nation.
Name of Mother: Jane Robson   a citizen of the   Chickasaw   Nation.

Postoffice   Franks I.T.

AFFIDAVIT OF MOTHER.

UNITED STATES OF AMERICA, Indian Territory, ⎫
       Southern   **DISTRICT.** ⎭

I,   Jane Robson   , on oath state that I am   about 23   years of age and a citizen by   blood   , of the   Chickasaw   Nation; that I am the lawful wife of Joe Robson   , who is a citizen, by blood   of the   Choctaw   Nation; that a male   child was born to me on   the 18^(th)   day of   June   , 1904; that said child has been named Charley Robson   , and was living March 4, 1905.

                                                                her
                                                     Jane x Robson
Witnesses To Mark: mark
    ⎰ TE Bunts
    ⎱ B.F. Talbott

Subscribed and sworn to before me this 29   day of   April   , 1905

                              JE Williams
                                   Notary Public.

38

BIRTH AFFIDAVIT.

DEPARTMENT OF THE INTERIOR.
COMMISSION TO THE FIVE CIVILIZED TRIBES.

IN RE APPLICATION FOR ENROLLMENT, as a citizen of the   Chickasaw   Nation, of   Charley Robeson   , born on the 18   day of June   , 1904

Name of Father: Joe Robeson   a citizen of the   Choctaw Nation.
Name of Mother: Jane Robeson   a citizen of the   Chickasaw Nation.

Postoffice   Franks Ind Ter

AFFIDAVIT OF MOTHER.

UNITED STATES OF AMERICA, Indian Territory, ⎫
     Sou   DISTRICT. ⎭

I,   Jane Robeson   , on oath state that I am   about 23   years of age and a citizen by   blood   , of the   Chickasaw   Nation; that I am the lawful wife of Joe Robeson   , who is a citizen, by blood   of the   Choctaw   Nation; that a   male   child was born to me on   the 18th day of   June   , 1904; that said child has been named Charley Robeson   , and was living March 4, 1905.

her
Jane x Robeson
mark

Witnesses To Mark:
    ⎰ C E Sevor
    ⎱ Jeff Stout

Subscribed and sworn to before me this 13   day of   July   , 1905

WH Burdeshaw
Notary Public.

AFFIDAVIT OF ATTENDING PHYSICIAN OR MID-WIFE.

UNITED STATES OF AMERICA, Indian Territory, ⎫
     Sou   DISTRICT. ⎭

I,   Marsa Harland   , a   midwife   , on oath state that I attended on Mrs.   Jane Robeson   , wife of   Joe Robeson   on the 18 day of   June   , 1904; that there was born to her on said date a   male   child; that said child was living March 4, 1905, and is said to have been named   Charley Robeson

her
Marsa x Harland
mark

Witnesses To Mark:
$\left\{\begin{array}{l}\text{Jeff Stout} \\ \text{C E Sevor}\end{array}\right.$

Subscribed and sworn to before me this 13   day of   July   , 1905

WH Burdeshaw
Notary Public.

Sou District
  Ind. Ter.

Be it known that on this 7th day of Aug 1905 personally appeared before me, Joe & Jane Robeson who after being duly sworn say that they want their child Charley Robeson, enrolled as a citizen of the Chickasaw Nation the Chickasaw Nation

his
Joe x Robeson
mark
her
Jane x Robeson
mark

Witness
  A.C. Craft
  C.E. Sevor

Sworn and subscribed to before me this 7th day of Aug. 1905

W.H. Burdeshaw
N.P. in and for Sou
Judicial Dis, Ind Ter.

Indian Territory
Chickasaw Nation
Southern Judicial District

I. Joe Robson, do solemnly swear that I am a Choctaw Indian by blood, that my Mother and Father were Choctaws by blood, that my Mother has been dead about 26 years and her name was Charity Robson, that my Father has been dead about 33 years and his name was Cat Robson. That I have selected an allotment in the Chickasaw Nation, that my roll name is Joe Robson and my roll number is 9432 as it appears upon my allotment certificate.

That my Wife was a Chickasaw Indian by blood, her Father and Mother were both Chickasaw Indians by blood. Her Mothers name was Benis Colbert, and has been dead about 1½ months and her Fathers name was Adam Lewis and he has been dead about 15 years.

My Wife was enrolled under her maiden name (Jane Lewis), but her allotment certificate was issued to Jane Roberson and she has selected an allotment in the

Chickasaw Nation and her roll number, as it appears up on her allotment certificate, is 1054.

his
Joe x Robson
mark

Wit.
   J.E. Terrell

Subscribed and sworn to before me, this the 3d. day of July 1905.

(Name Illegible)
Notary Public in and for the
Southern Judicial District Ind. Ter.

———————

Muskogee, Indian Territory, May 3, 1905.

Joe Robson,
   Franks, Indian Territory.

Dear Sir:

Receipt is hereby acknowledged of the affidavit of Jane Robson to the birth of Charley Robson, son of Joe and Jane Robson, June 18, 1904.

It is stated in the affidavit of the mother that she is a citizen by blood of the Chickasaw Nation, and that you are a citizen by blood of the Choctaw Nation. If this is correct you are requested to state the names under which you were enrolled, the names of your parents, and if either of you have selected an allotment in the Choctaw or Chickasaw Nation please give your roll numbers as they appear upon your allotment certificates.

Respectfully,

Chairman.

———————

9 -NB-517

Muskogee, Indian Territory, July 6, 1905.

Joe Robeson,
   Franks, Indian Territory.

Dear Sir:

There is inclosed you herewith for execution application for the enrollment of your infant child, Charley Robeson, born June 18, 1904.

The affidavit of your wife executed on April 29, 1905, which has heretofore been filed in this office, is signed Jane Robson. It appears from the records that she is enrolled under the name of Jane Robeson.

It further appears that you have not filed the affidavit of the physician or midwife who attended you wife at the birth of said child.

In having these affidavits executed care should be exercised to see that all names are written in full, as they appear in the body of the affidavit, and in the event that either of the persons signing the affidavit are unable to write, signatures by mark must be attested by two witnesses. Each affidavit must be executed before a Notary Public and the notarial seal and signature of the officer must be attached to each separate affidavit.

You are requested to give this matter your immediate attention as no further action can be taken relative to the enrollment of said child, until the evidence requested is supplied.

Respectfully,

LM-6-5

Commissioner.

9-NB-517

Muskogee, Indian Territory, July 8, 1905.

Joe Robson,
Franks, Indian Territory.

Dear Sir:

Receipt is hereby acknowledged of your letter of July 3, 1905, enclosing your affidavit relative to the enrollment of your wife which you offer in support of the application for the enrollment of your child Charley Robson and the same has been filed with the record in this case.

Respectfully,

Commissioner.

Applications for Enrollment of Chickasaw Newborn
Act of 1905   Volume VII

9-NB-517

Muskogee, Indian Territory, July 21, 1905.

Joe Robeson,
Franks, Indian Territory.

Dear Sir:

Receipt is hereby acknowledged of the affidavits of Jane Robeson and Marsa Harland to the birth of Charley Robeson, son of Joe and Jane Robeson, June 18, 1904, and the same have been filed with the record in this case.

You are further advised that it appears that you are a citizen by blood of the Choctaw Nation and that you[sic] wife, Jane Robeson, is a citizen by blood of the Chickasaw Nation.

Your attention is called to the provision of the Act of Congress approved June 28, 1898, as follows:

"The several tribes may, by agreement, determine the right of persons who for any reason may claim citizenship in two or more tribes, and to allotment of lands and distribution of moneys belonging to each tribe; but if no such agreement be made, then such claimant shall be entitled to such rights in one tribe only, and may elect in which tribe he will take such right; but if he fail or refuse to make such selection in due time, he shall be enrolled in the tribe with whom he has resided, and there be given such allotment and distributions, and not elsewhere."

It will therefore be necessary for you and your wife, Jane Robeson, to appear before a Notary Public or other officer authorized to administer oaths and by affidavit elect in which nation you desire to have said child enrolled, forwarding same, when properly executed, to this office.

Respectfully,

Commissioner.

9-NB-517

Muskogee, Indian Territory, August 11, 1905.

Joe Robeson,
     Franks, Indian Territory.

Dear Sir:

    Receipt is hereby acknowledged of the joint afficavit[sic] of yourself and your wife Jane Robeson electing to have your child Charley Robeson enrolled as a citizen by blood of the Chickasaw Nation and the same has been filed with the record in this case.

Respectfully,

Acting Commissioner.

9-NB-577

Muskogee, Indian Territory, September 20, 1905

Crawford & Bolen,
     Attorneys at Law,
          Ada, Indian Territory.

Gentlemen:

    Receipt is hereby acknowledged of your letter without date in which you state that you have been employed to file a contest for Charley Roberson[sic], an infant, and you request to be advised as to whether or not the enrollment of said child has been approved.

    In reply to your letter you are advised that the name of Charley Robeson has been placed upon a partial roll of new born citizens by blood of the Chickasaw Nation opposite number 550, which schedule was forwarded the Secretary of the Interior for approval on August 26, 1905. As soon as the Secretary approved the same you will be duly notified.

    Said child appears from our records to be the son of Joe Robeson, a Choctaw citizen, and Jane Robeson, a citizen by blood of the Chickasaw Nation.

Respectfully,

Commissioner.

Chic. N.B - 518
   (Julia Carney
   Born February 17, 1904)

BIRTH AFFIDAVIT.

DEPARTMENT OF THE INTERIOR.
COMMISSION TO THE FIVE CIVILIZED TRIBES.

IN RE APPLICATION FOR ENROLLMENT, as a citizen of the   Chickasaw   Nation, of   Julia Carnnay[sic]   , born on the   17th   day of February   , 1904

Name of Father: William Carnnay   a citizen of the   Chickasaw   Nation.
Name of Mother: Adaline Carnnay   a citizen of the   Chickasaw   Nation.

Postoffice   Cope Ind. Ty.

AFFIDAVIT OF MOTHER.

UNITED STATES OF AMERICA, Indian Territory,
   22ond Southern   DISTRICT.

I,   Adaline Carnnay   , on oath state that I am   27   years of age and a citizen by   blood   , of the   Chickasaw   Nation; that I am the lawful wife of   William Carnnay   , who is a citizen, by blood   of the   Chickasaw   Nation; that a Female   child was born to me on   17th   day of   ~~February~~ Jan   , 1904; that said child has been named   Julia Carnnay   , and was living March 4, 1905.

Adaline Carny[sic]
Witnesses To Mark:

Subscribed and sworn to before me this   28 day of   April   , 1905

T.C. Keller
Notary Public.

AFFIDAVIT OF ATTENDING PHYSICIAN OR MID-WIFE.

UNITED STATES OF AMERICA, Indian Territory,
   22ond Southern   DISTRICT.

I,   Roda Cass   , a midwife   , on oath state that I attended on Mrs. Adaline Carnnay   , wife of   William Carnnay   on the   17th   day of

45

Applications for Enrollment of Chickasaw Newborn
Act of 1905   Volume VII

~~February~~ Jan   , 1904; that there was born to her on said date a   Female   child;
that said child was living March 4, 1905, and is said to have been named Julia Carnnay

her
Roda x Cass
mark

Witnesses To Mark:
  - OH Luna
  - *(Name Illegible)*

Subscribed and sworn to before me this 28 day of   April   , 1905

T.C. Keller
Notary Public.

BIRTH AFFIDAVIT.   *No 81*

DEPARTMENT OF THE INTERIOR.
COMMISSION TO THE FIVE CIVILIZED TRIBES.

IN RE APPLICATION FOR ENROLLMENT, as a citizen of the   Chickasaw   Nation,
of   Julia Carney   , born on the 17th   day of Jan   , 1904

Name of Father: William Carney   a citizen of the   Chickasaw   Nation.
Name of Mother: Adline[sic] Carney   a citizen of the   Chickasaw   Nation.

Postoffice   Cope

AFFIDAVIT OF MOTHER.

UNITED STATES OF AMERICA, Indian Territory,
  Central   **DISTRICT.**

  I,   Adline Carney   , on oath state that I am 27   years of age and a citizen by
Blood   , of the   Chickasaw   Nation; that I am the lawful wife of   William
Carney   , who is a citizen, by   Blood   of the   Chickasaw   Nation; that a
Female   child was born to me on 17   day of   Jan   , 1904, that said child has
been named   Julia Carney   , and is now living.

Adelene[sic] Carny[sic]

Witnesses To Mark:

Subscribed and sworn to before me this 24th day of   Jan   , 1905.

E.J. Ball
Notary Public.

46

AFFIDAVIT OF ATTENDING PHYSICIAN OR MID-WIFE.

UNITED STATES OF AMERICA, Indian Territory, ⎫
    Central   DISTRICT. ⎭

I,   Rhoda Cass   , a   midwife   , on oath state that I attended on Mrs. Adline Carney   , wife of   William Carney   on the   17   day of   Jan , 1904; that there was born to her on said date a   Female   child; that said child is now living and is said to have been named   Julia Carney

                               Rhoda Cass

Witnesses To Mark:

    Subscribed and sworn to before me this   24   day of   Jan   , 1905.

                         E.J. Ball
                            Notary Public.

               Muskogee, Indian Territory, May 2, 1905.

William Carnnay,
    Cope, Indian Territory.

Dear Sir:

    Receipt is hereby acknowledged of the affidavits of Adaline Carnnay and Roda Cass to the birth of Julia Carnnay, daughter of William and Adaline Carnnay, February 17, 1904.

    It is stated in the affidavit of the mother that she is a citizen by blood of the Chickasaw Nation. If this is correct you are requested to state the name under which she was enrolled, the names of her parents, and if she has selected an allotment of the lands of the Choctaw or Chickasaw Nation please give her roll number as it appears upon her allotment certificate.

                     Respectfully,

                             Chairman.

(COPY)   7-537.

Cope, I. T.

May 23d, 1905.

Commission to the Five
    Civilized Tribes,
        Muskogee, I. T.

Gentlemen

in reply to your inquiry of Adaline Carneys[sic] former name. Upon the Commission roll you will find that her name is Adaline Dyer Daughter of Daniel Dyer   she made the application for her child as a new born baby, since ratification of the Treaty who is my wife and the Number of certificate are shows[sic] this 179 and she has selected as her allotment in the Chickasaw Nation near Post Office Viola I. T.
Hoping this will meet your approval

yours Respectfully,

William Carney.

9--57.

Muskogee, Indian Territory, May 31, 1905.

William Carney,
    Cope, Indian Territory.

Dear Sir:

Receipt is hereby acknowledged of your letter of May 23, giving information relative to the enrollment of Adeline Carney in the matter of the application for the enrollment of your child, Julia Carney, and this information has enabled us to identify her upon our records as an enrolled citizen by blood of the Chickasaw Nation, and the affidavits heretofore forwarded to the birth of Julia Carney have been filed with our records as an application for the enrollment of said child.

Respectfully,

Chairman.

Applications for Enrollment of Chickasaw Newborn
Act of 1905   Volume VII

Chic. N.B - 519
> *(Salina Jefferson*
> *Born August 1, 1904)*

9-4868
7-13579

DEPARTMENT OF THE INTERIOR,
COMMISSION TO THE FIVE CIVILIZED TRIBES.
SOUTH McALESTER, IND. TER. APRIL 26, 1905.

In the matter of the application for the enrollment of Salina Jefferson as a citizen by blood of the Chickasaw Nation.

Jacob James being first duly sworn testifies as follows:

EXAMINATION BY THE COMMISSION:

Q What is your name? A Jacob James.
Q How old are you? A Twenty-two.
Q What is your post office address? A Carbon.
Q Are you a citizen by blood of the Choctaw Nation? A Yes, sir.
Q Are you acquainted with Simeon Jefferson and his wife Mary Jefferson who have this day made application for their child Salina Jefferson? A Yes, sir.
Q How far do you live from Simeon Jefferson? A I live about [sic] mile and a half.
Q Do you know when their child was born? A Yes, sir, I went there next day.
Q When was this child born? A Born first day August.
Q First day of August of what year? A 1904.
Q Was this child living on March 4, 1905? A Yes, sir.

Witness excused.

Simeon Jefferson being first duly sworn testifies as follows:

EXAMINATION BY THE COMMISSION:

Q What is your name? A Simeon Jefferson.
Q How of are you Simeon? A Twenty-seven.
Q What is your post office address? A Carbon.
Q You have this day made application for your child Salina Jefferson; when was Salina born? A August 1, 1904.
Q Was Salina Jefferson living on March 4, 1905? A Yes, sir.
Q Of what nation is your wife a citizen? A Choctaw.
Q Of what nation are you a citizen? A Chickasaw.
Q In which nation do you desire to have your child Salina Jefferson enrolled?
A Chickasaw.

Witness excused.

Chas. T. Difendafer being first duly sworn states that the above and foregoing is a full, true and correct transcript of his stenographic notes taken in said cause on said date.

Chas. T. Difendafer

Subscribed and sworn to before me this 26th day of April 1905.

OL Johnson
Notary Public.

9-N.B.-519
O.L.J.

DEPARTMENT OF THE INTERIOR,
COMMISSIONER TO THE FIVE CIVILIZED TRIBES.

In the matter of the application for the enrollment of Salina Jefferson as a citizen by blood of the Chickasaw Nation.

D E C I S I O N .

It appears from the record herein that on April 26, 1905, application was made to the Commission to the Five Civilized Tribes for the enrollment of Salina Jefferson as a citizen by blood of the Chickasaw Nation.

It further appears from the record herein that said applicant was born on August 1, 1904, and is the daughter of Simeon Jefferson whose name appears as No. 4868 upon the final roll of citizens by blood of the Chickasaw Nation approved by the Secretary of the Interior September 22, 1904, and Mary Jefferson whose name appears as No. 13579 upon the final roll of citizens by blood of the Choctaw Nation approved by the Secretary of the Interior March 19, 1903; and that said applicant was living on March 4, 1905.

April 26, 1905, Simeon Jefferson, the father of said applicant, appeared before the Commission to the Five Civilized Tribes and under the provisions of Section twenty-one of the Act of Congress approved June 28, 1898 (30 Stats., 495), elected to have said child enrolled as a citizen by blood of the Chickasaw Nation.

I am, therefore, of the opinion that Salina Jefferson should be enrolled as a citizen by blood of the Chickasaw Nation, under the provisions of the Act of Congress approved March 3, 1905 (33 Stats., 1060), and it is so ordered.

Tams Bixby Commissioner.

Muskogee, Indian Territory.
FEB 19 1907

---

7 - 13579   9 - 4868

BIRTH AFFIDAVIT.

DEPARTMENT OF THE INTERIOR.
COMMISSION TO THE FIVE CIVILIZED TRIBES.

IN RE APPLICATION FOR ENROLLMENT, as a citizen of the   Chickasaw   Nation,
of   Salina Jefferson   , born on the 1   day of   August , 1904

Name of Father: Simeon Jefferson   a citizen of the   Chickasaw Nation.
Name of Mother: Mary Jefferson   a citizen of the   Choctaw Nation.

Postoffice   Carbon, I. T.

AFFIDAVIT OF MOTHER.

UNITED STATES OF AMERICA, Indian Territory, ⎫
    Central   **DISTRICT.** ⎭

    I,   Mary Jefferson   , on oath state that I am   24   years of age and a citizen
by   blood   , of the   Choctaw   Nation; that I am the lawful wife of   Simeon
Jefferson   , who is a citizen, by blood   of the   Chickasaw   Nation; that a
female   child was born to me on   1st   day of   August   , 1904; that said child has
been named   Salina Jefferson   , and was living March 4, 1905.

                         her
               Mary x Jefferson
Witnesses To Mark: mark
   ⎧ Chas. T. Difendafer
   ⎩ OL Johnson

Subscribed and sworn to before me this 26 day of   April   , 1905

              OL Johnson
              Notary Public.

This is to certify that I have this day joined in the Holy Bonds of Matrimony Simeon
Jefferson, a citizen of Tobucksy County, Choctaw Nation to Mary James, a citizen of the
same County & Nation
This the 4th day of November A.D. 1897.

              D.A. Bond
         The Minister of the Gospel

7-NB-1277.

Muskogee, Indian Territory, June 5, 1905.

Simeon Jefferson,
    Carbon, Indian Territory.

Dear Sir:

There is enclosed herewith for execution the affidavit of the attending physician or midwife in the matter of the enrollment of your infant child, Salina Jefferson, born August 1, 1904.

Before this matter can be finally determined it will be necessary that you secure the affidavit of the attending physician or midwife, which was omitted from the original application; but in the event that there was no one in attendance upon your wife at the time of birth of the applicant it will be necessary that you file in this office the affidavits of two persons, who are disinterested and not related to the applicant, who have actual knowledge of the facts that the child was born, the date of her birth; that she was living on March 4, 1905, and that Mary Jefferson is her mother.

In having this affidavit executed care should be exercised to see that all names are written in full, as they appear in the body of the affidavit, and in the event that the person signing the affidavit is unable to write, signature by mark must be attested by two witnesses. The affidavit must be executed before a Notary Public and the notarial seal and signature of the officer must be attached thereto.

This matter should receive your immediate attention, as no further action can be taken until this affidavit is filed with the Commission.

Respectfully,

VR 5-2.   [sic]

9-NB-519

Muskogee, Indian Territory, July 6, 1905.

Simeon Jefferson,
    Carbon, Indian Territory.

Dear Sir:

There is inclosed you herewith for execution an affidavit to be executed by the attending physician or mid wife to the birth of your infant child, Salina Jefferson, born August 1, 1904.

In the event that you cannot secure such affidavit, the affidavit of two disinterested persons who are not related to the applicant and who have actual knowledge of the facts, the exact date of her birth, that she was living on March 4, 1905, and that Mary Jefferson is her mother, is required.

The testimony of Jacob James to these facts has been filed in this office, it will therefore be necessary for you to furnish the affidavit of only one disinterested person.

This matter should receive your immediate attention as no further action can be taken relative to the enrollment of your child until the evidence requested is supplied.

Respectfully,

LM 6-4   Commissioner.

9-NB-519.

Muskogee, Indian Territory, August 17, 1905.

Simeon Jefferson,
    Carbon, Indian Territory.

Dear Sir:

On June 5, 1905, and again on July 6, 1905, this office addresses[sic] a letter to you requesting you to furnish in the matter of the enrollment of your minor daughter, Salina Jefferson, as a citizen by blood of the Chickasaw Nation, the affidavit of the attending physician or midwife at the birth of said child and each time forwarded you for such purpose a blank for proof of birth. You were advised that in case there was no attending physician or midwife when said child was born it would be necessary for you to furnish this office with the affidavit of an additional disinterested person as to the birth of said child. To said letters no response has been received.

You are again advised that it will be necessary for you to supply this office with such evidence and also with evidence of your marriage to Mary Jefferson, the mother of said child. Such evidence of marriage may consist of either the original or a certified copy of your marriage license and certificate or, in case you are unable to obtain the same, the affidavits of two eyewitnesses to your marriage.

You are advised that until this evidence is furnished the rights of the said Salina Jefferson as a citizen by blood of the Chickasaw Nation can not be finally determined.

Respectfully,

Acting Commissioner.

B C
Env.

Applications for Enrollment of Chickasaw Newborn
Act of 1905   Volume VII

9-NB-519

Muskogee, Indian Territory, October 23, 1906[sic].

Simeon Jefferson,
    Carbon, Indian Territory.

Dear Sir:

In the matter of the application for the enrollment of your child Selina[sic] Jefferson, as a new born citizen of the Chickasaw Nation, under the Act of Congress approved March 3, 1905, you are advised that it will be necessary that you forward the affidavit of the physician or midwife in attendance at the birth of this child or in the event no one was in attendance the affidavit of one disinterested witness who knows of the birth of this child, the names of her parents, and that she was living March 4, 1905. You should also forward evidence of your marriage to Mary Jefferson, the mother of this child. Repeated requests have heretofore been made for this evidence but no reply has heretofore been received and you are advised that the matter should receive your immediate attention in order that disposition may be made of the application for the enrollment of Selina Jefferson.

Respectfully,

Commissioner.

9-NB-519

Muskogee, Indian Territory, November 28, 1905.

Simeon Jefferson,
    Carbon, Indian Territory.

Dear Sir:

You have heretofore been advised that it would be necessary for you to furnish the affidavit of the attending physician or midwife at the birth of your child Selina Jefferson in the matter of the enrollment of said child, but up to this time no such evidence has been received.

You are again advised that you should at once forward such affidavit or in case there was no one in attendance at the birth of your child, the affidavit of one disinterested person as to the birth of said child, the date of its birth, the name of its mother, and whether or not the child was living March 4, 1905.

You should also forward evidence of your marriage to Mary Jefferson, the mother of this child.   Such evidence may consist of the original or a certified copy of the marriage license and certificate or in case you are unable to obtain the same, the evidence of two disinterested witnesses to your marriage. This matter should receive your prompt attention in order that disposition may be made of the application for the enrollment of this child.

Respectfully,

Acting Commissioner.

9-NB-519

Muskogee, Indian Territory, February 13, 1906.

Simeon Jefferson,
    Carbon, Indian Territory.

Dear Sir:

Your attention is invited to office letter of November 28, 1905, requesting an affidavit of the physician or mid wife in attendance at the birth of your child, Salina Jefferson, or in the event no one was in attendance, the affidavit of one disinterested person who has actual knowledge as to the birth of said child, the date of her birth, the name of her mother, and whether or not she was living on March 4, 1905.

Evidence of the marriage of Mary Jefferson, mother of Salina Jefferson was also requested, and until this evidence is received, no further action can be taken in the matter of the application for the enrollment of your child, Salina Jefferson.

Respectfully,

Acting Commissioner.

9-NB-519

Muskogee, Indian Territory, April 30, 1906.

Simeon Jefferson,
    Carbon, Indian Territory.

Dear Sir:

You are advised that no further action can be taken in the matter of the application for the enrollment of your child Selina Jefferson until the affidavit of the physician or midwife in attendance at the birth of this child is received or in the event no one was in

55

attendance the affidavit of one disinterested person who knows of the birth of said child, the date of her birth, the name of her mother and whether or not she was living March 4, 1905. Evidence of the marriage of Simeon and Mary Jefferson is also requested.

This matter should receive immediate attention.

Respectfully,

Commissioner.

———————

9-NB-519

Muskogee, Indian Territory, September 24, 1906.

J. S. Mullen,
Ardmore, Indian Territory.

Dear Sir:

Receipt is hereby acknowledged of your letter of September 10, 1906, asking if the affidavit required in the matter of the application for the enrollment of Selina Jefferson under the Act of Congress approved March 3, 1905, has ever been furnished.

In reply to your letter you are advised that the affidavit of the physician or midwife at the birth of Selina Jefferson, child of Simeon and Mary Jefferson, August 1, 1904, has not yet been received at this office and although numerous letters have been addressed to him advising him of the necessity of forwarding same. He has been advised that if no physician or midwife was in attendance at the birth of this child, the affidavit of one disinterested witness who knows of the birth of this child, the date of her birth, the names of her parents, and that she was living March 4, 1905, should be forwarded. Evidence of the marriage of Simeon and Mary Jefferson should also be forwarded in the matter of the enrollment of this child.

Respectfully,

Commissioner.

———————

9-NB-519

Muskogee, Indian Territory, November 2, 1906.

J. S. Mullen,
Ardmore, Indian Territory.

Dear Sir:

Receipt is hereby acknowledged of your letter of October 25, 1906, inclosing affidavit of Lyman Pusley to the birth of Salina Jefferson, child of Simeon and Mary Jefferson and the same is herewith returned for the reason that Lyman Pusley fails to state the date of the birth of this child in his affidavit. Please state the date of the birth in the affidavit. It also appears that the name of this child is Salina Jefferson instead of Selina Jefferson and you are requested in having the affidavit corrected to correct the Christian name of this child.

Copy of the marriage certificate between Simeon Jefferson and Mary James has been filed with the record in this case.

Please give this matter immediate attention.

Respectfully,

EB 2-2

Commissioner.

7-NB-1277

Muskogee, Indian Territory, January 12, 1907.

Simeon Jefferson,
Carbon, Indian Territory.

Dear Sir:

In the matter of the application for the enrollment of your minor child, Salina Jefferson, born August 1, 1904, you are advised that you should forward at once an affidavit of one other witness who knows of the date of the birth of said child, the names of her parents and that she was living March 4, 1905. This evidence should be forwarded so as to reach this office not later than January 17, 1907.

Respectfully,

Commissioner.

Applications for Enrollment of Chickasaw Newborn
Act of 1905   Volume VII

9-NB-519

Muskogee, Indian Territory, February 19, 1907.

Simeon Jefferson,
    Carbon, Indian Territory.

Dear Sir:

Inclosed herewith you will find a copy of the decision of the Commissioner to the Five Civilized Tribes, rendered February 19, 1907, granting the application for the enrollment of Salina Jefferson as a citizen by blood of the Chickasaw Nation.

You are hereby advised that the name of Salina Jefferson will be placed upon a schedule of citizens by blood of the Chickasaw Nation to be prepared for forwarding the Secretary of the Interior for his approval. You will be notified of Departmental action thereon.

Respectfully,
SIGNED

Tams Bixby
Commissioner.

Registered.
Incl. 9-NB-519

9-NB-519

COPY

Muskogee, Indian Territory, February 19, 1907.

Mansfield, McMurray & Cornish,
    Attorneys for Choctaw and Chickasaw Nations,
        South McAlester, Indian Territory.

Gentlemen:

Inclosed herewith you will find a copy of the decision of the Commissioner to the Five Civilized Tribes, rendered February 19, 1907, granting the application for the enrollment of Salina Jefferson as a citizen by blood of the Chickasaw Nation.

You are hereby advised that the name of Salina Jefferson will be placed upon a schedule of citizens by blood of the Chickasaw Nation to be prepared for forwarding the Secretary of the Interior for his approval. You will be notified of Departmental action thereon.

Respectfully,
SIGNED   *Tams Bixby*
Commissioner.

Registered.
Incl. 9-NB-519

Applications for Enrollment of Chickasaw Newborn
Act of 1905   Volume VII

<u>Chic. N.B - 520</u>
(Clifton Gaddis
Born March 17, 1904)

BIRTH AFFIDAVIT.

DEPARTMENT OF THE INTERIOR.
COMMISSION TO THE FIVE CIVILIZED TRIBES.

IN RE APPLICATION FOR ENROLLMENT, as a citizen of the   Chickasaw   Nation,
of   Clifton Gaddis   , born on the   17th   day of   March   , 1904

Name of Father: Will Gaddis   a citizen of the   Chickasaw   Nation.
Name of Mother: Salley Gaddis, nee Benton   a citizen of the   Chickasaw   Nation.

                                Postoffice   Mill Creek, Ind. Ter.

AFFIDAVIT OF MOTHER.

UNITED STATES OF AMERICA, Indian Territory, ⎫
   Southern Judicial   **DISTRICT.** ⎰

I,   Salley Gaddis, Nee Benton   , on oath state that I am   33 or about 33
years of age and a citizen by   blood   , of the   Chickasaw   Nation; that I am the
lawful wife of   Will Gaddis   , who is a citizen, by blood   of the   Chickasaw
Nation; that a   male   child was born to me on   17th day of   March   , 1904;
that said child has been named   Clifton Gaddis   , and was living March 4, 1905.
                                   her
                        Salley x Gaddis
Witnesses To Mark: mark
   ⎰ Richard Haley
   ⎱ B.R. Looney

Subscribed and sworn to before me this   11 day of   April   , 1905

                        James T. Walter
                        Notary Public.

59

AFFIDAVIT OF ATTENDING PHYSICIAN OR MID-WIFE.

UNITED STATES OF AMERICA, Indian Territory, ⎫
  Southern Judicial   **DISTRICT.** ⎭

I,   Mary Haley   , a mid-wife   , on oath state that I attended on Mrs.   Will Gaddis or Mrs Salley Gaddis   , wife of   Will Gaddis   on the 17th day of   March   , 1904; that there was born to her on said date a   male   child; that said child was living March 4, 1905, and is said to have been named Clifton Gaddis

Mary Haley

Witnesses To Mark:
  ⎧
  ⎩

Subscribed and sworn to before me this 11 day of   April   , 1905

James T. Walter
Notary Public.

Chic N.B.
    513   Choctaw 5485.
  "   520

Muskogee, Indian Territory, April 15, 1905.

Will Gaddis,
    Mill Creek, Indian Territory.

Dear Sir:

Receipt is hereby acknowledged of your letter without date, enclosing the affidavits of Sally Gaddis and Mary Haley to the birth of Clifton Gaddis, son of Will and Sally Gaddis, March 17, 1904, and the same have been filed with our records as an application for the enrollment of said child.

Respectfully,

Chairman.

Chic. N.B - 521
    (Foreman Brown
    Born April 8, 1904)

Applications for Enrollment of Chickasaw Newborn
Act of 1905   Volume VII

BIRTH AFFIDAVIT.

DEPARTMENT OF THE INTERIOR.
COMMISSION TO THE FIVE CIVILIZED TRIBES.

IN RE APPLICATION FOR ENROLLMENT, as a citizen of the   Chickasaw   Nation, of   Foreman Brown   , born on the 8th   day of   April   , 1904

Name of Father: Jerome Brown   a citizen of the   Chickasaw   Nation.
Name of Mother: Frances Brown   a citizen of the   Chickasaw   Nation.

Postoffice   Troy, I.T.

AFFIDAVIT OF MOTHER.

UNITED STATES OF AMERICA, Indian Territory,
     Southern   **DISTRICT.**

I,   Frances Brown   , on oath state that I am   20   years of age and a citizen by   blood   , of the   Chickasaw   Nation; that I am the lawful wife of   Jerome Brown   , who is a citizen, by   blood   of the   Chickasaw   Nation; that a male   child was born to me on   the 8th   day of April   , 1904; that said child has been named   Foreman Brown   , and was living March 4, 1905.

Frances Brown

Witnesses To Mark:

Subscribed and sworn to before me this 19th   day of   April   , 1905

JE Williams
Notary Public.

AFFIDAVIT OF ATTENDING PHYSICIAN OR MID-WIFE.

UNITED STATES OF AMERICA, Indian Territory,
     Southern   **DISTRICT.**

I,   Jincy Hamilton   , a   mid-wife   , on oath state that I attended on Mrs.   Frances Brown   , wife of   Jerome Brown   on the   8th   day of   April   , 1904; that there was born to her on said date a   male   child; that said child was living March 4, 1905, and is said to have been named   Foreman Brown

her
Jincy x Hamilton
mark

61

Witnesses To Mark:
   { A T Looney
   { Wilson Wolfe

Subscribed and sworn to before me this 8 day of   May   , 1905

W.F. Noble
Notary Public.

———————————

Muskogee, Indian Territory, May 16, 1905.

Jerome Brown,
     Troy, Indian Territory.

Dear Sir:

Receipt is hereby acknowledged of the affidavits of Frances Brown and Jency[sic] Hamilton to the birth of Foreman Brown, son of Jerome and Frances Brown, April 8, 1904.

It is stated in the affidavit of the mother that she is a citizen by blood of the Chickasaw Nation. If this is correct you are requested to state the name under which she was enrolled, the names of her parents, and if she has selected an allotment of the lands of the Choctaw or Chickasaw Nation please give her roll number as it appears upon her allotment certificate.

This matter should receive immediate attention in order that proper disposition may be made of the application for the enrollment of your child.

Respectfully,

Chairman.

———————————

Troy I. T. 5-25-1905

Mr. Tams Bixby,
     Muskogee, I. T.

Dear Sir:

Yours of the 16th inst received and in reply will say that my wife was enrolled under the name of Frances Pettigrew she has taken her allotment. Her mother name was Jencey Hamilton and her father was George Pettigrew he being a full blood Chickasaw her mother is also a full blood Chickasaw

Hoping this is satisfactory

I am yours truly,

Jerome Brown.

Chic. N.B - 522
> *(Benjamin C. Vaughan, Jr.*
> *Born August 21, 1902)*

W.F.
9-NB-522,

DEPARTMENT OF THE INTERIOR,
COMMISSION TO THE FIVE CIVILIZED TRIBES.

In the matter of the application for the enrollment of Benjamin C. Vaughan, Jr., as a citizen of the Chickasaw Nation.

--: D E C I S I O N :--

It appears from the record herein that on March 4, 1905 there was filed with the Commission application for the enrollment of Benjamin C. Vaughan, Jr., as a citizen of the Chickasaw Nation.

It further appears from the record herein and the records of the Commission that the applicant was born August 21, 1902 and is a son of Benjamin J. Vaughan, a recognized citizen by intermarriage of the Chickasaw Nation who was enrolled by this Commission as such in its decision of May 23, 1905 and Lizzie Vaughan, a white woman claiming no right to Chickasaw citizenship.

The Act of Congress approved March 3, 1905 (Public No. 212) among other things provides:

> "That the Commission to the Five Civilized Tribes is authorized for sixty days after the date of the approval of this act to receive and consider applications for enrollment of children born subsequent to September twenty-fifth, nineteen hundred and two, and prior to March fourth, nineteen hundred and five, and who were living on said latter date, to citizens by blood of the Choctaw and Chickasaw tribes of Indians whose enrollment has been approved by the Secretary of the Interior prior to the date of the approval of this act; and to enroll and make allotments to such children."

It is the opinion of this Commission that inasmuch as the applicant, Benjamin C. Vaughan, Jr., is not a child of a citizen by blood of the Chickasaw Nation the Commission is without authority to receive or consider the application for his enrollment as a citizen of the Chickasaw Nation and that, therefore, the Commission should decline to receive or consider such application, under the provision of law above quoted, and it is so ordered.

COMMISSION TO THE FIVE CIVILIZED TRIBES,

Tams Bixby
Chairman.

TB Needles
Commissioner.

C. R. Breckinbridge
Commissioner.

Muskogee, Indian Territory.
JUN 28 1906

(Copy)

BIRTH AFFIDAVIT.

DEPARTMENT OF THE INTERIOR.
COMMISSION TO THE FIVE CIVILIZED TRIBES.

IN RE APPLICATION FOR ENROLLMENT, as a citizen of the   Chickasaw   Nation, of   Benjamin C. Vaughn[sic], Jr.   , born on the 21st day of August , 1902

Name of Father: B. J. Vaughn   a citizen of the ....Nation.
Name of Mother: Lizzie Vaughn   a citizen of the   Chickasaw Nation.

Postoffice   Alex, I. T.

AFFIDAVIT OF MOTHER.

UNITED STATES OF AMERICA, Indian Territory, ⎱
    Southern   **DISTRICT.** ⎰

   I,   Lizzie Vaughn   , on oath state that I am   27   years of age and a citizen by ...., of the ....Nation; that I am the lawful wife of B J Vaughn   , who is a citizen, by Intermarriage   of the   Chickasaw   Nation; that a   male child was born to me on   21st day of   August   , 1902; that said child has been named   Benjamin C. Vaughn Jr   , and ~~was living March 4, 1905~~. is now living

(signed)   Lizzie Vaughan

Witnesses To Mark:
    ⎧ (Seal)
    ⎩

Subscribed and sworn to before me this 13   day of   April   , 1904

Alger Melton
Notary Public.

AFFIDAVIT OF ATTENDING PHYSICIAN OR MID-WIFE.

UNITED STATES OF AMERICA, Indian Territory, ⎫
   So.   **DISTRICT.** ⎭

    I,   B[sic].M. Johnson[sic]   , a   Physician   , on oath state that I attended on Mrs.   Vaughn   , wife of   B J Vaughn   on the 21   day of   August , 1902; that there was born to her on said date a   male   child; that said child ~~was living March 4, 1905~~, and is said to have been named Benjamin C. Vaughn Jr. is now living

D.M. Johnston

Witnesses To Mark:

⎰
⎱ (Seal)

Subscribed and sworn to before me this 9 day of   April   , 1904

Alger Melton
Notary Public.

9-NB-522.

Muskogee, Indian Territory, June 28, 1905.

B. J. Vaughn[sic],   **COPY**
    Alex, Indian Territory.

Dear Sir:

    Enclosed herewith you will find a copy of the decision of the Commission to the Five Civilized Tribes, rendered June 28, 1905, declining to receive or consider the application for the enrollment of Benjamin C. Vaughn, Jr., as a citizen of the Chickasaw Nation.

    The decision, with the record of proceedings in the case, is this day transmitted to the Secretary of the Interior for review. The final decision of the Secretary will be made known to you as soon as this office is informed of the same.

Respectfully,

SIGNED

Tams Bixby
Chairman.

Registered.
  Enc. 9-Nb[sic]-522.

9-NB-522.

Muskogee, Indian Territory, June 28, 1905.

Mansfield, McMurray & Cornish,   **COPY**
    Attorneys for Choctaw and Chickasaw Nations,
      South McAlester, Indian Territory.

Gentlemen:

    Enclosed herewith you will find a copy of the decision of the Commission to the Five Civilized Tribes, rendered June 28, 1905, declining to receive or consider the application for the enrollment of Benjamin C. Vaughn, Jr., as a citizen of the Chickasaw Nation.

    The decision, with the record of proceedings in the case, is this day transmitted to the Secretary of the Interior for review. The final decision of the Secretary will be made known to you as soon as this office is informed of the same.

Respectfully,

SIGNED

Tams Bixby
Chairman.

Enc. -9 NB 522.

Muskogee, Indian Territory, June 28, 1905.

The Honorable,   **COPY**
    The Secretary of the Interior.

Sir:

    There is herewith transmitted the record of proceedings in the matter of the application for the enrollment of Benjamin C. Vaughan, Jr., as a citizen of the Chickasaw Nation, including the decision of the Commission, dated June 28, 1905, declining to receive or consider said application.

Respectfully,

SIGNED

Tams Bixby
Chairman.

Through the
Commissioner of Indian Affairs.

2 Enc. 9 NB 522.

J.W.H.

FHE.

DEPARTMENT OF THE INTERIOR,

D.C. 50034-1905   WASHINGTON.
I.T.D. 13888-1905   October 30, 1905.

L.R.S.

Commissioner to the Five Civilized Tribes,
    Muskogee, Indian Territory.

Sir:

June 28, 1905, the Commission to the Five Civilized Tribes transmitted the record of proceedings in the matter of the application for the enrollment of Benjamin C. Vaughan, Jr., as a citizen of the Choctaw[sic] Nation, together with its decision of the same date, declining to receive or consider said application.

It seems that this applicant is the minor child of Benjamin J. Vaughan, whose enrollment case was the subject of departmental letter to the Commission to the Five Civilized Tribes of April 1, 1905. From your letter of October 11, 1905, which was also transmitted by the Indian Office with the papers in the case, it appears that the name of the said Benjamin J. Vaughan was placed upon a schedule of the Chickasaw Nation which was approved by the Department subsequently to the date of the approval of the act of March 3, 1905 (33 Stat., 1048). It further appears that the said Benjamin C. Vaughan, Jr., was born in the Chickasaw Nation August 21, 1902. Both parents are white persons.

On June 28, 1905, the Commission to the Five Civilized Tribes held that inasmuch as the applicant is not a child of a citizen <u>by</u> <u>blood</u> of the Chickasaw Nation, the Commission was without authority to receive or consider his application. Accordingly, it declined to receive or consider the same. This decision was rendered under that provision of the act of March 3, 1905, which reads as follows:

Applications for Enrollment of Chickasaw Newborn
Act of 1905   Volume VII

"That the Commission to the Five Civilized Tribes is authorized for sixty days after the date of the approval of this act to receive and consider applications for enrollment of children born subsequent to September twenty-fifth, nineteen hundred and two, and prior to March fourth, nineteen hundred and five, and who were living on said latter date, to citizens by blood of the Choctaw and Chickasaw tribes of Indians whose enrollment has been approved by the Secretary of the Interior prior to the date of the approval of this act; and to enroll and make allotments to such children."

Reporting in the matter October 21, 1905, the Indian Office discussed the rights of the applicant, both under the said act of March 3, 1905, and under the act of July 1, 1902 (32 Stat., 641). Concurring in the views of the Commission as to the construction of the first mentioned of said acts, and expressing the opinion that inasmuch as no application was filed for the child within the time limit provided by section 34 of the last mentioned act, it concluded that he is not entitled to enrollment.

On behalf of the applicant a brief was filed by his attorney, in which the position is taken that said act of March 3, 1905, is not applicable in this case, but that Benjamin C. Vaughan Jr., should be enrolled in accordance with sections 27 and 28 of the act of July 1, 1902, supra. Reliance is placed in this brief upon said sections, because the father of the applicant belonged to the class known as "court citizens", concerning whom section 27 provided:

"That no person claiming right to enrollment and allotment and distribution of tribal property, by virtue of a judgment of the United States court in the Indian Territory under the act of June 10 1896 (29 Stats., 321), and which right is contested by legal proceedings instituted under the provisions of this agreement, shall be enrolled or receive allotment of lands of distribution of tribal property until his right thereto has been finally determined."

Inasmuch as the applicant was born prior to the ratification of the agreement, section 28 is relied upon in said brief as authority for his enrollment. It is contended that as Benjamin J. Vaughan, the applicant's father, was under a legal disability during the ninety days immediately following the ratification of the Choctaw-Chickasaw agreement, an application on behalf of his son during that period was impossible, and onsequently[sic] that the time limit, so named, prescribed by section 34 of the agreement, did not run against said applicant.

In connection with the said decision of the Commission to the Five Civilized Tribes of June 28, 1905, reference is made to the approved opinion of the Assistant Attorney General of September 1, 1905, in the Chickasaw enrollment case of George McKinney. In said opinion the Assistant Attorney General advised that notwithstanding the fact that George McKinney was born to a white person, he was not barred from enrollment simply because the act of March 3, 1905, provides only for the enrollment of children born to citizens "by blood" of the Choctaw and Chickasaw tribes of Indians. In view of said opinion it is not apparent at this time that the decision of the Commission to the Five Civilized Tribes should be affirmed. The Department concurs, however, in the opinion expressed by the Indian Office that the applicant is barred from enrollment by section 34 of the act of July 1, 1902. The argument of the applicant's attorney is considered unsound. The provision of said section 27 upon which he relies relates to court citizens, who necessarily must have been in existence during the period when the Commission to the Five Civilized Tribes was exercising its jurisdiction under said act of June 10, 1896. Only persons then in existence could possibly be considered as parties to cases pending before the citizenship court under said act of July 1, 1901. While this time limit is no doubt arbitrary and works a hardship upon the applicant, his misfortune is no greater than that of Esau Wolf, a full blood Chickasaw, and others, who were barred from enrollment simply because their application were made too late. While the Department considers that the applicant is not barred from enrollment for the reasons stated by the Commission to the Five Civilized Tribes and by the Indian Office in connection with the act of March 3, 1905, it concludes that under said act there is another reason which at this time renders his enrollment impossible. As noted above, the approval of his father's enrollment by the Secretary of the Interior was not given until after the approval of the act last mentioned. Accordingly, under the approved opinion of the Assistant Attorney General dated July 21, 1905, relative to the Creek freedman case of William Durant, et al., the applicant is not, under the strict letter of the law, entitled to enrollment. Final decision will not, however, be rendered at this time, under this provision of the law, inasmuch as it was advised in said opinion that "final action" in the William Durant and similar cases "be withheld until the matter can be presented to the Congress with request for such further action as may be proper and necessary to avoid the apparent inequalities and injustice necessarily growing out of the law as it now stands."

You are request to advise the parties in interest hereof.

Respectfully,
Thos. Ryan
First Assistant Secretary.

Through the
Commissioner of Indian Affairs.

9-NB-522

Muskogee, Indian Territory, November 10, 1905.

B. J. Vaughan,
Alex, Indian Territory.

Dear Sir:

You are hereby advised that on October 30, 1905, the Secretary of the Interior directed that further action be withheld in the matter of the enrollment of your child Benjamin C. Vaughan jr[sic]., as a citizen of the Chickasaw Nation the Chickasaw Nation until the matter can be presented to Congress with request for such further action as may be proper and necessary to avoid the apparent inequality and injustice growing out of the law as it now stands.

You are therefore advised that in accordance with the above instruction no action will be taken in the matter of the enrollment of this child until this office is further directed by the Department.

Respectfully,

Commissioner.

9-NB-522

Muskogee, Indian Territory, November 10, 1905.

Mansfield, McMurray & Cornish,
    Attorneys for Choctaw and Chickasaw Nations,
        South McAlester, Indian Territory.

Gentlemen:

For your information there is inclosed herewith copy of Departmental letter of October 30, 1905 (I.T.D. 13888-1905) instructing that final action in the matter of the application for the enrollment of Benjamin C. Vaughan, Jr., as a citizen of the Chickasaw Nation be withheld until the matter can be presented to Congress with request for such further action as may be proper and necessary to avoid the apparent inequality and injustice growing out of the law as it now stands.

You are therefore advised that in accordance with the above instructions no action will be taken in the matter of the enrollment of this child until this office is further directed by the Department.

Respectfully,

Commissioner.

EB 5-10.

Chic. N.B - 523
    (Winnie Ruby Reynolds
    Born October 12, 1900)
    (Bessie Jewel Reynolds
    Born March 13, 1902)
    (Minnie Myrtle Reynolds
    Born January 21, 1904)

W.F.

9-NB-523.

DEPARTMENT OF THE INTERIOR,
COMMISSION TO THE FIVE CIVILIZED TRIBES.

In the matter of the application for the enrollment of Winnie Ruby Reynolds, Minnie Myrtle Reynolds and Bessie Jewel Reynolds as citizens of the Chickasaw Nation.

--: D E C I S I O N :--

It appears from the record herein that on April 10, 1905 there were filed with the Commission application for the enrollment of Winnie Ruby Reynolds, Minnie Myrtle Reynolds and Bessie Jewel Reynolds as citizens of the Chickasaw Nation.

It further appears from the record herein and the records of the Commission that the applicants Winnie Ruby Reynolds, Minnie Myrtle Reynolds and Bessie Jewel Reynolds were born on October 12, 1900, March 13, 1902 and January 21, 1904, respectively, and are children of Charles A. Reynolds, a recognized and enrolled citizen by intermarriage of the Chickasaw Nation whose name appears opposite number 526 upon the final roll of citizens by intermarriage of the Chickasaw Nation, approved by the Secretary of the Interior November 16, 1904, and Maud Reynolds, a citizen of the United States.

The Act of Congress approved March 3, 1905 (Public No. 212) No. 212) among other things provides:

"That the Commission to the Five Civilized Tribes is hereby authorized for sixty days after the date of the approval of this act to receive and consider applications for enrollment of infant children born prior to September twenty-fifth, nineteen hundred and two, and who were living on said date, to citizens by blood of the Choctaw and Chickasaw tribes of Indians whose enrollment has been approved by the Secretary of the Interior prior to the date of the approval of this act; and to enroll and make allotments to such children."

"That the Commission to the Five Civilized Tribes is authorized for sixty days after the date of the approval of this act to receive and consider applications for enrollment of children born subsequent to September twenty-fifth, nineteen hundred and two, and prior to March fourth, nineteen hundred and five, and who were living on said latter date, to citizens by blood of the Choctaw and Chickasaw tribes of Indians whose enrollment has been approved by the Secretary of the Interior prior to the date of the approval of this act; and to enroll and make allotments to such children."

It is the opinion of this Commission that, inasmuch as Winnie Ruby Reynolds, Minnie Myrtle Reynolds, and Bessie Jewel Reynolds as not children of a citizen by blood of the Chickasaw Nation, the Commission is without authority to receive or consider said applications, under the provisions of law above quoted, and it is so ordered.

COMMISSION TO THE FIVE CIVILIZED TRIBES,

Tams Bixby
Chairman.
TB Needles
Commissioner.
C. R. Breckinbridge
Commissioner.

Muskogee, Indian Territory.
JUN 28 1905

(Copy)

BIRTH AFFIDAVIT.

DEPARTMENT OF THE INTERIOR.
COMMISSION TO THE FIVE CIVILIZED TRIBES.

IN RE APPLICATION FOR ENROLLMENT, as a citizen of the   Chickasaw   Nation,
of   Winnie Ruby Reynolds   , born on the   12   day of   October   , 1900

Name of Father: Charles A Reynolds   a citizen of the   Chickasaw   Nation.
Name of Mother: Maud Reynolds   a citizen of the   Chickasaw   Nation.

Postoffice   Chickasha, I.T.

AFFIDAVIT OF MOTHER.

UNITED STATES OF AMERICA, Indian Territory,
     Southern   **DISTRICT.**

     I,   Maud Reynolds   , on oath state that I am   24   years of age and a citizen
by   blood   , of the   United States   Nation; that I am the lawful wife of
Charles A. Reynolds   , who is a citizen, by   Marriage   of the   Chickasaw
Nation; that a   female   child was born to me on   12   day of   October   , 1900;
that said child has been named   Winnie Ruby Reynolds   , and was living March 4,
1905.

(signed)   Maud Reynolds

Witnesses To Mark:

     Subscribed and sworn to before me this 5th   day of   April   , 1905
Seal

JE Williams
Notary Public.

72

AFFIDAVIT OF ATTENDING PHYSICIAN OR MID-WIFE.

UNITED STATES OF AMERICA, Indian Territory, ⎫
    Southern   **DISTRICT.** ⎬

       I, Martha A. Foreman   , a Mid-wife   , on oath state that I attended on Mrs.   Maud Reynolds   , wife of   Charles A. Reynolds   on the 12   day of October   , 1900; that there was born to her on said date a   female   child; that said child was living March 4, 1905, and is said to have been named Winnie Ruby Reynolds

                          (signed) Martha A. Foreman

Witnesses To Mark:

    { Seal

    Subscribed and sworn to before me this 8 day of   April   , 1905

                          J.L. Lindsey
                                 Notary Public.

(Copy)

BIRTH AFFIDAVIT.

DEPARTMENT OF THE INTERIOR.
COMMISSION TO THE FIVE CIVILIZED TRIBES.

       IN RE APPLICATION FOR ENROLLMENT, as a citizen of the   Chickasaw   Nation, of   Minnie Myrtle Reynolds   , born on the 13 day of March , 1902

Name of Father: Charles A Reynolds   a citizen of the   Chickasaw Nation.
Name of Mother: Maud Reynolds   a citizen of the   Chickasaw Nation.

                    Postoffice   Chickasha

AFFIDAVIT OF MOTHER.

UNITED STATES OF AMERICA, Indian Territory, ⎫
    Southern   **DISTRICT.** ⎬

       I,   Maud Reynolds   , on oath state that I am 24   years of age and a citizen by   blood   , of the   United States   Nation; that I am the lawful wife of Charles A. Reynolds   , who is a citizen, by Marriage   of the   Chickasaw Nation; that a   female   child was born to me on 13   day of   March   , 1902; that said child has been named Minnie Myrtle Reynolds   , and was living March 4, 1905.

                    (signed) Maud Reynolds

Witnesses To Mark:

{

Subscribed and sworn to before me this 5th day of   April   , 1905

Seal

JE Williams
Notary Public.

AFFIDAVIT OF ATTENDING PHYSICIAN OR MID-WIFE.

UNITED STATES OF AMERICA, Indian Territory,
Southern   DISTRICT.

I, J Hampton Stumm   , a Physician   , on oath state that I attended on Mrs.   Maud Reynolds   , wife of   Charles A. Reynolds   on the 13   day of March   , 1902; that there was born to her on said date a   female   child; that said child was living March 4, 1905, and is said to have been named Minnie Myrtle Reynolds

(Signed) Dr. J. Hampton Stumm

Witnesses To Mark:

{ Seal

Subscribed and sworn to before me this 8 day of   April   , 1905

Stephen Brown
Notary Public.

(Copy)

BIRTH AFFIDAVIT.

DEPARTMENT OF THE INTERIOR.
COMMISSION TO THE FIVE CIVILIZED TRIBES.

IN RE APPLICATION FOR ENROLLMENT, as a citizen of the   Chickasaw   Nation, of   Bessie Jewel Reynolds   , born on the 21 day of January   , 1904

Name of Father: Charles A Reynolds   a citizen of the   Chickasaw Nation.
Name of Mother: Maud Reynolds   a citizen of the   Chickasaw Nation.

Postoffice   Chickasha, I.T.

AFFIDAVIT OF MOTHER.

UNITED STATES OF AMERICA, Indian Territory, ⎫
Southern   **DISTRICT.** ⎰

I,   Maud Reynolds   , on oath state that I am   24   years of age and a citizen by   blood   , of the   United States   Nation; that I am the lawful wife of Charles A. Reynolds   , who is a citizen, by Marriage   of the   Chickasaw Nation; that a   female   child was born to me on 21   day of   January   , 1904; that said child has been named   Bessie Jewel Reynolds   , and was living March 4, 1905.

(Signed) Maud Reynolds

Witnesses To Mark:

{

Subscribed and sworn to before me this 5th   day of   April   , 1905
Seal

JE Williams
Notary Public.

AFFIDAVIT OF ATTENDING PHYSICIAN OR MID-WIFE.

UNITED STATES OF AMERICA, Indian Territory, ⎫
Southern   **DISTRICT.** ⎰

I, J Hampton Stumm   , a Physician   , on oath state that I attended on Mrs.   Maud Reynolds   , wife of   Charles A. Reynolds   on the 21   day of January   , 1904; that there was born to her on said date a   female   child; that said child was living March 4, 1905, and is said to have been named Bessie Jewel Reynolds

(Signed) Dr. J. Hampton Stumm

Witnesses To Mark:

{ Seal

Subscribed and sworn to before me this 8th day of   April   , 1905

Stephen Brown
Notary Public.

9-1591.

Muskogee, Indian Territory, April 17, 1905.

Charles A. Reynolds,
    Chickasha, Indian Territory.

Dear Sir:

Receipt is hereby acknowledged of the affidavits of Maud Reynolds and Martha A. Foreman to the birth of Winnie Ruby Reynolds; also the affidavits of Maud Reynolds and Dr. J. Hampton Stumm to the birth of Minnie Myrtle Reynolds and Bessie Jewel Reynolds, children of Charles A. and Maud Reynolds, October 12, 1900, and March 13, 1902 and January 21, 1904, respectively.

It appears from our records that you are an intermarried citizen of the Chickasaw Nation and your wife, Maud Reynolds, is a citizen of the United States, and as the Act of Congress approved March 3, 1905, authorizes the Commission for a period of sixty days from that date to receive applications for the enrollment of children born to enrolled citizens by blood of the Choctaw and Chickasaw Nations prior to March 4, 1905, you will see that the Commission is withour[sic] authority to enroll your children by a non-citizen mother.

        Respectfully,

              Chairman.

9-NB-523.

Muskogee, Indian Territory, June 28, 1905.

Charles A. Reynolds,   **COPY**
    Chickasha, Indian Territory.

Dear Sir:

Enclosed herewith you will find a copy of the decision of the Commission to the Five Civilized Tribes, rendered June 28, 1905, declining to receive or consider the application for the enrollment of Winnie Ruby Reynolds, Minnie Myrtle Reynolds and Bessie Jewel Reynolds as citizens of the Chickasaw Nation.

The decision, with the record of proceedings in the case, is this day transmitted to the Secretary of the Interior for review. The final decision of the Secretary will be made known to you as soon as this office is informed of the same.

Respectfully,

SIGNED   *Tams Bixby*
Chairman.

Registered.
Enc. 9-NB-523.

9-NB-523.

Muskogee, Indian Territory, June 28, 1905.

Mansfield, McMurray & Cornish,   **COPY**
    Attorneys for Choctaw and Chickasaw Nations,
        South McAlester, Indian Territory.

Gentlemen:

Enclosed herewith you will find a copy of the decision of the Commission to the Five Civilized Tribes, rendered June 28, 1905, declining to receive or consider the application for the enrollment of Winnie Ruby Reynolds, Minnie Myrtle Reynolds and Bessie Jewel Reynolds as citizens of the Chickasaw Nation.

The decision, with the record of proceedings in the case, is this day transmitted to the Secretary of the Interior for review. The final decision of the Secretary will be made known to you as soon as this office is informed of the same.

Respectfully,

SIGNED   *Tams Bixby*
Chairman.

Enc. --9-NB-523.

Muskogee, Indian Territory, June 28, 1905.
COPY

The Honorable,
    The Secretary of the Interior,

Sir:

There is transmitted herewith the record of proceedings in the matter of the applications for the enrollment of Winnie Ruby Reynolds, Minnie Myrtle Reynolds and Bessie Jewel Reynolds as citizens of the Chickasaw Nation, including the decision of the Commission, dated June 28, 1905, declining to receive or consider said applications.

Respectfully,

SIGNED   *Tams Bixby*
Chairman.

Through the
Commissioner of Indian Affairs.

2 Enc. 9-NB-523.

DEPARTMENT OF THE INTERIOR,
OFFICE OF INDIAN AFFAIRS,
WASHINGTON. July 25, 1905.

Land.
50898-1905.

The Honorable,
The Secretary of the Interior.

Sir:

I have the honor to enclose a report from the Commission to the Five Civilized Tribes, dated June 28, 1905, transmitting the record of the application made July 10, 1905, for enrollment as citizens of the Chickasaw Nation by Winnie Ruby, Minnie Myrtle and Bessie Jewel Reynolds.

June 28, 1905, the Commission decided adversely to the applicants.

The record shows that the applicants were born October 12, 1900, March 13, 1902 and January 21, 1904, respectively, and are children of Charles A Reynolds, a recognized and enrolled citizen by intermarriage of the Chickasaw Nation, whose name appears opposite No. 525 upon the final roll of citizens by intermarriage of the Chickasaw Nation approved by the Department November 16, 1904, and Maud Reynolds, a citizen of the United States.

In view of the record and of the act of March 3, 1905 (33 Stats., 1071) the approval of the Commission's decision adverse to the applicants is recommended.

Very respectfully,
C. F. Larrabee
Acting Commissioner.

M. M. M.
W.

DEPARTMENT OF THE INTERIOR,
WASHINGTON.   GR

LLB

D C   50030-1905.   October 28, 1905.
I T D   9214-1905.

LRS

Commissioner to the Five Civilized Tribes,
 Muskogee, Indian Territory.

Sir:

  June 28, 1905, the Commission to the Five Civilized Tribes transmitted the record of the application made April 10, 1905, under the act of March 3, 1905, (33 Stat., 1048-1071), for the enrollment of Winnie Ruby Reynolds, Minnie Myrtle Reynolds, and Bessie Jewel Reynolds, infants born, respectively, October 12, 1900, March 13, 1902 and January 21, 1904, as citizens by blood of the Chickasaw Nation, including the decision of the Commission of same date declining to receive or consider said applications on the ground that the above named applicants are not the children of a citizen by blood of the Chickasaw Nation, and therefore the Commission is without authority to receive or consider the same.

  July 25, 1905, the Acting Commissioner of Indian Affairs reporting thereon, recommended that the decision of the Commission, declining to receive or consider said applications, on grounds stated, be affirmed. A copy of his letter is inclosed.

  The Department concurs in the recommendation made and the decision of the Commission to the Five Civilized Tribes dated June 28, 1905, declining to receive or consider the applications for the enrollment of Winnie Ruby Reynolds, Minnie Myrtle Reynolds and Bessie Jewel Reynolds as citizens by blood of the Chickasaw Nation is hereby affirmed.

       Respectfully,
        E. A. Hitchcock,
         Secretary.
         T.R.

1 inclosure.

9-NB-523

Muskogee, Indian Territory, November 8, 1905.

Charles A. Reynolds,
   Chickasha, Indian Territory.

Dear Sir:

You are hereby notified that the Secretary of the Interior under date of October 28, 1905, affirmed the decision of the Commission to the Five Civilized Tribes, dated June 28, 1905, declining to receive or consider the application for the enrollment of Winnie Ruby Reynolds, Minnie Myrtle Reynolds and Bessie Jewel Reynolds as citizens of the Chickasaw Nation.

Respectfully,

Commissioner.

9-NB-523

Muskogee, Indian Territory, November 8, 1905.

Mansfield, McMurray & Cornish,
   Attorneys for Choctaw and Chickasaw Nations,
      South McAlester, Indian Territory.

Gentlemen:

You are hereby notified that the Secretary of the Interior under date of October 28, 1905, affirmed the decision of the Commission to the Five Civilized Tribes, dated June 28, 1905, declining to receive or consider the application for the enrollment of Winnie Ruby Reynolds, Minnie Myrtle Reynolds and Bessie Jewel Reynolds as citizens of the Chickasaw Nation.

Respectfully,

Commissioner.

Chic. N.B - 524
   (May Bell Porter
   Born February 7, 1905)

CHICKASAW   524

NEW BORN

ACT OF CONGRESS APPROVED MARCH 30, 1905.

May Bell Porter
(Born February 7, 1905)

CANCELLED

Record transferred to Chickasaw   New Born #22

ACT OF CONGRESS APPROVED APRIL 26, 1906.

JUL 13 1906

Chic. N.B - 525
(Velma Polk
Born April 28, 1905)

CHICKASAW   525

NEW BORN

ACT OF CONGRESS APPROVED MARCH 30, 1905.

Velma Polk
(Born April 28, 1905)

CANCELLED

Record transferred to
CHICKASAW   NEW BORN No 311

ACT OF CONGRESS APPROVED APRIL 26, 1906.

AUG 8- 1906

Chic. N.B - 526
(Young Love
Born April 1, 1903)

DEPARTMENT OF THE INTERIOR,
COMMISSION TO THE FIVE CIVILIZED TRIBES.

Record in the matter of the application for enrollment as a citizen by blood of the Chickasaw Nation of:

YOUNG LOVE   9-NB-526.

———————

W.F.
9-NB-526.

DEPARTMENT OF THE INTERIOR,
COMMISSION TO THE FIVE CIVILIZED TRIBES.

In the matter of the application for the enrollment of Young Love as a citizen by blood of the Chickasaw Nation.

---oOo---

It appears from the record herein that on May 1, 1905 there was filed with the Commission application for the enrollment of Young Love as a citizen by blood of the Chickasaw Nation.

It further appears from the record herein and the records of the Commission that the applicant was born April 1, 1903; that he is a son of Edward Davis Love, a recognized and enrolled citizen by blood of the Chickasaw Nation whose name appears as number 3609 upon the final roll of citizens by blood of the Chickasaw Nation, approved by the Secretary of the Interior December 12, 1902, and Mary Caroline Love, a recognized and enrolled citizen by intermarriage of the Chickasaw Nation; and that said applicant died October 25, 1904.

The Act of Congress approved March 3, 1905 (Public No. 212) No. 212) among other things provides:

"That the Commission to the Five Civilized Tribes is authorized for sixty days after the date of the approval of this act to receive and consider applications for enrollment of children born subsequent to September twenty-fifth, nineteen hundred and two, and prior to March fourth, nineteen hundred and five, and who were living on said latter date, to citizens by blood of the Choctaw and Chickasaw tribes of Indians whose enrollment has been approved by the Secretary of the Interior prior to the date of the approval of this act; and to enroll and make allotments to such children."

It is, therefore, hereby ordered that the application for the enrollment of Young Love as a citizen by blood of the Chickasaw Nation be dismissed in accordance with the order of the Commission of March 31, 1905.

COMMISSION TO THE FIVE CIVILIZED TRIBES,

Applications for Enrollment of Chickasaw Newborn
Act of 1905   Volume VII

Tams Bixby
Commissioner.

Muskogee, Indian Territory.
JUN 28 1905

BIRTH AFFIDAVIT.

DEPARTMENT OF THE INTERIOR.
COMMISSION TO THE FIVE CIVILIZED TRIBES.

IN RE APPLICATION FOR ENROLLMENT, as a citizen of the   Chickasaw   Nation, of   Young Love   , born on the 1 day of April , 1903

Name of Father: Edward Davis Love   a citizen of the   Chickasaw   Nation.
Name of Mother: Mary Caroline Love   a citizen of the   Chickasaw   Nation.

Postoffice   Mead, I.T.

AFFIDAVIT OF MOTHER.

UNITED STATES OF AMERICA, Indian Territory,
      Central   DISTRICT.

I,   Mary Caroline Love   , on oath state that I am   about 36   years of age and a citizen by   intermarriage   , of the   Chickasaw   Nation; that I am the lawful wife of   Edward Davis Love   , who is a citizen, by   blood   of the Chickasaw   Nation; that a   male   child was born to me on   the 1st day of April   , 1903; that said child has been named   Young Love   , and was living ~~March 4, 1905~~ Oct 25 1904 - and Died Oct 25- 1904

Mary Caroline Love
Witnesses To Mark:

Subscribed and sworn to before me this 30 day of   April   , 1905

E.Q. Franklin
Notary Public.

Applications for Enrollment of Chickasaw Newborn
Act of 1905   Volume VII

AFFIDAVIT OF ATTENDING PHYSICIAN OR MID-WIFE.

UNITED STATES OF AMERICA, Indian Territory, ⎫
   Central   DISTRICT. ⎭

    I,   Mrs. J.A. Pittman   , a   midwife   , on oath state that I attended on Mrs. Mary Caroline Love   , wife of Edward Davis Love   on the 1 day of April   , 1903; that there was born to her on said date a   male   child; that said child was ~~living March 4, 1905~~, and is said to have been named Young Love
Oct 25 - 1904 and Died Oct 25 1904

                                 Mrs. J A Pittman midwife

Witnesses To Mark:

    Subscribed and sworn to before me this 29 day of April   , 1905

                        E.Q. Franklin
                             Notary Public.

                                 9--1239.

           Muskogee, Indian Territory, May 4, 1905.

Edward Davis Love,
    Mead, Indian Territory.

Dear Sir:

    Receipt is hereby acknowledged of the affidavits of Mary Carline[sic] Love and Mrs. J. A. Pittman to the birth of Young Love, son of Edward Davis and Mary Caroline Love, April 1, 1903.

    It appears from the affidavits that this child died October 25, 1904.   Under the provisions of the act of Congress approved March 3, 1905, the Commission is authorized for a period of sixty days from that date to receive applications for the enrollment of children born to enrolled citizens by blood of the Choctaw and Chickasaw Nations between September 25, 1902 and March 4, 1905, and living on the latter date.

    You will therefore see that the Commission is without authority to enroll your child.
                     Respectfully,

                             Chairman.

9-NB-526.

Muskogee, Indian Territory, June 28, 1905.

Edward Davis Love,
    Mead, Indian Territory.

Dear Sir:

    Inclosed herewith you will find a copy of the order of this Commission, dated June 28, 1905, dismissing the application for the enrollment of Young Love as a citizen by blood of the Chickasaw Nation.

           Respectfully,

              SIGNED   *Tams Bixby*

Registered.   Chairman.
Incl. 9-NB-526.

9-NB-526.

Muskogee, Indian Territory, June 28, 1905.

Mansfield, McMurray & Cornish,   **COPY**
    Attorneys for Choctaw and Chickasaw Nations,
        South McAlester, Indian Territory.

Gentlemen:

    Inclosed herewith you will find a copy of the order of this Commission, dated June 28, 1905, dismissing the application for the enrollment of Young Love as a citizen by blood of the Chickasaw Nation.

           Respectfully,

           SIGNED   *Tams Bixby*
                    Chairman.

Incl. 9-NB-526.

Chic. N.B - 527
     (Luther Bell Smith
     Born April 3, 1905)

CHICKASAW   527

NEW BORN

ACT OF CONGRESS APPROVED MARCH 30, 1905.

Luther Bell Smith
(Born April 3, 1905)

CANCELLED

Record transferred to Chickasaw   New Born   *(Illegible)*

ACT OF CONGRESS APPROVED APRIL 26, 1906.

JUL 13 1906

Chic. N.B - 528
　　　(Lawrence C. Kinney
　　　Born March 26, 1905)

W.F.
9-NB-528.

DEPARTMENT OF THE INTERIOR,
COMMISSION TO THE FIVE CIVILIZED TRIBES.

In the matter of the application for the enrollment of Lawrence C. Kinney as a citizen by blood of the Chickasaw Nation.

--: D E C I S I O N :--

It appears from the record herein that on May 1, 1905 there was filed with the Commission application for the enrollment of Lawrence C. Kinney as a citizen by blood of the Chickasaw Nation.

It further appears from the record herein and the records of the Commission that the applicant was born March 26, 1905 and is a son of James Kinney, a recognized and enrolled citizen by blood of the Chickasaw Nation whose name appears opposite number 1878 upon the final roll of citizens by blood of the Chickasaw Nation, approved by the Secretary of the Interior December 12, 1902, and Oda Ellen Kinney, a noncitizen.

The Act of Congress approved March, 3, 1905 (Public No. 212) among other things provides:

86

Applications for Enrollment of Chickasaw Newborn
Act of 1905   Volume VII

"That the Commission to the Five Civilized Tribes is authorized for ninety days after the date of the approval of this act to receive and consider applications for enrollment of infant children born subsequent to September twenty-fifth, nineteen hundred and two, and prior to March fourth, nineteen hundred and five, and living on said latter date, to citizens of the Choctaw and Chickasaw tribes of Indians whose enrollment has been approved by the Secretary of the Interior prior to the date of the approval of this act, and to enroll and make allotments to such children."

It is the opinion of this Commission that, inasmuch as the said Lawrence C. Kinney was not born prior to March 4, 1905, the Commission is without authority to receive or consider the application for his enrollment as a citizen by blood of the Chickasaw Nation and that, therefore, the Commission should decline to receive or consider such application, under the provision of law above quoted and it is so ordered.

COMMISSION TO THE FIVE CIVILIZED TRIBES,

Tams Bixby
Chairman.
TB Needles
Commissioner.
C. R. Breckinbridge
Commissioner.

Muskogee, Indian Territory.
JUN 28 1905

BIRTH AFFIDAVIT.

DEPARTMENT OF THE INTERIOR.
COMMISSION TO THE FIVE CIVILIZED TRIBES.

IN RE APPLICATION FOR ENROLLMENT, as a citizen of the   Chickasaw   Nation, of   Lawrence C. Kinney   , born on the 26th   day of   March   , 1905

Name of Father: James C Kinney   a citizen of the   Chickasaw Nation.
Name of Mother: Oda Ellen Kinney   a citizen of the   Chickasaw Nation.

Postoffice   Sulphur Ind Ter

AFFIDAVIT OF MOTHER.

UNITED STATES OF AMERICA, Indian Territory, ⎫
  Southern   DISTRICT. ⎰

I,   Oda Ellen Kinney   , on oath state that I am 18   years of age and a citizen by   intermarriage   , of the   Chickasaw   Nation; that I am the lawful wife of   James C Kinney   , who is a citizen, by Blood   of the   Chickasaw

87

Applications for Enrollment of Chickasaw Newborn
Act of 1905   Volume VII

Nation; that a   Male   child was born to me on   26th   day of   March   , 1905; that said child has been named   Lawrence C Kinney   , and was living March 4, 1905.

Oda Ellen Kinney

Witnesses To Mark:

{

Subscribed and sworn to before me this   29th day of   April   , 1905

My Commission Expires June 27, 1907   AD Goodenough
Notary Public.

AFFIDAVIT OF ATTENDING PHYSICIAN OR MID-WIFE.

UNITED STATES OF AMERICA, Indian Territory, }
    Southern   **DISTRICT.** }

I,   J Lee Borden   , a   MD   , on oath state that I attended on Mrs.   Oda Ellen Kinney   , wife of   James C Kinney   on the   26th   day of March   , 1905; that there was born to her on said date a   male   child; that said child was living March 4, 1905, and is said to have been named Lawrence C Kinney

J Lee Borden M.D.

Witnesses To Mark:

{

Subscribed and sworn to before me this   29th day of   April   , 1905

My Commission Expires June 27, 1907   AD Goodenough
Notary Public.

9-NB-528.

Muskogee, Indian Territory, June 28, 1905.

James Kinney,   **COPY**
    Sulphur, Indian Territory.

Dear Sir:

Enclosed herewith you will find a copy of the decision of the Commissioner to the Five Civilized Tribes, rendered June 28, 1905, declining to receive or consider the application for the enrollment of Lawrence C. Kinney as a citizen by blood of the Chickasaw Nation.

88

The decision, with the record of proceedings in the case, is this day transmitted to the Secretary of the Interior for review. The final decision of the Secretary will be made known to you as soon as this office is informed of the same.

Respectfully,

SIGNED

Tams Bixby
Chairman.

Registered.
Enc. 9-NB-528.

9-NB-528.

Muskogee, Indian Territory, June 28, 1905.

Mansfield, McMurray & Cornish,   **COPY**
      Attorneys for Choctaw and Chickasaw Nations,
            South McAlester, Indian Territory.

Gentlemen:

Enclosed herewith you will find a copy of the decision of the Commissioner to the Five Civilized Tribes, rendered June 28, 1905, declining to receive or consider the application for the enrollment of Lawrence C. Kinney as a citizen by blood of the Chickasaw Nation.

The decision, with the record of proceedings in the case, is this day transmitted to the Secretary of the Interior for review. The final decision of the Secretary will be made known to you as soon as this office is informed of the same.

Respectfully,

SIGNED

Tams Bixby
Chairman.

Enc. 9-NB-528.

Muskogee, Indian Territory, June 28, 1905.

The Honorable,   **COPY**
      The Secretary of the Interior.

Sir:

There is herewith transmitted the record of proceedings in the matter of the application for the enrollment of Lawrence C. Kinney as a citizen by blood of the

Chickasaw Nation, including the decision of the Commission, dated June 29, 1905, declining to receive or consider said application.

Respectfully,

CHNOIS   *Tams Bixby*

Chairman.

Through the
Commissioner of Indian Affairs.

2 Enc. 9-NB-528.

DEPARTMENT OF THE INTERIOR,
OFFICE OF INDIAN AFFAIRS,
WASHINGTON. July 25, 1905.

Land.
50894-1905.

The Honorable,
The Secretary of the Interior.

Sir:

I have the honor to enclose a report from the Commission to the Five Civilized Tribes, dated June 28, 1905, transmitting the record of the application for enrollment as a citizen by blood of the Chickasaw Nation of Lawrence C. Kinney.

June 28, 1905, the Commission decided adversely to the applicants.

The record shows that the applicant was born March 26, 1905, is a son of James Kinney, a recognized and enrolled citizen by blood of the Chickasaw Nation whose name appears opposite No. 1878 of a final roll of citizens by blood of the Chickasaw Nation approved by the Department December 12, 1902, and Oda Ellen Kinney, a non-citizen.

In view of the record and of the act of March 3, 1905 (33 Stats., 1071) the approval of the Commission's decision adverse to the applicant is recommended.

Very respectfully,
C. F. Larrabee
Acting Commissioner.

M M M
W

DEPARTMENT OF THE INTERIOR,
WASHINGTON.   GR

LLB

D C   50031-1905.   October 28, 1905.
I T D   9002-1905.

LRS

Commissioner to the Five Civilized Tribes,
    Muskogee, Indian Territory.

Sir:

June 28, 1905, the Commission to the Five Civilized Tribes transmitted the record of the application made May 1, 1902, under the act of March 3, 1905, (33 Stat., 1048-1071), for the enrollment of Lawrence C. Kinney, an infant, born March 26, 1905, as a citizen by blood of the Chickasaw Nation, including the decision of the Commission dated June 28, 1905, declining to receive or consider said application, on the ground that the said Lawrence C. Kinney was not born prior to March 4, 1905, and the Commission is therefore without authority to receive or consider the same.

July 22, 1905, the Acting Commissioner of Indian Affairs reporting thereon, recommended that the decision of the Commission declining to receive or consider said application be affirmed. A copy of his letter is inclosed.

The Department concurs in the recommendation made and the decision of the Commission to the Five Civilized Tribes dated June 28, 1905, declining to receive or consider the application for the enrollment of Lawrence C. Kinney, an infant, as a citizen by blood of the Chickasaw Nation is hereby affirmed.

                          Respectfully,
                              E. A. Hitchcock,
                                  Secretary. T.R.

1 inclosure.

9-NB-528

Muskogee, Indian Territory, November 8, 1905.

James Kinney,
    Sulphur, Indian Territory.

Dear Sir:

You are hereby notified that the Secretary of the Interior under date of October 28, 1905, affirmed the decision of the Commission to the Five Civilized Tribes, dated June 28, 1905, declining to receive or consider the application for the enrollment of Lawrence C. Kinney as a citizen by blood of the Chickasaw Nation.

Respectfully,

Commissioner.

9-NB-528

Muskogee, Indian Territory, November 8, 1905.

Mansfield, McMurray & Cornish,
    Attorneys for Choctaw and Chickasaw Nations,
        South McAlester, Indian Territory.

Gentlemen:

You are hereby notified that the Secretary of the Interior under date of October 28, 1905, affirmed the decision of the Commission to the Five Civilized Tribes, dated June 28, 1905, declining to receive or consider the application for the enrollment of Lawrence C. Kinney as a citizen by blood of the Chickasaw Nation.

Respectfully,

Commissioner.

COPY

Muskogee, Indian Territory, November 13, 1906[sic].

The Honorable,
  The Secretary of the Interior.

Sir:

June 28, 1905, the Commission to the Five Civilized Tribes rendered its decision declining to receive or consider the application of Laurence[sic] C. Kinney for enrollment as a new born citizen of the Chickasaw Nation under the act of Congress approved March 3, 1905, for the reason that said child was born subsequent to March 3, 1905 and October 28, 1905, this action was approved by the Department.

In view of the provision of Section 2 of the Act of Congress approved April 26, 1906, I have the honor to request the return of the record in this case for readjudication under said act.

Respectfully,
SIGNED

Tams Bixby
Commissioner.

Through the Commissioner
  of Indian Affairs.

9-NB-528

Muskogee, Indian Territory, January 2, 1907.

James Kinney,
  Sulphur, Indian Territory.

Dear Sir:

In the matter of the application for the enrollment of your minor son, Lawrence C. Kinney, as a citizen by blood of the Chickasaw Nation, you are advised that the Department on December 20, 1906, returned the record in the matter of said application for readjudication under the provisions of Section 520 of the Act of Congress approved April 26, 1906 (34 Stats., 137).

It will, therefore, be necessary for you to forward this office at the earliest possible date a new affidavit of birth, and for this purpose a blank is enclosed. It will also be necessary for you to forward this office either the original or a certified copy of your certificate of marriage to Oda Ellen Kinney, the mother of said child.

Respectfully,

Commissioner.

Encl. B. A.

9-NB-528

Muskogee, Indian Territory, January 25, 1907.

James C. Kinney,
    Sulphur, Indian Territory.

Dear Sir:

In the matter of the application for the enrollment of your child Lawrence C. Kinney as a minor citizen of the Chickasaw Nation under the Act of Congress approved April 26, 1906, there is enclosed herewith a blank upon which you should forward at once affidavits showing the birth of this child and that he was living March 4, 1906.

This matter should recieved[sic] immediate attention and this information should be forwarded so as to reache[sic] this office not later thatn[sic] January 29, 1907.

Respectfully,

B.C.   Commissioner.

Chic. N.B - 529
    (Frank Flemmons
    Born February 22, 1905)

BIRTH AFFIDAVIT.

DEPARTMENT OF THE INTERIOR.
COMMISSION TO THE FIVE CIVILIZED TRIBES.

IN RE APPLICATION FOR ENROLLMENT, as a citizen of the   Chickasaw   Nation, of   Frank Flemmons   , born on the   22   day of   Feby   , 1905

Name of Father: Baily Flemmons   a citizen of the   Chickasaw   Nation.
Name of Mother: Annie Viola Flemmons   a citizen of the   Chickasaw   Nation.

Postoffice   Kemp Ind Ter

Applications for Enrollment of Chickasaw Newborn
Act of 1905   Volume VII

AFFIDAVIT OF MOTHER.

UNITED STATES OF AMERICA, Indian Territory, ⎱
    Central   DISTRICT. ⎰

    I,   Annie Viola Flemmons   , on oath state that I am   19   years of age and a citizen by   Birth   , of the   Chickasaw   Nation; that I am the lawful wife of Baily Flemmons   , who is a citizen, by   Marriage   of the   Chickasaw Nation; that a   male   child was born to me on 22   day of Feby   , 1905; that said child has been named   Frank Flemmons   , and was living March 4, 1905.

                                          Annie Viola Flemmons

Witnesses To Mark:

           {

    Subscribed and sworn to before me this 8 day of   April   , 1905

                              S T Johns
                                 Notary Public.

AFFIDAVIT OF ATTENDING PHYSICIAN OR MID-WIFE.

UNITED STATES OF AMERICA, Indian Territory, ⎱
    Central   DISTRICT. ⎰

    I,   S J Grizell   , a   mid wife   , on oath state that I attended on Mrs.   Annie Viola   , wife of   Baily Flemmons   on the 22 day of Feby   , 1905; that there was born to her on said date a   male   child; that said child was living March 4, 1905, and is said to have been named Frank Flemmons

                                 S J Grizell

Witnesses To Mark:

           {

    Subscribed and sworn to before me this 8 day of   April   , 1905

                              S T Johns
                                 Notary Public.

Applications for Enrollment of Chickasaw Newborn
Act of 1905   Volume VII

Muskogee, Indian Territory, April 15, 1905.

Baily Flemmons,
    Kemp, Indian Territory.

Dear Sir:

Receipt is hereby acknowledged of the affidavits of Annie Viola Flemmons and S. J. Grizele[sic] to the birth of Frank Flemmons, son of Baily and Annie Viola Flemmons February 22, 1905.

It is stated in the affidavit of the mother that she is a citizen by blood of the Chickasaw Nation. If this is correct you are requested to state the name under which she is enrolled, the names of her parents, and if she has selected an allotment of the lands of the Choctaw or Chickasaw Nation please give her roll number as it appears upon her allotment certificate.

Respectfully,

Chairman.

———————

Muskogee, Indian Territory, May 29, 1905.

Baily Flemmons,
    Kemp, Indian Territory.

Dear Sir:

Referring to the application for the enrollment of your child, Frank Flemmons, a letter was addressed to you on April 15, 1905, asking information which would enable us to identify the mother of this child upon our records.

Before further consideration can be given this application it will be necessary for you to state the name under which your wife, Annie Viola Flemmons, was enrolled, the names of her parents, and if she has selected an allotment of the lands of the Choctaw or Chickasaw Nation, give her roll number as the same appears upon her allotment certificate.

This matter should receive immediate attention.

Respectfully,

Chairman.

———————

Applications for Enrollment of Chickasaw Newborn
Act of 1905   Volume VII

Kemp, Indian Territory, June 5, 1905.

Commission to the Five Civilized Tribes,
Muskogee, I. T.

Sir;-

I will say to you in reply to your letter of the 29 ult. that Frank Flemmons is not my child, I married his mother Annie Viola Powell and in about six weeks the said Frank Flemmons was born I then left her and have not been back about her since.

Yours truly,
Baily Flemmons,
Per O. R. Fowler
Atty.

Chickasaw 1631

Muskogee, Indian Territory, June 13, 1905.

Bailey[sic] Flemmons,
Kemp, Indian Territory.

Dear Sir:

Receipt is hereby acknowledged of your letter of June 5, stating that you are not the father of Frank Flemmons, and this information has been made a matter of record in his case.

Respectfully,

Chairman.

Chic. N.B - 530
*(Waunita Reagan
Birthdate not given.)*

CHICKASAW   **530**
NEW BORN
ACT OF CONGRESS APPROVED MARCH 30, 1905.

Waunita Reagan

DECISION RENDERED **July 29 1905**

ACTION SUSPENDED BY
SECRETARY OF INTERIOR
July 3 1905

CANCELLED

Record transferred to
CHICKASAW   NEW BORN Card #93
ACT OF CONGRESS APPROVED APRIL 26, 1906.

Chic. N.B - 531
 (Daisy Williford
 Born January 10, 1901)
 (Fred Clark Williford
 Born November 22, 1903)

W.F.
9-NB-531.

DEPARTMENT OF THE INTERIOR,
COMMISSION TO THE FIVE CIVILIZED TRIBES.

In the matter of the application for the enrollment of Daisy Williford and Fred Clark Williford as citizens of the Chickasaw Nation.

--: D E C I S I O N :--

It appears from the record herein that on June 5, 1905 there were filed with the Commission applications for the enrollment of Daisy Williford and Fred Clark Williford as citizens of the Chickasaw Nation.

It further appears from the record herein and the records of the Commission that the applicants Daisy Williford and Fred Clark Williford were born on January 10, 1901 and November 22, 1903, respectively, and are the children of Joe Williford and Nannie Williford, white persons and recognized and enrolled citizens by intermarriage of the Chickasaw Nation whose names appear opposite numbers and , respectively, upon the final roll of citizens by blood of the Choctaw Nation, approved by the Secretary of the

Interior; and that said applicant died numbers 504 and 505, respectively, upon the final roll of citizens by intermarriage of the Chickasaw Nation, approved by the Secretary of the Interior October 25, 1904.

The Act of Congress approved March 3, 1905 (Public No. 212) among other things provides:

"That the Commission to the Five Civilized Tribes is hereby authorized for sixty days after the date of the approval of this act to receive and consider applications for enrollment of infant children born prior to September twenty-fifth, nineteen hundred and two, and who were living on said date, to citizens by blood of the Choctaw and Chickasaw tribes of Indians whose enrollment has been approved by the Secretary of the Interior prior to the date of the approval of this act; and to enroll and make allotments to such children."

"That the Commission to the Five Civilized Tribes is authorized for sixty days after the date of the approval of this act to receive and consider applications for enrollment of children born subsequent to September twenty-fifth, nineteen hundred and two, and prior to March fourth, nineteen hundred and five, and who were living on said latter date, to citizens by blood of the Choctaw and Chickasaw tribes of Indians whose enrollment has been approved by the Secretary of the Interior prior to the date of the approval of this act; and to enroll and make allotments to such children."

It is, therefore, the opinion of this Commission that inasmuch as the applications for the enrollment of Daisy Williford and Fred Clark Williford were not received by the Commission within the time prescribed by the Act of Congress approved March 3, 1905 and inasmuch as said applicants are not the children of a citizen by blood of the Chickasaw Nation the Commission is without authority to receive or consider the applications for their enrollment as citizens of the Chickasaw Nation and that the Commission should decline to receive or consider said applications, under the provisions of law above quoted, and it is so ordered.

COMMISSION TO THE FIVE CIVILIZED TRIBES,

Tams Bixby
Chairman.
TB Needles
Commissioner.
C. R. Breckinbridge
Commissioner.

Muskogee, Indian Territory.
JUN 29 1905

Applications for Enrollment of Chickasaw Newborn
Act of 1905   Volume VII

DEPARTMENT OF THE INTERIOR.
COMMISSION TO THE FIVE CIVILIZED TRIBES.

IN RE APPLICATION FOR ENROLLMENT, as a citizen of the   Chickasaw   Nation,
of   Daisy Williford   , born on the 10th day of Jany.   , 1901

Name of Father: Joe Williford   a citizen of the   Chickasaw Nation.
Name of Mother: Nannie Williford   a citizen of the   Chickasaw Nation.

Postoffice   Woodford, I. T.

AFFIDAVIT OF MOTHER.

UNITED STATES OF AMERICA, Indian Territory, }
    Southern   **DISTRICT.** }

I,   Nannie Williford   , on oath state that I am   39   years of age and a citizen
by   Intermarriage   , of the   Chickasaw   Nation; that I am the lawful wife of
Joe Williford   , who is a citizen, by Intermarriage   of the   Chickasaw
Nation; that a   Female   child was born to me on the 10th   day of   Jany.   ,
1901; that said child has been named   Daisy Williford   , and was living March 4,
1905.

Nannie Williford

Witnesses To Mark:
  { Sallie A. Dalley
  { Lizzie Williford

Subscribed and sworn to before me this 1st day of   June   , 1905

SEAL   M. F. Moss
                                   Notary Public.

AFFIDAVIT OF ATTENDING PHYSICIAN OR MID-WIFE.

UNITED STATES OF AMERICA, Indian Territory, }
    Southern   **DISTRICT.** }

I,   Sallie A. Dalley   , a Midwife   , on oath state that I attended on
Mrs. Nannie Williford   , wife of Joe Williford   on the 10th day of   Jany.   ,
1901; that there was born to her on said date a   Female   child; that said child was
living March 4, 1905, and is said to have been named Daisy Williford

Sallie A. Dalley

Witnesses To Mark:
{ Lizzie Williford
{ Effie Boyd

Subscribed and sworn to before me this 1st day of   June   , 1905

SEAL   M. F. Moss
                                                    Notary Public.

(COPY)

BIRTH AFFIDAVIT.

DEPARTMENT OF THE INTERIOR.
COMMISSION TO THE FIVE CIVILIZED TRIBES.

IN RE APPLICATION FOR ENROLLMENT, as a citizen of the   Chickasaw   Nation, of   Fred Clark Williford   , born on the 22d day of Nov. , 1903

Name of Father: Joe Williford   a citizen of the   Chickasaw Nation.
Name of Mother: Nannie Williford   a citizen of the   Chickasaw Nation.

Postoffice   Woodford

AFFIDAVIT OF MOTHER.

UNITED STATES OF AMERICA, Indian Territory, }
   Southern   DISTRICT. }

I, Nannie Williford   , on oath state that I am 39   years of age and a citizen by   Intermarriage   , of the   Chickasaw   Nation; that I am the lawful wife of Joe Williford   , who is a citizen, by Intermarriage   of the   Chickasaw Nation; that a   Male   child was born to me on the 22d   day of Nov.   , 1903; that said child has been named   Fred Clark Williford   , and was living March 4, 1905.

                                          Nannie Williford
Witnesses To Mark:
{ Sallie A. Dalley
{ Lizzie Williford

Subscribed and sworn to before me this 1st day of   June   , 1905

SEAL   M. F. Moss
                                                    Notary Public.

Applications for Enrollment of Chickasaw Newborn
Act of 1905 Volume VII

AFFIDAVIT OF ATTENDING PHYSICIAN OR MID-WIFE.

UNITED STATES OF AMERICA, Indian Territory, ⎫
    Southern   DISTRICT. ⎭

    I,   Sallie A. Dalley   , a Midwife   , on oath state that I attended on Mrs. Nannie Williford   , wife of Joe Williford   on the 22d day of   Nov.   , 1903; that there was born to her on said date a   Male   child; that said child was living March 4, 1905, and is said to have been named   Fred Clark Williford

Sallie A. Dalley

Witnesses To Mark:
  ⎰ Geneva Mclain
  ⎱ Lizzie Williford

    Subscribed and sworn to before me this 1st day of   June   , 1905

SEAL   M. F. Moss
                                    Notary Public.

(COPY)

9-NB-531

Muskogee, Indian Territory, June 29, 1905.

Joe Williford,   **COPY**
    Woodford, Indian Territory.

Dear Sir:

    Inclosed herewith you will find a copy of the decision of the Commission to the Five Civilized Tribes, rendered June 29, 1905, declining to receive or consider the application for the enrollment of your minor children, Daisy and Fred Clark Williford, as citizens of the Chickasaw Nation.

    The decision, with the record of proceedings in the case is this day transmitted to the Secretary of the Interior for review. The final decision of the Secretary will be made known to you as soon as this office is informed of the same.

Respectfully,
SIGNED

Tams Bixby

Registered.   Chairman.
Incl. 9-NB-531.

Applications for Enrollment of Chickasaw Newborn
Act of 1905   Volume VII

9-NB-531

Muskogee, Indian Territory, June 29, 1905.

Mansfield, McMurray & Cornish,   **COPY**
    Attorneys for Choctaw and Chickasaw Nations,
        South McAlester, Indian Territory.

Gentlemen:

Inclosed herewith you will find a copy of the decision of this Commission, rendered June 29, 1905, declining to receive or consider the application for the enrollment of Daisy Williford and Fred Clark Williford as citizens of the Chickasaw Nation.

The decision, with the record of proceedings in the case is this day transmitted to the Secretary of the Interior for review. The final decision of the Secretary will be made known to you as soon as this office is informed of the same.

Respectfully,
SIGNED

Tams Bixby
Chairman.

Incl. 9-NB-531.

Muskogee, Indian Territory, June 29, 1905.

The Honorable,   **COPY**
    The Secretary of the Interior.

Sir:

There is herewith transmitted the record of proceedings in the matter of the application for the enrollment of Daisy Williford and Fred Clark Williford as citizens of the Chickasaw Nation, including the decision of the Commission, dated June 29, 1905, declining to receive or consider said application.

Respectfully,
SIGNED

Tams Bixby
Through the   Chairman.
    Commissioner of Indian Affairs.

2 Incl. 9-NB-531.

DEPARTMENT OF THE INTERIOR,
OFFICE OF INDIAN AFFAIRS,
WASHINGTON. July 25, 1905.

Land.

50902-1905.

The Honorable,
The Secretary of the Interior.

Sir:

I have the honor to enclose a report from the Commission to the Five Civilized Tribes, dated June 29, 1905, transmitting the record of the application for enrollment as citizens of the Chickasaw Nation of Daisy and Fred Clark Williford.

June 29, 1905, the Commission decided adversely to both applicants.

The record shows that the applicants were born on January 10, 1901, and November 22, 1903, respectively, and are the children of Joe and Nannie Williford, <u>white persons</u> whose names appear as Nos. 504 and 505, respectively, on the final roll of citizens by intermarriage of the Chickasaw Nation approved by the Department October 25, 1904.

In view of the record and of the act of March 3, 1905 (33 Stats., 1071) the approval of the Commission's decision adverse to the applicant in[sic] recommended.

Very respectfully,
C. F. Larrabee
Acting Commissioner.

M.M.M.
W.

J.P.
DEPARTMENT OF THE INTERIOR,

WASHINGTON.

D.C. 45445-1905.

L.L.B.

I.T.D. 9224-1905.

September 26, 1905.

L.R.S.

Commissioner to the Five Civilized Tribes,
Muskogee, Indian Territory.

Sir:

June 29, 1905, the Commission to the Five Civilized Tribes transmitted the record in the matter of the applications for enrollment as citizens of the Chickasaw Nation of Daisy and Fred Clark Williford.

Applications for Enrollment of Chickasaw Newborn
Act of 1905   Volume VII

Reporting July 25, 1905, the Indian Office recommended that the Commission's decision, declining to receive or consider said applications be approved. A copy of its letter is inclosed.

The Department concurs in said recommendation, and the Commission's decision is hereby affirmed, on the ground that the applications were not presented in the time required by the act of March 3, 1905 (33 Stat., 1048-1071).

Respectfully,
Thos Ryan
Acting Secretary.

1 inclosure.

9-NB-531

Muskogee, Indian Territory, October 6, 1905.
COPY

Joe Williford,
Woodford, Indian Territory.

Dear Sir:

You are hereby notified that the Secretary of the Interior under date of September 26, 1905, affirmed the decision of the Commission to the Five Civilized Tribes, dated June 29, 1905, declining to receive or consider the application for the enrollment of your minor children, Daisy and Fred Clark Williford, as citizens of the Chickasaw Nation.

Respectfully,
SIGNED

Tams Bixby
Commissioner.

9-NB-531.

COPY

Muskogee, Indian Territory, October 6, 1905.

Mansfield, McMurray & Cornish,
Attorneys for Choctaw and Chickasaw Nations,
South McAlester, Indian Territory.

Gentlemen:

You are hereby notified that the Secretary of the Interior under date of September 26, 1905, affirmed the decision of the Commission to the Five Civilized Tribes, dated June 29, 1905, declining to receive or consider the application for the enrollment of Daisy Williford and Fred Clark Williford, as citizens of the Chickasaw Nation.

Respectfully,

SIGNED

Tams Bixby

Commissioner.

Chic. N.B - 532

    (Audra Ethel Skinner
    Born February 28, 1903)

AFFIDAVIT OF ATTENDING PHYSICIAN OR MID-WIFE.

UNITED STATES OF AMERICA, Indian Territory, ⎫
    Central   **DISTRICT.** ⎭

    I,   J.N. Taylor   , a   physician   , on oath state that I attended on Mrs. Wm L. Skinner   , wife of   Wm L. Skinner on the 28   day of February   , 1903; that there was born to her on said date a   female   child; that said child is now living and is said to have been named Ethel Skinner

Jas. N. Taylor, M.D.

Witnesses To Mark:

    {

    Subscribed and sworn to before me this 17 day of February   , 1905.

Claude C. *(Illegible)*

Notary Public.

BIRTH AFFIDAVIT.

DEPARTMENT OF THE INTERIOR.
COMMISSION TO THE FIVE CIVILIZED TRIBES.

    IN RE APPLICATION FOR ENROLLMENT, as a citizen of the   Chickasaw   Nation, of   Audra Ethel   , born on the 28 day of February , 1903

Name of Father: William Lee Skinner   a citizen of the   Chickasaw Nation.
Name of Mother: Permelia Skinner   a citizen of the   Chickasaw Nation.

Postoffice   Kemp

106

AFFIDAVIT OF MOTHER.

UNITED STATES OF AMERICA, Indian Territory, ⎫
    Central   DISTRICT. ⎭

I, Permelia Skinner , on oath state that I am 24 years of age and a citizen by Blood , of the Chickasaw Nation; that I am the lawful wife of William Lee Skinner , who is a citizen, by intermarriage of the Chickasaw Nation; that a female child was born to me on 28 day of February , 1903, that said child has been named Audra Ethel , and is now living.

Permelia Skinner

Witnesses To Mark:
    ⎰ Vina Lee Reynolds
    ⎱ J.K. Kemp

Subscribed and sworn to before me this 19 day of January , 1905.

S M Mead
Notary Public.

AFFIDAVIT OF ATTENDING PHYSICIAN OR MID-WIFE.

UNITED STATES OF AMERICA, Indian Territory, ⎫
                    DISTRICT. ⎭

I, ... , a .... , on oath state that I attended on Mrs. .... , wife of .... on the .... day of .... , 1............ ; that there was born to her on said date a .... child; that said child is now living and is said to have been named ....

Witnesses To Mark:
    ⎰ Vina Lee Reynolds
    ⎱ W.L. Skinner

Subscribed and sworn to before me this.............day of .... , 190....

Notary Public.

DEPARTMENT OF THE INTERIOR.
COMMISSION TO THE FIVE CIVILIZED TRIBES.

In the matter of the death of   Audra Ethel Skinner
a citizen of the   Chickasaw   Nation, who formerly resided at or near   Kemp   , Ind.
Ter., and died on the   17 day of   April   , 1904

AFFIDAVIT OF RELATIVE.

UNITED STATES OF AMERICA, Indian Territory,⎫
   Central   DISTRICT. ⎬

I, Permelia Skinner   , on oath state that I am   25   years of age and a
citizen by blood   , of the Chickasaw Nation; that my postoffice address is   Kemp   ,
Ind. Ter.; that I am   Mother   of   Audra Ethel Skinner   who was a citizen, by blood
of the   Chickasaw   Nation and that said   Audra Ethel Skinner   died on the   17
day of   Apil[sic]   , 1904

                              Permelia Skinner

Witnesses To Mark:

Subscribed and sworn to before me this   28   day of   June   , 1905.
Central

                        O.R. Fowler
                               Notary Public.

AFFIDAVIT OF ACQUAINTANCE.

UNITED STATES OF AMERICA, Indian Territory, ⎫
   Central   DISTRICT. ⎬

I,   Amanda Dillingham   , on oath state that I am   58   years of age, and a
citizen by   by blood   of the   Chickasaw   Nation; that my postoffice address is   Kemp   ,
Ind. Ter.; that I was personally acquainted with   Audra Ethel Skinner   who was a
citizen, by   blood   , of the   Chickasaw   Nation; and that said   Audra Ethel Skinner
died on the   17   day of   April   , 1904   her
                         Amanda x Dillingham
Witnesses To Mark: mark
   ⎰ J.A. Farnsworth
   ⎱ *(Name Illegible)*

Subscribed and sworn to before me this   28   day of   June   , 1905.
Central

                         O.R. Fowler
                               Notary Public.

9-1238

Muskogee, Indian Territory, June 9, 1905.

O. R. Fowler,
    Kemp, Indian Territory.

Dear Sir:

    Receipt is hereby acknowledged of your letter of June 3, 1905, asking for a blank for the purpose of making proof of the death of Audra Ethel Skinner who was born February 28, 1903 and died April 19, 1904.

    In compliance with your request there is inclosed herewith blank for the purpose of making proof of death of the above named child.

Respectfully,

Chairman.

D C

9-NB-532.

Muskogee, Indian Territory, June 20, 1905.

Permelia Skinner,
    Kemp, Indian Territory.

Dear Madam:

    In the matter of the application for the enrollment of your daughter Audra Ethel Skinner as a citizen by blood of the Chickasaw Nation it appears from your affidavit on file with the records of the Commission that said child is dead.

    For the purpose of making her death a matter of record there is inclosed herewith a blank for proof of birth which you are requested to have properly executed and return to the Commission as early as practicable.

    You will note that there is a blank for the affidavit of a friend and an acquaintance of the deceased. In having the same executed be careful to see that all blanks are properly filled, all names written in full and that the notary public, before whom the affidavits are acknowledged, attaches his name and seal to each affidavit.

Respectfully,

Chairman.

D C
Env.

9-NB-532

COPY

Muskogee, Indian Territory, August 23, 1905.

W. L. Skinner,
      Kemp, Indian Territory.

Dear Sir:

    You are hereby advised that it appearing from the records of this office, that your child, Audra Ethel Skinner, died prior to March 4, 1905, the Commissioner to the Five Civilized Tribes on August 23, 1905, dismissed the application for the enrollment of said child as a citizen by blood of the Chickasaw Nation.

Respectfully,
SIGNED

Tams Bixby
Commissioner.

9-NB-532

COPY

Muskogee, Indian Territory, August 23, 1905.

Mansfield, McMurray & Cornish,
      Attorneys for Choctaw and Chickasaw Nations,
            South McAlester, Indian Territory.

Gentlemen:

    You are hereby advised that it appearing from the records of this office that Audra Ethel Skinner died prior to March 4, 1905, the Commissioner to the Five Civilized Tribes on August 23, 1905, dismissed the application for the enrollment of said child as a citizen by blood of the Chickasaw Nation.

Respectfully,
SIGNED

Tams Bixby
Commissioner.

Chic. N.B - 533
(Cordie Marie Thurston
Born November 9, 1904)

7-N. B.-533
O.L.J.

DEPARTMENT OF THE INTERIOR,
COMMISSIONER TO THE FIVE CIVILIZED TRIBES.

In the matter of the application for the enrollment of Cordie Marie Thurston as a citizen by blood of the Chickasaw Nation.

D E C I S I O N .

It appears from the record herein that on March 28, 1905, application was made to the Commission to the Five Civilized Tribes for the enrollment of Cordie Marie Thurston as a citizen by blood of the Chickasaw Nation, under the provisions of the Act of Congress approved March 3, 1905 (33 Stats., 1060).

It further appears from the record herein and from the records in the possession of this office, that said applicant was born November 9, 1904, and is the daughter of Roxie Thurston, a non-citizen, and David Jeff Thurston whose name appears as No. 587 upon the final roll of citizens by blood of the Chickasaw Nation approved by the Secretary of the Interior, December 12, 1902, and that said applicant was living on March 4, 1905.

I am, therefore, of the opinion that Cordie Marie Thurston should be enrolled as a citizen by blood of the Chickasaw Nation, under the provisions of the Act of Congress approved March 3, 1905 (33 Stats., 1060), and it is so ordered.

Tams Bixby
Commissioner.

Muskogee, Indian Territory.
FEB 8 1907

BIRTH AFFIDAVIT.

DEPARTMENT OF THE INTERIOR.
COMMISSION TO THE FIVE CIVILIZED TRIBES.

Chickasaw

IN RE APPLICATION FOR ENROLLMENT, as a citizen of the ~~Choctaw~~ Nation, of   Cordie Marie Thurston   , born on the 9th   day of   November   , 1904

Name of Father: David Jeff Thurston   a citizen of the   Chickasaw   Nation.
Name of Mother: Roxie Thurston   a citizen of the United States Nation.

Postoffice   Houston, I. T.

Applications for Enrollment of Chickasaw Newborn
Act of 1905   Volume VII

AFFIDAVIT OF MOTHER.

UNITED STATES OF AMERICA, Indian Territory,
Central   DISTRICT.

I,   Roxie Thurston   , on oath state that I am   years of age and a citizen ~~by~~
.... , of the   United States   ~~Nation~~; that I am the lawful wife of   David
Jeff Thurston   , who is a citizen, by blood   of the   Chickasaw   Nation;
that a   female   child was born to me on the 9th   day of November   , 1904;
that said child has been named   Cordie Marie Thurston   , and was living March 4,
1905.

Roxie Thurston

Witnesses To Mark:

Subscribed and sworn to before me this 28th day of   March   , 1905

Wirt Franklin
Notary Public.

Child present.

AFFIDAVIT OF ATTENDING PHYSICIAN OR MID-WIFE.

UNITED STATES OF AMERICA, Indian Territory,
Central   DISTRICT.

I,   L. M. Sackett   , a physician   , on oath state that I attended on
Mrs. Roxie Thurston   , wife of David Jeff Thurston   on the 9th   day of
November   , 1904; that there was born to her on said date a   female   child; that
said child was living March 4, 1905, and is said to have been named   Cordie Marie
Thurston

L. M. Sackett M.D.

Witnesses To Mark:
LM Sackett M.D.

Subscribed and sworn to before me this .... day of ...., 1905.

....
Notary Public.

112

No.

Certificate of Record
of Marriages.

𝔘nited 𝔖tates of 𝔄merica,
  The Indian Territory,   } sct.
   Central   *District.*

I,   E. J. Fannin   Clerk
of the United States Court, in the Indian Territory
and District aforesaid, do hereby CERTIFY, that the
License for and Certificate of the Marriage of

Mr.   Jeff D. Thurston   and

M   Roxie King   was

filed in my office in said Territory and District the
   28"   day of   July
A.D., 190 4 , and duly recorded in Book   11
of Marriage Record, Page   236

WITNESS my hand and Seal of said Court, at
    So McAlester
this   28"   day of   July
A.D. 190 4

    EJ Fannin

              Clerk.
By   WC Donnelly   Deputy.

P. O. ....

UNITED STATES OF AMERICA,
INDIAN TERRITORY, CENTRAL DISTRICT.

At South McAlester.

I, E. J. Fannin, Clerk of the United
States Court within and for the Central District, Indian Territory, hereby certify that the
within and foregoing is a true copy of the Marriage License issued by me July 13th 1904,
to Jeff D. Thurston and Roxie King, and the minister's return made on the Certificate
thereto attached, as the same appears of record in my Office in Vol. "11" of Marriage
records at page 236 thereof.
In Testimony Whereof I hereunto set my hand and affix the seal of said Court, at my
Office in South McAlester, I.T., this the 18th day of April A.D. 1905.

EJ Fannin   Clerk of the U.
S. Court for Central Dist., I.T.
By   JB Rose   Deputy Clerk.

No.   4323

ₘARRIAGE LICENSₑ

United States of America,   The Indian Territory,
                                             Central   DISTRICT, SS.

𝕿o any 𝕻erson 𝖆uthorized by 𝕷aw to 𝕾olemnize 𝕸arriage, 𝕲reeting:

*You are hereby commanded to Solemnize the Rite and publish the Banns of Matrimony
between Mr.*   Jeff D. Thurston
of   Wilburton   *in the Indian Territory, aged*   23   *years,*
and M iss Roxie King   *of*   Wilburton
in the Indian Territory., aged   18   *years, according to law, and do you officially
sign and return this License to the parties therein named.*

WITNESS my hand and official seal, this   13th
day
          of   July   *A. D. 190* 4

E.J. Fannin
Clerk of the United States Court.

WC Donnelly   *Deputy*

Certificate of Marriage.

𝖀nited 𝕾tates of 𝖆merica, ⎫
  The Indian Territory, ⎬ *ss.*
    Central   *District.* ⎭   *I,*   G.T. Dawson

a   Ordain Minister   *, do hereby certify, that on the*   20   *day*
of   July   *A. D. 190* 4 *, I did, duly and according to law, as commanded in the
foregoing License, solemnize the Rite and publish the Banns of Matrimony between the
parties therein named.*

Witness my hand, this   20   *day of*   July   *A. D. 190* 4

My credentials are recorded in the office of the Clerk of *the United States Court in the Indian Territory,* *Central District, Book* **C** *, Page* **22**	G.T. Dawson *a* Ordain Minister

Note—This License and Certificate of Marriage must be returned to the Office of the Clerk of the United States Court of the Indian Territory, from whence it was issued, within sixty days from the date thereof, or the party to whom the License was issued will be liable in the amount of the One Hundred Dollars ($100.00)

Chick - 9 - NB - 533
Testimony of Mary Walton

What is your name - Mary Walton
What is your age - 37
What is your P.O. - Houston, I.T.
Are you acquainted with Roxie Thurston - Yes
Has Roxie any children - Yes one
What is the childs[sic] name - Marie
How do you know Roxie is the mother of Marie
I have seen her nursing Marie and I suppose she was
Is Marie still living - Yes
Who is she living with - With her mother grand mother and grand father
Are you any relation to any of the Thurston
No sir
Have you any interest in the enrollment of this child - No sir

Mary Walton

SEAL

Subscribed and sworn to before me this 2nd day of February 1907

JL Gary
Notary Public.

Testimony of Roxie Thurston

What is your name Roxie Thurston
What is your P O Houston, I T
How old are you - 21
What is your Husbands[sic] name - Jeff Thurston
Have you any children [sic] just one
What is her name - Cordie Marie
Is that child living - Yes sir
Where was you married to Jeff Thurston
Wilberton[sic]
Where was this child born - Wilburton
Who was the physician attend you when Marie was born - Dr L.M. Sackett

Where did you get the licence[sic] to be married
South McAlester
Were you married under US. Laws
Yes sir
Has Marie been living with you since she was born and is now living - Yes sir

Roxie Thurston

Seal

Subscribed and sworn to before me this 2nd day of January 1907

J L Gary
Notary Public.

Chick - 9 - NB - 533
Testimony of W J Pearson

What is your name   W J Pearson
How old are you - 30
What is your P.O. Houston, IT
Are you acquainted with David Jeff Thurston
I have see[sic] him
What is his wifes[sic] name - Roxie
Have they any children - Yes one
What is her name - They call it Marie
Is Marie living - She was living 2 days ago
Do you know if Jeff Thurston is the father of Marie - no sir I do not but everybody knows them says he is
Is Jeff Thurston and his wife living together
No Sir - Where is Jeff Thurston living - Dont[sic] know
Who is this child Marie living with -
She is living with her mother and Roxie is living with her father
Are you any relation to Jeff Thurston or Roxie Thurston - No sir
Have you any interest in the enrollment of this child - None what ever

Seal

Subscribed and sworn to before me this 1st day of February 1907

JL Gary
Notary Public.

Muskogee, Indian Territory, August 4, 1905.

Chief Clerk,
> Chickasaw Land Office,
>> Ardmore, Indian Territory

Dear Sir:

Refer to duplicate Chickasaw New Born Roll Card No. 533, in the possession of your office, under the head of "Remarks" is the following notation:

"Application for enrollment of No. 1, received June 20, 1905."

Please change said notation to read "March 28, 1905: instead of June "20, 1905."

Respectfully,

Commissioner.

9-NB-533

Muskogee, Indian Territory, August 24, 1905.

David Jeff Thurston,
> Houston, Indian Territory.

Dear Sir:

In the matter of the application for the enrollment of your minor daughter, Cordie Marie Thurston, as a citizen by blood of the Chickasaw Nation, it will be necessary for you to furnish this office with your affidavit and the affidavit of L. M. Sackett, the physician who attended your wife, Roxie Thurston, at the birth of said child. The affidavit of the said L. M. Sackett, which is now on file in said case, is defective inasmuch as the notary public before whom the same was sworn to, if sworn to at all, neglected to affix his name and seal to the affidavit.

For the purpose of securing the proof above requested, there is enclosed herewith blank for proof of birth, which you are requested to have executed and returned to this office.

There is on file in this case a certified copy of the marriage license and certificate, showing marriage between Jeff D. Thurston and Roxie King, from which it appears that said parties were married July 20, 1904. It is noted from the proof of birth on file that the child, Cordie Marie Thurston, for whom application is made, was born November 9, 1904, about four months after said marriage.

The mother of said child being a non-citizen, it will be necessary for you to furnish this office, before the rights of your said daughter can be finally determined, evidence showing whether or not you and the said Roxie King lived and cohabited together prior to said marriage, and if so, for how long, and whether or not said Cordie Marie Thurston is your child.   Such evidence should consist of your affidavit, the affidavit of your said wife, and the affidavits of not less than two disinterested persons who are personally acquainted with the facts in the case.

This matter should have your immediate attention.

Respectfully,

Commissioner.

JYM-24-1

9- NB 533

Muskogee, Indian Territory, September 1, 1905.

Jefferson Kuincy,
Heavener, Indian Territory.

Dear Sir:

I am in receipt of your letter of August 27th, in which you desire to be informed if the child of Mrs. Roxie Thurston has been enrolled as a citizen of the Chickasaw Nation.

In reply to your letter you are advised that on March 28, 1905, application was made to the Commission to the Five Civilized Tribes for the enrollment of Cordie Marie Thurston, born September 9, 1904. The father of this child appears from the records of this office to be a citizen by blood of the Chickasaw Nation and the mother a non-citizen white woman.

No disposition has yet been made of the application for the enrollment of this child, but when same is acted upon, the father will be advised thereof.

Respectfully,

Commissioner.

9-NB-533

Muskogee, Indian Territory, November 28, 1905.

David Jeff Thurston,
    Houston, Indian Territory.

Dear Sir:

    Referring to the application for the enrollment of your infant child Cordie Marie Thurston your attention is invited to office letter of August 24, 1905, and you are again advised that it will be necessary to forward proof requested therein before further action can be taken in the matter of the enrollment of said child.

                Respectfully,

                        Acting Commissioner.

9-NB-533

Muskogee, Indian Territory, February 13, 1906.

David Jeff Thurston,
    Houston, Indian Territory.

Dear Sir:

    In the matter of the enrollment of your child, Cordie Marie Thurston as a new born citizen of the Chickasaw Nation, you are advised that it will be necessary for you and your wife, Roxie Thurston to appear at this office for the purpose of testifying relative to the right to enrollment of said child.

    This matter should receive your immediate attention as no further action can be taken in the matter of the application for the enrollment of Cordie Marie Thurston until such hearing. Notice of the time of taking such testimony must first be served on the attorneys for the Choctaw and Chickasaw Nations.

                Respectfully,

                        Acting Commissioner.

9-NB-533

Muskogee, Indian Territory, April 3, 1907.

Quincy Jefferson,
      Heavener, Indian Territory.

Dear Sir:

Receipt is hereby acknowledged of your letter of March 27, 1907, in which you state that J. J. King has asked you to write in regard to the approval of the enrollment of Cordey[sic] Maree[sic] Thurston by the Secretary of the Interior.

In reply to your letter you are advised that Cordie Marie Thurston has been enrolled and her enrollment as a new born citizen of the Chickasaw Nation under the Act of March 3, 1905, was approved by the Secretary of the Interior March 2, 1907.

Respectfully,

Acting Commissioner.

7-NB-533.

COPY
Muskogee, Indian Territory, February 8, 1907.

David Jeff Thurston,
      Houston, Indian Territory.

Dear Sir:

Inclosed herewith you will find a copy of the decision of the Commissioner to the Five Civilized Tribes, rendered February 8, 1907, granting the application for the enrollment of Cordie Marie Thurston as a citizen by blood of the Chickasaw Nation.

You are hereby advised that the name of Cordie Marie Thurston will be placed upon the next schedule of citizens by blood of the Chickasaw Nation to be submitted to the Secretary of the Interior for his approval.

Respectfully,
SIGNED   *Tams Bixby*
Commissioner.

Registered.
Incl. 7NB-533

Applications for Enrollment of Chickasaw Newborn
Act of 1905   Volume VII

7-NB-533.

Muskogee, Indian Territory, February 8, 1907.

Mansfield, McMurray & Cornish,
    Attorneys for Choctaw and Chickasaw Nations,
       South McAlester, Indian Territory.

Gentlemen:

    Inclosed herewith you will find a copy of the decision of the Commissioner to the Five Civilized Tribes, rendered February 8, 1907, granting the application for the enrollment of Cordie Marie Thurston as a citizen by blood of the Chickasaw Nation.

    You are hereby advised that the name of Cordie Marie Thurston will be placed upon the next schedule of citizens by blood of the Chickasaw Nation to be submitted to the Secretary of the Interior for his approval.

Respectfully,

SIGNED   *Tams Bixby*
              Commissioner.

Registered.
Incl. 7-NB-533

Chic. N.B - 534
    (Minerva B. Thompson
    Born November 26, 1903)

BIRTH AFFIDAVIT.

DEPARTMENT OF THE INTERIOR.
COMMISSION TO THE FIVE CIVILIZED TRIBES.

IN RE APPLICATION FOR ENROLLMENT, as a citizen of the   Choctaw[sic]   Nation, of   Minerva B. Thompson   , born on the 26th   day of Nov , 1903

Name of Father: Robt Thompson   a citizen of the   Choctaw   Nation.
Name of Mother: Nettie Thompson   a citizen of the   Choctaw   Nation.

Postoffice   Kiowa Ind Ter

121

Applications for Enrollment of Chickasaw Newborn
Act of 1905   Volume VII

UNITED STATES OF AMERICA, Indian Territory, ⎫
Central   DISTRICT. ⎭

I,   Nettie Thompson   , on oath state that I am   24   years of age and a citizen by   Blood   , of the   Choctaw   Nation; that I am the lawful wife of Robt Thompson   , who is a citizen, by Blood   of the   Choctaw   Nation; that a   Female   child was born to me on   26th   day of   November   , 1903; that said child has been named Minerva B Thompson   , and was living March 4, 1905.

Nettie Thompson

Witnesses To Mark:
{

Subscribed and sworn to before me this 8th day of   April   , 1905

C.E. Culbertson
Notary Public.

UNITED STATES OF AMERICA, Indian Territory, ⎫
Central   DISTRICT. ⎭

I,   Dr S.W. Jackson   , a Physician   , on oath state that I attended on Mrs. Nettie Thompson   , wife of   Robt Thompson   on the 26th   day of November   , 1903; that there was born to her on said date a   Female   child; that said child was living March 4, 1905, and is said to have been named   Minerva B. Thompson

S.W. Jackson M.D.

Witnesses To Mark:
{

Subscribed and sworn to before me this 4th day of   April   , 1905

C.E. Culbertson
Notary Public.

County of Atoka ⎫
15th District   ⎬   This to certify that thereon I, Robert Thompson am a citizen by
Indian Territory ⎭   blood of the Chickasaw Nation and my wife Nettie Thompson is
                     a citizen by blood of the Choctaw Nation. Now therefore I, Robert
                     Thompson and my wife Nettie Thompson mutually join and agree
to have our child Minerva B. Thompson enrolled in the Chickasaw Nation.

Robert Thompson
Nettie Thompson

Subscribed & sworn to this 23rd day of June 1905 before me a Notary Public to Centl Dist
Indian Territory

HB Rowley
Notary Public.

NEW BORN AFFIDAVIT

No ....

CHOCTAW ENROLLING COMMISSION

IN THE MATTER OF THE APPLICATION FOR ENROLLMENT as a citizen of the Chickasaw
Nation, of   Minerva B. Thompson   born on the 26th day
of   November   190 3

Name of father Robt. R. Thompson   a citizen of   Chickasaw   Nation,
final enrollment No. 1977
Name of mother Nettie Thompson   a citizen of   Choctaw   Nation,
final enrollment No.   12404

Kiowa I.T.   Postoffice.

AFFIDAVIT OF MOTHER

UNITED STATES OF AMERICA ⎫
    INDIAN TERRITORY   ⎬
DISTRICT   Central   ⎭

I   Nettie Thompson   , on oath state that I am   24   years of
age and a citizen by   Blood   of the   Choctaw   Nation, and as such have been
placed upon the final roll of the   Choctaw   Nation, by the Honorable Secretary of the
Interior my final enrollment number being   12404   ; that I am the lawful wife of Robt. R.
Thompson   , who is a citizen of the   Chickasaw   Nation, and as such has been
placed upon the final roll of said Nation by the Honorable Secretary of the Interior, his final

123

enrollment number being   1977   and that a   Female   child was born to me on the   26th
day of   November   190 3; that said child has been named   Minerva B Thompson   , and
is now living.

Nettie Thompson

WITNESSETH:

Must be two witnesses { L.W. McMorries
who are citizens   { M E Crisp

Subscribed and sworn to before me this, the   25th   day of   Feby   , 190 5

C.E. Culbertson
Notary Public.

My Commission Expires: 12/2/05

Affidavit of Attending Physician or Midwife

UNITED STATES OF AMERICA, ⎫
    INDIAN TERRITORY,   ⎬
Central   DISTRICT ⎭

I,   Dr S.W. Jackson   a   Physician
on oath state that I attended on Mrs.   Nettie Thompson
wife of   Robt R Thompson   on the   26th   day of
.   Nov.   , 190 3, that there was born to her on said date a   Female   child, that said
child is now living, and is said to have been named   Minerva B. Thompson

S.W. Jackson   M. D.

Subscribed and sworn to before me this the   25th   day of   Feby   1905

C.E. Culbertson
Notary Public.

WITNESSETH:

Must be two witnesses { L.W. McMorries
who are citizens and {
know the child.   { M E Crisp

We hereby certify that we are well acquainted with   Dr S.W. Jackson
a   Physician   and know   him   to be reputable and of good standing in the
community.

Must be two citizen { L.W. McMorries
witnesses.   { ME Crisp

124

7-NB-794.

Muskogee, Indian Territory, June 7, 1905.

Robert Thompson,
    Kiowa, Indian Territory.

Dear Sir:

Referring to the application for the enrollment of your infant child, Minerva B. Thompson, born November 26, 1903, it appears that you are a citizen by blood of the Chickasaw Nation while your wife is a citizen by blood of the Choctaw Nation.

Your attention is called to the provision of the Act of Congress approved June 28, 1898, as follows:

The several Tribes may, by agreement, determine the right of persons who for any reason may claim citizenship in two or more tribes, and to allotment of lands and distribution of moneys belonging to each tribe; but if no such agreement be made, then such claimant shall be entitled to such rights in one tribe only, and may elect in which tribe he will take such right; but if he fail or refuse to make such selection in due time, he shall be enrolled in the tribe with whom he has resided, and there be given such allotment and distributions, and not elsewhere.

It will therefore be necessary for you and your wife to appear before a Notary Public or other officer authorized to administer oaths and by affidavit elect in which nation you desire to have said child enrolled, forwarding same, when properly executed, to the Commission.

                    Respectfully,

                            Commissioner in Charge.

Choctaw N B 794

Muskogee, Indian Territory, June 28, 1905.

Robert Thompson,
    Kiowa, Indian Territory.

Dear Sir:

Receipt is hereby acknowledged of the joint affidavit of yourself and your wife, Nettie Thompson, electing to have your child, Minerva B. Thompson, enrolled as a citizen by blood of the Chickasaw Nation, and the same has been filed with our records in the matter of the enrollment of said child.

Respectfully,

Chairman.

Chic. N.B - 535
(Lula A. Byrd
Born March 11, 1905)

CHICKASAW 535

NEW BORN

ACT OF CONGRESS APPROVED MARCH 30, 1905.

Lula A. Byrd
(Born March 11, 1905)

CANCELLED

Record transferred to
Chickasaw   New Born   #186

ACT OF CONGRESS APPROVED APRIL 26, 1906.

JUL 13 1906

Chic. N.B - 536
(Nicholas Bean
Born September 2, 1904)

Applications for Enrollment of Chickasaw Newborn
Act of 1905   Volume VII

9-NB-536.

Department of the Interior,
Commissioner to the Five Civilized Tribes.
Muskogee, Indian Territory, April 25, 1906.

In the matter of the application for the enrollment of Nicholas Bean as a citizen by blood of the Chickasaw Nation.

FELIN BEAN, being first duly sworn, testified as follows through interpreter, Burney Jones:

Examination by the Commissioner:

Q What is your name? A Felin Bean.
Q How old are you? A Going on thirty-six years old.
Q What is your postoffice? A Oakman.
Q Are you a citizen by blood of the Chickasaw Nation? A Yes.
Q You have been finally enrolled and selected your allotment? A Yes, sir.

The witness is identified upon Chickasaw Field Card, No. 225, opposite No. 728.

Q What is the name of your wife? A Abby Bean.
Q How old is she? A Going on twenty-four.
Q Is she a Choctaw by blood? A Yes sir.
Q Selected her allotment? A Yes sir.
Q Is she living? A Yes sir.

Abby Bean is identified upon Choctaw Field Care No. 30, opposite No. 50.

Q When were you first married to Abby Bean? A 1902.
Q What month? A About May.
Q In the spring? A Yes sir.
Q You remember what day? A No, I don't remember what day.
Q Who married you? A Benjamin.
Q What is his full name? A Charley Benjamin.
Q What was he? A Preacher
Q Choctaw preacher? A Choctaw preacher.
Q Is he living? A Dead.
Q When did he die? A I don't know what certain day he died.
Q What year? A About a year and a half or two years.
Q About two years ago? A Yes sir.
Q Who was present when you married Abby Bean? A These two fellows, Simeon Sheilds[sic] and Henry Sheilds.

127

Applications for Enrollment of Chickasaw Newborn
Act of 1905   Volume VII

Q Are they Choctaws or Chickasaws? A Chickasaws by blood.

Q Where were you married? A Married in the Choctaw Nation.

Q At what place? A Place called Citra.

Q At whose house? A William Jackson.

Q Have you lived with Abby Bean ever since? A Yes sir.

Q Were you afterwards married to her again under United States law? A Yes sir.

Q Where were you married? A I married right at home there.

Q What place? A Ada.

Q Who married you then? A Howard--I. W. Howard.

Q Was he a preacher? A Yes sir.

Q White preacher? A Yes sir.

Q What year was this? A 1905. December 10th

Q Did you get a license the first time you were married? A No, I never got any license.

Q Just married by a preacher? A Yes sir.

Q When was your son, Nicholas Bean, born? A Born in 1904.

Q What month and day? A September 2nd.

Q September 2nd or September 3rd? You have September 3rd in your affidavit?
A September 2.

Q Where were you living when this child was born? A Living right close to Ada.

Q Is this child living? A Yes sir.

Q Living at your home now? A Yes sir.

Q   In case that Nicholas Bean is entitled to enrollment both as a Choctaw and a Chickasaw, in what nation do you want him to be enrolled? A Chickasaw.

Q Did Charley Benjamin have any one place where he preached, or did he preach all over? A All over.

Q What kind of a preacher was he? A Missionary preacher.

Q What church did he belong to? A Baptist.

(Witness excused.)

SIMEON SHEILDS[sic], being first duly sworn, testified as follows through interpreter Burney Jones.

Examination by the Commissioner:

Q What is your name? A Simeon Shields.

Q How old are you? A Thirty-two.

Q What is your postoffice? A Allen, I. T.

Q Are you acquainted with Felin Bean? A Yes sir.

Q Are yoy[sic] related to him? A Yes sir.

Q How? [sic] Felin Bean is my nephew.

Q Are you acquainted with Abby Bean? A Yes sir.

Q How long have you known her? A Known her all my life.

Q Do you know anything about whether or not Felin Bean was married to Abby Bean?
A I heard they was married, but never seen them. I wasn't present.

Q Do you know who married them? A I heard that Charley Benjamin married them. I wasn't present and didn't see them.

128

Q How long have Felin Bean and Abby Bean lived together? A Lived together four or five years.

Q Did he live with her before he married her? A Yes sir.

Q Have Felin Bean and Abby Bean any other children? A Only that one.

Q When was this child, Nicholas Bean, born? A I don't know just the exact date, but I know them well.

Q Have Felin Bean and Abby Bean lived together all the time for the last four or five years? A Yes sir.

Q How far away from them have you lived for the last four or five years? A Felin Bean's wife's father lived right at me, about two or three hundred yards away. Sometime[sic] they came there and stayed, but then they lived about fifteen miles from me.

Q How long has Charley Benjamin been dead? A About two years.

Q Did you know him well? A Yes sir, I know him well. He used to preach around in the Chickasaw Nation.

Q Is this child, Nicholas Bean, living? A Yes sir.

Q Were you present when Charley Benjamin married Felin Bean and Abby Bean? A I wasn't present.

(Witness excused.)

HENRY SHIELDS, being first duly sworn, testified as follows through interpreter Burney Jones.

Examination by the Commissioner:

Q What is your name? A Henry Shields.

Q How old are you? A About thirty years.

Q Postoffice? A Allen, I. T.

Q Are you a citizen by blood of the Chickasaw Nation? A Yes sir.

Q How much? A About full blood.

Q Are you acquainted with Felin Bean? A Yes sir.

Q How long have you known him? A Were kind of raised together.

Q Are you related to Felin Bean? A Yes sir.

Q Do you know Abby Bean? A Yes sir.

Q How long have you known her? A From childhood up.

Q Do you know when that child, Nicholas Bean, was born? A Yes sir.

Q When? A 1905.

Q Sure it was 1905? A 1904.

Q What month? A September. In about September.

Q Were they living near you when this child was born? A Yes sir, right close. I seen them nearly every other day or so.

Q Do you know whether or not Felin Bean and Abby Bean were married by Charley Benjamin? A I heard that Charley Benjamin married them, but I wasn't present, but everybody else said they was married.

Q Did you know Charley Benjamin? A Yes sr.

Q How long had you known him? A Somewhere about fifteen years.

Q What was Charley Benjamin? A He was a preacher, Choctaw preacher.

Q Is he living? A He is dead.

Q When did he die? A About two years ago.

Q Has Abby Bean been living with any other man besides Felin Bean since 1902?
A No sir.

Q Are Felin Bean and Abby Bean living together now? A Yes sir.

(Witness excused.)

FELIN BEAN, being recalled, testified through interpreter Burney Jones, as follows:

Examination by the Commissioner:

Q Did Charley Benjamin give you a certificate of marriage in writing when he married you? A No sir.

Q He didn't? A No sir.

Q Who saw you married? A These two fellows saw me married.

Q They say they were not there? A Yes, there was a whole lot of them.

Q Who were they? A William Jackson and his wife.

Q At whose house were you married? A William Jackson.

Q Was William Jackson's wife there? A Yes sir.

Q What is her name? A Mollie Jackson.

(Witness excused.)

Lenora B. Ashton, as stenographer to the Commissioner to the Five Civilized Tribes, upon oath states that she reported the testimony taken in the above cause on the 25th day of April, 1906, and that the above and foregoing is a true and correct translation of her stenographic notes at said time.

Lenora B. Ashton

Subscribed and sworn to before me this 25th day of April, 1906.

(Name Illegible)
Notary Public.

BIRTH AFFIDAVIT.   *No 65*

DEPARTMENT OF THE INTERIOR.
COMMISSION TO THE FIVE CIVILIZED TRIBES.

IN RE APPLICATION FOR ENROLLMENT, as a citizen of the   Chickasaw   Nation, of   Nicholas Bean   , born on the   3rd[sic]   day of   Sept   , 1904

Name of Father: Felin Bean   a citizen of the   Chickasaw   Nation.
Name of Mother: Abby Bean   a citizen of the   Choctaw   Nation.

Postoffice   Ada, I.T.

AFFIDAVIT OF MOTHER.

UNITED STATES OF AMERICA, Indian Territory, ⎫
       Southern   DISTRICT. ⎭

I,   Abbey[sic] Bean   , on oath state that I am   22   years of age and a citizen by   blood   , of the   Choctaw   Nation; that I am the lawful wife of   Felin Bean   , who is a citizen, by   blood   of the   Chickasaw   Nation; that a male   child was born to me on   3rd day of   September   , 1904, that said child has been named   Nicholas Bean   , and is now living.

                              her
                          Abby x Bean
Witnesses To Mark: mark
  ⎰ *(Name Illegible)*
  ⎱ A W White

Subscribed and sworn to before me this   6th day of   January   , 1905.

                    Tom D. McKeown
                        Notary Public.

AFFIDAVIT OF ATTENDING PHYSICIAN OR MID-WIFE.

UNITED STATES OF AMERICA, Indian Territory, ⎫
       Southern   DISTRICT. ⎭

I,   C. W. McMillan   , a   Physician   , on oath state that I attended on Mrs.   Abby Bean   , wife of   Felin Bean   on the   3rd day of September , 1904; that there was born to her on said date a   male   child; that said child is now living and is said to have been named   Nicholas Bean

                    C.W. McMillan M.D.

131

Witnesses To Mark:

{

Subscribed and sworn to before me this 6th day of   January , 1905.

Tom D. McKeown
Notary Public.

BIRTH AFFIDAVIT.

DEPARTMENT OF THE INTERIOR,
COMMISSIONER TO THE FIVE CIVILIZED TRIBES.

ENROLLMENT OF MINORS.   ACT OF CONGRESS, APPROVED APRIL 26, 1906.

IN RE APPLICATION FOR ENROLLMENT, as a citizen of the   Chocktaw[sic]   Nation,
of   Nickles[sic] Bean   , born on the   2   day of   September , 1904

Name of Father: Fealin[sic] Bean   a citizen of the Chicksaw[sic]Nation.
Name of Mother: Abby Bean ne Jackson   a citizen of the   Chocktaw   Nation.

Tribal enrollment of father Chicksaw   Tribal enrollment of mother Chocktaw

Postoffice   Ada I.T.

AFFIDAVIT OF MOTHER.

UNITED STATES OF AMERICA, Indian Territory, }
Southern   District.

I,   Abby Bean Ne Jackson   , on oath state that I am   23
years of age and a citizen by   Blood   , of the   Chocktaw   Nation; that I am
the lawful wife of   Fealin Bean   , who is a citizen, by   Blood   of the   Chicksaw
Nation; that a   male   child was born to me on 2   day of   September   , 1904 , that
said child has been named   Nickles Bean   , and was living March 4, 1906.

her
Abby x Bean ne Jackson
mark

WITNESSES TO MARK:
{ Adline Jackson
{ B.P. Ford

Subscribed and sworn to before me this 25   day of   September , 1906.

B.P. Ford
Notary Public.

132

AFFIDAVIT OF ATTENDING PHYSICIAN OR MID-WIFE.

UNITED STATES OF AMERICA, Indian Territory, }
     Southern   District. }

    I,   Chas W. McMillan   , a   Physician   , on oath state that I attended on Abby Bean ne Jackson   , wife of Fealin Bean on the 2 day of Sept , 190 4; that there was born to her on said date a   male   child; that said child was living March 4, 1906, and is said to have been named Nicholas Bean

                                     Chas W. McMillan

WITNESSES TO MARK:

   {

Subscribed and sworn to before me this 24 day of Sept   , 1906.

                          B.P. Ford
                              Notary Public.

T. J. CHAMBLESS
DEALER IN
DRY GOODS, GROCERIES, SHOES, CLOTHING
xxxxxxxxxxxx **AND IMPLEMENTS** xxxxxxxxxxxx

                             ADA, I. T. _____1908

Ind Ter }
So Dist }
       Personally appeared before me a Notary Public for the aforesaid District H.G. Richmond who after being duly sworn by me states upon his oath that he was present and saw Felin Bean married to his wife Abbie[sic] Bean - in the fall of 1905 I am personally acquainted

Given under my hand this April 14 1905

                           H.G. Richmond

Subscribed and sworn to before me this 14th day of April 1906

                        BK McKinley
                        Notary Public So Dist
                              Ind Terry

So District
Chickasaw Nation }
Indian Terry   Be it known that on this date the 7th day of April 1906 before me the undersigned a Notary Public in and for So District Ind. Terry. personally appeared one W.B. Seaton who after being duly sworn by me states upon oath the he saw the marriage ceremony performed between Felian[sic] Bean and Abbie[sic] Bean

Signed - W.B. Seaton

Subscribed and sworn to before me this 7th day of April 1906.

BK McKinley
Notary Public   So Dist
Indian Terry

TOM D. M^cKEOWN.
ATTORNEY AND COUNSELLOR
ADA, IND. TER.

OFFICE IN
CITIZENS' NATIONAL BANK BUILDING

IN RE ENROLLMENT OF NICHOLAS BEAN.

United States of America
  Southern District
Indian Territory.   Felin Bean being duly sworn on oath says I am the father of Nicholas Bean and I am a member of the Chickasaw Tribe of Indians and it is my desire that Nicholas Bean be enrolled as a member of the Chickasaw Tribe of Indians.

Felin Bean

Subscribed and sworn to before me this 11th day of July A.D. 1905.

Tom D McKeown
Notary Public

AFFIDAVIT OF MOTHER.

United States of America
  Southern District
Indian Territory.   Abbey Bean, nee Jackson, being duly sworn on oath says I am the wife of Felin Bean, and that my maiden name was Abby Jackson, and I am enrolled as a member of the Choctaw Nation and it is my desire that Nicholas Bean be enrolled as a member of the Chickasaw Tribe.

Witness to mark
Tom D. McKeown
Felin Bean

her
Abby x Bean
mark

Applications for Enrollment of Chickasaw Newborn
Act of 1905 Volume VII

Subscribed and sworn to before me this 11th day of July A.D. 1905.

Tom D McKeown
Notary Public

(The below typed as given.)

(Copy)

5/18--1905 Oakman, I. T.

Commission to the five civilized tribes muskogee I.T.
the Note Publick in filling out the Name of my wife abby Bean
Her name is on Role and filed as abby Jackson, York Jackson, father. filed in chickasaw
Role 50   if this is not corect any thing else Required Please let me at once   very
Respectfully

Felin Bean.

(Copy)

Ada I.T.   May 19th, 1905.

To the Commission to the Five Civilized Tribes,
Muskogee, I. T.

Gentlemen:-

In the Matter of the enrollment of Nicholas Bean, son of Felin and Abby Bean; beg to say that Abby Bean, is a citizen of the Choctaw Nation and enrolled as Abby Jackson, and her roll number, Choctaw by blood No. 50 and she has selected her allotment.

Yours respectfully,

Tom D. McKeown.

COPY.   MARRIAGE LICENSE.
No. 1035.

UNITED STATES OF AMERICA,)
)
INDIAN TERRITORY,   ) ss.   To Any Person Authorized by Law to
)
SOUTHERN DISTRICT.   )   Solemnize Marriage, Greeting:- -

YOU ARE HEREBY COMMANDED to solemnize the Rite and publish the Banns of Matrimony between Mr. <u>Felin Bean</u> of <u>Oakman</u> in the Indian Territory, aged <u>36</u>

135

years, and <u>Miss Abby Jackson</u> of <u>Oakman</u> in the Indian Territory, aged <u>24</u> years, according to laws and do you officially sign and return this license to the parties therein named.

WITNESS my hand and official Seal, this <u>9"</u> day of <u>December</u> A. D. 1905.

C. M. Campbell
Clerk of the United States Court.

By A. H. Constant, Deputy.

CERTIFICATE OF MARRIAGE.

UNITED STATES OF AMERICA,)

INDIAN TERRITORY,   ) ss.

SOUTHERN DISTRICT.   )   I, <u>I. W. Howard, Francis I. T.</u> do hereby

certify that on the _____ day of _____ A. D. 190_, I did duly and according to law, as commanded in the foregoing License, solemnize the Rite and publish the Banns of Matrimony between the parties therein named.

WITNESS my hand this <u>10</u> day of <u>Dec.</u> A. D. 1905.

My credentials are recorded in the office of the Clerk of the United States Court, Indian Territory, Southern District, at Ardmore, Book <u>A</u> , Page <u>91</u>.

I. W. Howard
a minister of g

CERTIFICATE OF RECORD OF MARRIAGE.

UNITED STATES OF AMERICA,)
INDIAN TERRITORY,   ) sct.
SOUTHERN DISTRICT.   )

I, C. M. CAMPBELL, Clerk of the United States Court, in the Territory and District aforesaid, do hereby certify that the License for and Certificate of Marriage of Mr. <u>Felin Bean</u> and M <u>Abby Jackson</u> were filed in my office in said Territory and District the <u>13</u> day of <u>December</u> A. D. 1905, and duly recorded in Book <u>2</u> of Marriage Record, Page <u>536</u>.

Witness my hand and Seal of said Court, at Ardmore, this 13 day of December A.D. 1905.

C. M. Campbell
Clerk.

Filed at Ardmore,
Dec. 13, 1905, - P.M.
C. M. Campbell, Clerk and
Exofficio Recorded, District No. 21, Ind. Ter.

I, Lenora B. Ashton, as stenographer to the Commissioner to the Five Civilized Tribes, upon oath state that I made the foregoing copy, and that the same is a true and complete copy of the original transcript.

Lenora B. Ashton

Subscribed and sworn to before me this 25th day of April, 1906.

Edward Merrick
Notary Public.

Department of the Interior.
Commissioner to the Five Civilized Tribes.

In Re-application of Nicholas Bean,

to be enrolled as a new born	)) Affidavit of Father.)
citizen of the Chickasaw Nation.	)

United States of America   )
Southern District,   )   ss.
Indian Territory   )

Felin Bean, being duly sworn on oath;- Says that I am the father of Nicholas Bean, and that his mother is enrolled as a member of the Choctaw Nation, by blood, and her name on the roll of the Choctaw Nation is Abby Jackson, No. 50.

Affiant says he and Abby Jackson were married by a Choctaw Preacher in the year 1902, at the residence of William Jackson, in the Choctaw Nation, near Citra, Indian Territory.

Affiat[sic] furhter[sic] says that Nicholas Bean was born to them by reason of said marriage.

137

Affiant says that when the question of this child came up that he discovered that the preacher Charlie Benjamin, who is now dead, was not a liscenced[sic] preacher, and that he and his wife were re-married under the United States Law, in force in the Indian Territory.

Affiant furhter[sic] says that he and his wife are living together and that the child is still living.

Felin Bean

Subscribed and sworn to before me this 23rd day of April 1906.

Jno. P. Crawford
Notary Public.

Muskogee, Indian Territory, May 4, 1905.

Felin Bean,
    Ada, Indian Territory.

Dear Sir:

Receipt is hereby acknowledged of the affidavits of Abby Bean and C. W. McMillan to the birth of Nicholas Bean, son of Felin and Abby Bean, September 3[sic], 1904.

It is stated in the affidavit of the mother that she is a citizen by blood of the Choctaw Nation. If this is correct you are requested to state the name under which she was enrolled, the names of her parents, and if she has selected an allotment of the lands of the Choctaw or Chickasaw Nation please give her roll number as it appears upon her allotment certificate.

Respectfully,

Chairman.

Muskogee, Indian Territory, May 18, 1905.

Felin Bean,
    Ada, Indian Territory.

Dear Sir:

Receipt is hereby acknowledged of your letter of May 10, 1905, asking when you will be allowed to file for your child Nicholas Bean born September 2, 1904.

Applications for Enrollment of Chickasaw Newborn
Act of 1905   Volume VII

In reply to your letter you are informed that on May 4, 1905, a letter was addressed to you stating that it would be necessary for you to give the name under which the mother of this child was enrolled, the names of her parents, and if she had selected an allotment of the lands of the Choctaw or Chickasaw Nation to give her roll number as it appeared upon her allotment certificate. This matter should receive immediate attention in order that proper disposition may be made of the application for the enrollment of this child.

Respectfully,

Chairman.

7--30.

Muskogee, Indian Territory, May 24, 1905.

Tom D. McKeown,
    Ada, Indian Territory.

Dear Sir:

Receipt is hereby acknowledged of your letter of May 19, in the matter of the enrollment of Nicholas Bean, son of Felin and Abby Bean, in which you state that Abby Bean is a citizen of the Choctaw Nation and enrolled as Abby Jackson and her roll number is 50.

In reply to your letter you are advised that this information has enabled us to identify Abby Jackson upon our records as a citizen by blood of the Choctaw Nation, and the affidavits heretofore forwarded to the birth of Nicholas Bean, have been filed with our records as an application for the enrollment of said child.

Respectfully,

Chairman.

7--30.

Muskogee, Indian Territory, May 24, 1905.

Felin Bean,
    Oakman, Indian Territory.

Dear Sir:

Receipt is hereby acknowledged of your letter of May 18, stating that your wife, Abbie Bean, was enrolled and selected her allotment as Abby Jackson, that she is the daughter of York Jackson and her roll number is 50.

This information has enabled us to identify Abby Bean upon our records as an enrolled citizen by blood of the Chickasaw Nation, and the affidavits heretofore forwarded to the birth of Nicholas Bean, have been filed with our records as an application for the enrollment of said child.

Respectfully,

Chairman.

_____

7-NB-1453.

Muskogee, Indian Territory, June 15, 1905.

Felin Bean,
    Ada, Indian Territory.

Dear Sir:

Referring to the application for the enrollment of your infant child, Nicholas Bean, it appears that you are a citizen by blood of the Chickasaw Nation, while you wife is a citizen by blood of the Choctaw Nation.

Your attention is called to the provision of the Act of Congress approved June 28, 1898, as follows:

The several Tribes may, by agreement, determine the right of persons who for any reason may claim citizenship in two or more tribes, and to allotment of lands and distribution of moneys belonging to each tribe; but if no such agreement be made, then such claimant shall be entitled to such rights in one tribe only, and may elect in which tribe he will take such right; but if he fail or refuse to make such selection in due time, he shall be enrolled in the tribe with whom he has resided, and there be given such allotment and distributions, and not elsewhere.

140

It will therefore be necessary for you and your wife to appear before a Notary Public or other officer authorized to administer oaths and by affidavit elect in which nation you desire to have said child enrolled, forwarding same when properly executed, to the Commission.

Respectfully,

Chairman.

7-NB-1453

Muskogee, Indian Territory, July 18, 1905.

Tom D. McKeown,
    Attorney at Law,
        Ada, Indian Territory.

Dear Sir:

Receipt is hereby acknowledged of your letter of July 11, 1905, enclosing affidavits of Felin and Abbie Bean electing to have their son Nicholas Bean enrolled as a citizen by blood of the Chickasaw Nation and the same have been filed with the record in this case.

Respectfully,

Commissioner.

9-NB-536.

Muskogee, Indian Territory, August 17, 1905.

Felin Bean,
    Ada, Indian Territory.

Dear Sir:

In the matter of the application for the enrollment of your minor son Nicholas Bean as a citizen by blood of the Chickasaw Nation it will be necessary for you to furnish this office evidence of your marriage to Abby Bean, nee Jackson, the mother of said child. Such evidence of marriage may consist either of the original or a certified copy of your marriage license and certificate or, in case you are unable to obtain same, this office will accept the affidavits of two eyewitnesses to your marriage relative thereto.

Respectfully,

Acting Commissioner.

9-NB-536

Muskogee, Indian Territory, October 27, 1905.

Felin Bean,
    Oakman, Indian Territory.

Dear Sir:

Receipt is hereby acknowledged of your letter of October 21, 1905, asking when you can file for your child Nicholas Bean.

In reply to your letter you are advised that in order that disposition may be made of the application for the enrollment of your child Nicholas Bean, you should forward at once either the original or a certified copy of the license and certificate between yourself and your wife Addie[sic] Jackson. This evidence of marriage was reqeusted[sic]sic] August 17, 1905, but no reply to this request has yet been received.

Respectfully,

Commissioner.

9-NB-536

Muskogee, Indian Territory, November 28, 1905.

Felin Bean,
    Ada, Indian Territory.

Dear Sir:

In the matter of the enrollment of your child Nicholas Bean you are again advised that it will be necessary for you to furnish evidence of your marriage to Abby Bean, the mother of said child. If you are unable to secure the original marriage license and certificate or a certified copy thereof you should forward the affidavits of two or more disinterested witnesses to your marriage. This matter should receive your immediate attention as no further action can be taken in the matter of the enrollment of your child until this evidence has been furnished.

Respectfully,

Acting Commissioner.

9-NB-536

Muskogee, Indian Territory, March 29, 1906.

Fellin[sic] Bean,
    Oakman, Indian Territory.

Dear Sir:

Receipt is hereby acknowledged of your letter of March 12, 1906, asking if your infant child Nicholas Bean is entitled to enrollment and allotment.

In reply to your letter you are advised that the application for the enrollment of your child Nicholas Bean has not yet been passed upon and you are requested to forward at once evidence of marriage of yourself and Abbie Bean, the mother of this child. Upon receipt of this evidence of marriage, the matter of the enrollment of your child will receive further consideration.

If you secured no license and will forward the certificate of the minister who performed the ceremony between yourself and your wife or affidavits of the persons who were present at said marriage, the same will receive consideration in the matter of the enrollment of this child.

        Respectfully,

        Acting Commissioner.

REFER IN REPLY TO THE FOLLOWING:
9-NB-536

DEPARTMENT OF THE INTERIOR,
COMMISSIONER TO THE FIVE CIVILIZED TRIBES.

Muskogee, Indian Territory, April 12, 1906.

Felin Bean,
    Oakman, Indian Territory.

Dear Sir:

Receipt is hereby acknowledged of the affidavit of W. B. Seaton to the effect that he witnessed the marriage ceremony between Felin Bean and Abbie Bean and the same has been filed with the record in the matter of the enrollment of your child Nicholas Bean. You should also forward the affidavit of another disinterested witness to your marriage in the matter of the enrollment of said child.

Respectfully,
W^m.O. Beall
Acting Commissioner.

9-NB-536.

Muskogee, Indian Territory, April 25, 1906.

Tom D. McKeown,
Ada, Indian Territory.

Dear Sir:

Receipt is hereby acknowledged of your letter of April 23, 1906, enclosing the affidavit of Felin Bean, wherein he states that he was married to Abby Bean in 1902, by Charley Benjamin, a Choctaw preacher, who is now dead. Said affidavit has been filed with the record in the matter of the application for the enrollment of Nicholas Bean, minor child of Felin Bean and Abby Bean, as a citizen by blood of the Chickasaw Nation.

Respectfully,

Commissioner.

25-536.

Muskogee, Indian Territory, September 6, 1906.

Felin Bean,
Oakman, Indian Territory.

Dear Sir:

Receipt is hereby acknowledged of your letter of August 27, 1906, requesting to be advised of the status of the application for the enrollment of your minor son, Nicholas Bean, an applicant for enrollment as a citizen by blood of the Chickasaw Nation.

On your appearance before this office on April 25, 1906, you were furnished an affidavit relative to your marriage, which was to be signed by William Jackson and his wife, and to be returned to this office at an early date, and as yet the same has not been received. Until this matter is attended to no further action can be taken in the matter of the application for the enrollment of said child.

Respectfully,

Acting Commissioner.

9-NB-536

Muskogee, Indian Territory, October 10, 1906.

Felin Bean,
     Ada, Indian Territory.

Dear Sir:

You were heretofore furnished an affidavit to be signed by William and Mollie Jackson to the marriage of yourself and Abby Bean in May 1902 to be used as evidence in the matter of the enrollment of your child Nicholas Bean but the same has not been received.

There is inclosed herewith another copy of this affidavit which you are requested to have executed and returned to this office at once.

Respectfully,

EB 1-10

Commissioner.

9-NB-536.

Muskogee, Indian Territory, March 7, 1907.

Yoch[sic] Jackson,
     Allen, Indian Territory.

Dear Sir:

Your letter of February 4, addressed to the United States Indian Agent, has been by him referred to this office for appropriate action. Therein you ask if Nicholas Bean, child of Abbie Bean, has been enrolled.

In reply you are advised that on February 1, 1907, the Secretary of the Interior approved the enrollment of Nicholas Bean as a new born citizen of the Chickasaw Nation under the Act of Congress approved March 3, 1905.

Respectfully,

Commissioner.

Chic. N.B - 537
>   *(Lida Lois Milligan*
>   *Born February 13, 1903)*

CHICKASAW

5*(corner torn)*

NEW BORN

ACT OF CONGRESS APPROVED MARCH 30, 1905.

Lida Lois Milligan
(Born Feby 13, 1903)

CANCELLED

Record transferred to
CHICKASAW   NEW BORN   No 308

ACT OF CONGRESS APPROVED APRIL 26, 1906.

AUG 8- 1906

Chic. N.B - 538
>   *(Emma Lavers*
>   *Born October 28, 1903)*

DEPARTMENT OF THE INTERIOR,
COMMISSIONER TO THE FIVE CIVILIZED TRIBES.

Durant, Indian Territory, January 17, 1907.

_____oOOo_____

In the matter of the application for the enrollment, as a citizen by blood of the Chickasaw Nation, of Emma Lavers, New Born Card Number 538.

Testimony taken in Sulphur, Indian Territory, January 15, 1907, at home of Amanda Palmer.

Applications for Enrollment of Chickasaw Newborn
Act of 1905 Volume VII

AMANDA PALMER, being duly sworn, by Lacey P. Bobo, Notary Public in and for the Southern District of Indian Territory, testified as follows:

BY THE COMMISSIONER:

Q Are you a duly enrolled citizen by blood of the Chickasaw Nation? A Yes, sir.
Q How does your name appear upon the roll?
A I think it was Henderson, but they changed it to Palmer, Amanda Palmer.
Q How old are you? A 23.
Q What is your post office address? A Sulphur, Indian Territory formerly Sugden.

Witness is identified as a Chickasaw by blood, Roll No. 2800.

Q Did you ever give birth to a female child afterwards named Emma Lavers?
A Yes, sir.
Q Who was the father of said child? A J.O. Lavers--Over ton[sic] Lavers.
Q At the time of the birth of this child, were you the wife of J.O. or Overton Lavers?
A No, sir.
Q When was Emma Lavers born?
A In 1903--October 28th.
Q How old was this child when it died?
A Two years old.
Q Where did the child die?
A At this town--herein Sulphur.
Q Who attended the child as physician during its last illness?
A Dr. Ponder.
Q Is this Dr. Ponder a white man or an Indian? A White man.
Q How long after his last visit until the child died?
A He was there with her when she died.
Q Where is the child buried? A She is buried about two miles east of here.
Q Did an undertaker assist in the burial of the child?
A We bought the coffin already made from Mr. Weems.
Q Where is Mr. Weems place of business?
A Over on the west side of town.
Q Do you know the day of the week this child died?
A Thursday.
Q What time of day? A Thursday night at 19 o'clock.
Q When was she buried? A She was buried Saturday after she died.
Q When did she die? A March 4, 1905.
Q Are you positive this child died on Thursday and was buried on Saturday?
A Yes, I think I am.
Q How long has she been dead? A A year.
Q You are also positive she died on March 4, 1905, are you? A Yes, sir.
Q Have you any record of her death? A No, sir.
Q Was the child able to walk and talk when she died? A She could not talk but she was walking.

Q Who else in this town would know when this child died? A Mrs. Colbert was there when she died and went to the burial.

Q What Mrs. Colbert was that? A Dixie Colbert's wife.

Q It appears from the records of the Commission to the Five Civilized Tribes that you made affidavit before A. A. Chapman that this child was born the 28th day of October 1904--

A Well, he was mistaken, it was in 1903.

Q Said affidavit further set forth that the child was living the 22nd day of April 1905--

A I do not know anything about that affidavit.

Q You remember appearing before A. A. Chapman, Notary Public, do you not?

A Yes, sir, it has been two years now.

Q Was the child dead when you went before Chapman? A No, sir she was living.

Q It appears from the records of the Commission to the Five Civilized Tribes that before T. M[sic]. Gafford, Notary Public in and for the Southern District of Indian Territory, you made affidavit that Emma Lavers died on the 4th day of March 1906: This is wrong and it should be 1905? A yes, sir.

Q Amanda, were there any other deaths in Sulphur about the time you child died?

A No, sir, I do not know anything about that.

Q Where does this Notary Public, T. M[sic]. Gafford, live?

A He lives right here at Sulphur.

Q You are certain it was in the month of March this child died? A Yes, sir.

Q And it was two years ago this coming March? A Yes, sir.

Witness Excused.

Testimony taken in the office of A. V. Ponder, M. D., Sulphur, Indian Territory, January 15, 1907.

A. V. Ponder, M. D., being duly sworn, by Lacey P. Bobo, Notary Public in and for the Southern District of Indian Territory, testified as follows:

BY THE COMMISSIONER:

Q What is your name? A A. V. Ponder.

Q What is your post office? A Sulphur, I. T.

Q How old are you? A I am 50 years old.

Q What is your profession? A I am a physician.

Q How long have you practiced? A About 30 years, but I have been in Sulphur only five years.

Q During your practice, have you ever attended the family of Overton Lavers?

A Yes, sir.

Q Do you know one Amanda Palmer who has resided some time with Overton Lavers?

A Yes, sir.

Q Did you ever attend one of her children? A Yes, sir, the one that died.

Q What was the sex of this child? A It was a girl.

Applications for Enrollment of Chickasaw Newborn
Act of 1905   Volume VII

Q Do you recollect the age of the child? A No, sir, I have heard it but have forgotten.

Q Are you able to state when this baby girl of Amanda Palmer's died by reference to your case book? A It was some time in December 1905, as shown by my book, I do not remember the exact date.

Q Did you understand this child of Amanda Palmer's was the illegitimate child of Overton Lavers?

A No, sir, I do not know anything about that.   My book shows that I visited Amanda Palmer and Baby on the 2nd, 3rd, 4th, 5th and 6th days of December 1905, the child was taken sick on the 11th day of November and I visited it on up until the 6th day of December and that was the last visit I made.

Q Were you present when the child died? A No, sir, I was there in a few minutes after it died, I got in just afterwards. I have been out and had not been gone long when they 'phoned me, and when I returned I went over there but it was dead.

Q How old was this child at the time of her death? A I do not know, I suppose it was tow or two and a half, somewhere along there, it was just a small baby.

Q By reference to your case-book, you state that a little daughter of Amanda Palmer's died in the month of December 1905? A Yes, sir.

Q When next subsequent to the death of this little girl did you attend this Overton Lavers' family? A I was there next on the 4th of March.

Q What member of Overton's family did you attend that time? A One of his boys named Ben--that's where that woman got it mixed up, she has not got much of a memory anyhow.

Testimony taken in the home of M. C. Weems, Sulphur, Indian Territory, January 15, 1907.

M. C. WEEMS, being duly sworn, by Lacey P. Bobo, Notary Public in and for the Southern District of Indian Territory, testified as follows:

BY THE COMMISSIONER:

Q State your name, age and post office, please?
A M. C. Weems, I am 61 years old and my post office is Sulphur, I. T.

Q What is your business or occupation? A I have always been in the furniture business until I was burned out in December last year, I am in the real estate business now.

Q Prior to the time you were burned out in December last year, did you conduct an undertaking establishment in connection with your furniture business? A Yes, sir.

Q Are you acquainted with Amanda Palmer, a Chickasaw woman?

A I know her when I meet her, I could not say I was very well acquainted with her.

Q With whom does she make her home in Sulphur? A Overton Lavers

Q Did you ever as undertaker bury a child for this woman? A Just one.

Q When was that child buried? A December 8, 1905.

Q To whom did you charge the coffin? A I did not charge it at all, they paid cash for it; we always kept a record of everything to keep track of our business, and that was a cash item but we made a record of it in this book.

Witness here produces undertaker's book showing that Overton Lavers was furnished on December 8, 1905, with one child's coffin; amount, $12.50.

Q Do you know this child's name? A No, sir, I do not know it, I never asked.
Q Did you know the sex of the child? A No, sir.
Q You know it was an Indian baby? A Yes, it was an Indian.
Q How long had the child been a corpse when you buried it? A It died in the evening the second day before I buried it--I think it died in the morning and has been dead two nights which would make it about 48 hours, something like that when we buried it.

At home of Amanda Palmer.

AMANDA PALMER re-examined.

Q You gave testimony before this party this morning stating that your daughter Emma died March 4, 1905?
A I got a letter from the Commission stating the child died March 4th.

Witness produces letter from the Commissioner to the Five Civilized Tribes, under date of December 14, 1906, in which it is stated that "it appears from the records of this office that your daughter, Emma Lavers, died prior to march 4, 1906 . . . ."

Witness states that she understood the words "prior to" to mean that the child Emma Lavers died on the 4th day of March, and that if she did not have to listen to what other said she could tell the right date when the child died.

Q You are expected to tell the truth regardless of what others say or advise you to say-- now, when did this child of yours, Emma Lavers, die?
A December 7, 1905.
Q How long has the child been dead? A Just a year.
Q You remember and state positively that this child died December 7, 1905, are you Amanda? A Yes, sir.
Q Why did you state that this child died March 4, 1905, in testimony taken this morning?
A Because Overton Lavers said if I would make it march 4, 1905, he thought I would get the child on the roll; I do not know who saw him and told him that.
Q From the records of the Commission to the Five Civilized Tribes it appears that before one T. M[sic]. Gafford, Notary Public, in and for the Southern District of Indian Territory, you, as mother, of Sulphur, Indian Territory, together with Mary Ann Cobb, acquaintance, of Davis, Indian Territory, made affidavit that you daughter, Emma Lavers, died on the 4th day of March, 1906: When you made this affidavit before T. M[sic]. Gafford, you knew the child died before March 4, 1906?
A Yes, sir.
Q You just made said affidavit simply because you thought the child would not be enrolled unless it was shown to be living then? A Yes, sir.

Q Did you tell the Notary Public before whom you appears, Mr. Gafford, that the child died before March 4, 1906? A I do not know whether Gafford knew anything about it or not; I told him the child died March 4, 1905. I do not know whether he knew anything about it or not.

Q When you went down before Chapman to make an affidavit about this, did Mary Ann Cobb to with you?

A No, sir, but Chapman went down there and saw her after I made that affidavit, she was not with me.

Q When you made affidavit in the matter of the application for the enrollment of your daughter, Emma Lavers, as a citizen of the Chickasaw Nation, before A. A. Chapman, do you remember what time of the year you appeared? A 1905, in April.

Q Had the sixty days after March 4, 1905, during which the Commission had authority to receive applications for new borns expired? A No, sir.

Q How much did it like of having expired? A Well, Chapman said when I made that that it did not expire until May 2nd.

Q Do you remember how many days before May 2nd it was you made this application?

A I made the application on the 24th day of April, 1905.

Witness Excused.

W. P. Covington, being duly sworn, states that the above and foregoing is a full, true and correct transcript of his stenographic notes taken in said case on said date.

W.P. Covington

Subscribed and sworn to before me, this 19 day of Jany. 1907.

Lacey P Bobo
Notary Public.

9-N.B.-538.
O.L.J.

DEPARTMENT OF THE INTERIOR,
COMMISSIONER TO THE FIVE CIVILIZED TRIBES.

In the matter of the application for the enrollment of Emma Lavers as a citizen by blood of the Chickasaw Nation.

D E C I S I O N .

It appears from the record herein that application was duly made for the enrollment of Emma Lavers as a citizen by blood of the Chickasaw Nation within the time limited by the provisions of Section One of the Act of Congress approved April 26, 1906 (34 Stats., 137).

It further appears from the records in the possession of this office that the applicant, Emma Lavers, was born October 28, 1904, and is the illegitimate child of Amanda Palmer, a recognized and enrolled citizen by blood of the Chickasaw Nation, whose name appears as No. 2800 upon the final roll of citizens by blood of the Chickasaw Nation approved by the Secretary of the Interior December 12, 1902, and that said applicant died on March 4, 1906.

I am, therefore, of the opinion that Emma Lavers should be enrolled as a citizen by blood of the Chickasaw Nation, under the provisions of the Act of Congress approved March 3, 1905 (33 Stats., 1060), and it is so ordered.

Tams Bixby   Commissioner.

Muskogee, Indian Territory.
 JAN 10 1907

Muskogee, Indian Territory, January 24 1907.

In the matter of the application for the enrollment of Emma Lavers as a citizen of the Chickasaw Nation

Service of a copy of the decision of the Commissioner to the Five Civilized Tribes rendered January 10 1907, together with the customary fifteen days within which to protest against the said decision is hereby waived.

Mansfield McMurray & Cornish
Atteys for the Choctaw and Chickasaw Nation[sic].

BIRTH AFFIDAVIT.

DEPARTMENT OF THE INTERIOR,
COMMISSION TO THE FIVE CIVILIZED TRIBES.

IN RE Application for Enrollment, as a citizen of the Chickasaw Nation, of Emma Lavers , born on the 28th day of October ,1904

Name of Father: J O Lavers   a citizen of the Chickasaw Nation.
Name of Mother: Amanda Palmer (Suggs) a citizen of the Chickasaw Nation.

Post-Office: Sugden I.T.

Applications for Enrollment of Chickasaw Newborn
Act of 1905   Volume VII

AFFIDAVIT OF MOTHER.

UNITED STATES OF AMERICA, ⎫
INDIAN TERRITORY. ⎬
Southern   District. ⎭

I,   Amanda Palmer (Suggs)   , on oath state that I am about 22   years of age and a citizen by   Blood   , of the Chickasaw   Nation; that I am the ~~lawful~~ Cohort wife of   J O Lavers   , who is a citizen, by   Blood   of the Chickasaw   Nation; that a Female   child was born to me on   28th   day of   October   , 1904 , that said child has been named   Emma Lavers   , and is now living.

Amanda Palmer Suggs

WITNESSES TO MARK:
{ A.A. Chapman
{ Lewis Seely

Subscribed and sworn to before me this 22nd *day of*   April   , 1905.

A.A. Chapman
NOTARY PUBLIC.

AFFIDAVIT OF ATTENDING PHYSICIAN OR MID-WIFE.

UNITED STATES OF AMERICA, ⎫
INDIAN TERRITORY. ⎬
Southern   District. ⎭

I,   Mollie Keel   , a   mid wife   , on oath state that I attended on Mrs. Amanda Palmer (Suggs   , ~~wife~~ Cohort of   J O Lavers   on the   28th   day of October   , 190 4; that there was born to her on said date a   female   child; that said child is now living and is said to have been named   Emma Lavers

her
Mollie x Keel
mark

WITNESSES TO MARK:
{ A.A. Chapman
{ Lewis Seely

Subscribed and sworn to before me this 25th   *day of*   April   , 1905.

A.A. Chapman
NOTARY PUBLIC.

153

DEPARTMENT OF THE INTERIOR.
COMMISSION TO THE FIVE CIVILIZED TRIBES.

———

In the matter of the death of   Emma Lavers
a citizen of the   Chickasaw   Nation, who formerly resided at or near   Sulphur   , Ind.
Ter., and died on the   4th day of   March , 1906

———

AFFIDAVIT OF RELATIVE.

UNITED STATES OF AMERICA, Indian Territory, ⎫
    Southern   **DISTRICT.** ⎭

    I,   Amanda Palmer   , on oath state that I am   26   years of age and a
citizen by Blood   , of the Chickasaw Nation; that my postoffice address is   Sulphur   ,
Ind. Ter.; that I am   The Mother   of   Emma Lavers   who was a citizen, by Blood ,
of the Chickasaw   Nation and that said   Emma Lavers   died on the   4th day of
March   , 1906

                  Amanda Palmer

Witnesses To Mark:
    {

    Subscribed and sworn to before me this   21st day of   December   , 1906

               T.F. Gafford
My Commission Expires June 21, 1908.   Notary Public.

———

AFFIDAVIT OF ACQUAINTANCE.

UNITED STATES OF AMERICA, Indian Territory, ⎫
    Southern   **DISTRICT.** ⎭

    I,   Mary Ann Cobb   , on oath state that I am   39   years of age, and a citizen
by Blood   of the Chickasaw   Nation; that my postoffice address is   Davis   , Ind. Ter.;
that I was personally acquainted with   Emma Lavers   who was a citizen, by Blood ,
of the   Chickasaw Nation; and that said   Emma Lavers   died on the   4th day of
March   , 1906

            Mrs Mary Ann Cobb

Witnesses To Mark:
    {

    Subscribed and sworn to before me this   21st day of   December   , 1906

               T.F. Gafford
My Commission Expires June 21, 1908.   Notary Public.

———

Muskogee, Indian Territory, May 15, 1905.

A. A. Chapman,
    Ravia, Indian Territory.

Dear Sir:

Receipt is hereby acknowledged of your letter of April 30, and replying to that part thereof which refers to the affidavits to the birth of Emma Lavers, you are advised that the information contained therein is not sufficient to enable us to identify Emma Lavers upon our records. If you will state the name under which Amanda Palmer was enrolled and her roll number as it appears upon her allotment certificate, the matter will receive further consideration.

You are advised, however, that the affidavits were not received until May 5, 1905, which was subsequent to the sixty days within which the Commission was authorized to receive applications for the enrollment of children.

Respectfully,

Chairman.

––––––––––

(COPY)

Ravia, I. T.   May 16, 1905.

Commission to the 5 Civilized Tribes,
    Muskogee, I. T.

Gentlemen:

Your May 15th, 1905, recd. replying to your inquiry Amanda Palmer Was Enrolled as the daughter of Campbell Henderson. I cannot give her number as it appears upon her allotment certificate, she having moved to Sugden I. T. is the cause of her delay in getting her midwife's affidavit of her child Emma birth-- this child is the full sister to Maud Lavers who was enrolled by your Commission in 1903 if I remember correctly. I can write her and get her Number in case you do not identify her as Amenda[sic] Henderson. She married Charles Palmer who died some years ago. She then became the common wife of J. O. Lavers and Maude[sic] Lavers was born and enrolled, then she gave birth to this child, Emma Lavers.

Trusting this will be plain to you, i[sic] am yours truly

A. A. Chapman.

––––––––––

Applications for Enrollment of Chickasaw Newborn
Act of 1905   Volume VII

9--936.

Muskogee, Indian Territory, May 23, 1905.

A. A. Chapman,
   Ravia, Indian Territory.

Dear Sir:

Receipt is hereby acknowledged of your letter of May 16, giving information relative to the enrollment of Amanda Palmer, which has enabled us to identify her upon our records as a citizen by blood of the Chickasaw Nation.

You are advised, however, that the affidavits heretofore forwarded to the birth of Emma Lavers, daughter of Amanda Palmer, were not received at this office until May 5, 1905, which was subsequent to the expiration of the sixty days in which the Commission was authorized by the act of Congress approved March 3, 1905, to received applications for the enrollment of children born to enrolled citizens by blood of the Choctaw and Chickasaw Nations.

You will therefore see that the Commission is now without authority to enroll Emma Lavers.

Respectfully,

Chairman.

9-NB-538

Muskogee, Indian Territory, March 24, 1906.

Amanda Suggs,
   Sulphur, Indian Territory.

Dear Madam:

Receipt is hereby acknowledged of your letter of March 10, 1906, relative to the enrollment of your child Emma Lavers.

In reply to your letter you are advised that the affidavits to the birth of your child Emma Lavers was received at this office May 5, 1905, and under the act of Congress approved March 3, 1905, the time within which applications for enrollment as citizens of the Choctaw and Chickasaw Nations could be received expired May 2, 1905 and this office was without authority to enroll your child Emma Lavers. In event of additional legislation on this subject the matter of the enrollment of your child will receive consideration.

Respectfully,

Acting Commissioner.

9-NB-538

Muskogee, Indian Territory, June 9, 1906.

A. A. Chapman,
　　Ravia, Indian Territory.

Dear Sir:

Receipt is hereby acknowledged of your letter of May 22, 1906, in which you refer to the application for the enrollment of Emma Lavers and state that you thought you mailed same within the time provided by the act of Congress approved March 3, 1905; that this child died prior to march 4, 1906 but was living March 4, 1905, and you ask if there is any chance for her enrollment.

In reply to your letter you are advised that the affidavits to the birth of Emma Lavers were not received at this office until May 5, 1905, three days after the expiration of the time within which the Commission to the Five Civilized Tribes could receive applications for enrollment under the act of March 3, 1905.

The act of Congress approved April 26, 1906, only provides for the enrollment of those children of Choctaw and Chickasaw citizens who were living March 4, 1906.

Respectfully,

Commissioner.

9-NB-538

Muskogee, Indian Territory, August 21, 1906.

Amanda Palmer,
　　Sulphur, Indian Territory.

Dear Madam:

Receipt is hereby acknowledged of your letter of July 30, 1906, relative to the application made for the enrollment of your child in 1905 in which you state that you hope this is sufficient to enroll this child.

In reply to your letter you are advised that the application for the enrollment of your child Emma Lavers, born October 28, 1904, was not received at this office until May 5, 1905, although the letter bore date April 13, 1905.

It appearing from a letter of A. A. Chapman that Emma Lavers died prior to march 4, 1906, she would not be entitled to enrollment under the act of Congress approved April 26, 1906.

For the purpose of making the death of this child a matter of record there is inclosed blank form for proof of death which please have executed and returned to this office as early as practicable.

Respectfully,

Commissioner.

D. C.

9NB538

Muskogee, Indian Territory, December 27, 1906.

Amanda Palmer,
    Sulphur, Indian Territory.

Dear Madam:

Receipt is hereby acknowledged of your affidavit and the affidavit of Mary Ann Cobb to the death of your child, Emma Lavers, which occurred March 4, 1906, and the same have been filed with the record in the matter of the enrollment of this child.

Respectfully,

Acting Commissioner.

9-NB-538

COPY
Muskogee, Indian Territory, January 10, 1907.

Amanda Palmer,
    Sulphur, Indian Territory.

Dear Madam:

Inclosed herewith you will find a copy of the decision of the Commissioner to the Five Civilized Tribes, rendered January 10, 1907, granting the application for the enrollment of Emma Lavers as a citizen by blood of the Chickasaw Nation.

The attorneys for the Choctaw and Chickasaw Nations have been furnished a copy of the decision and have been allowed fifteen days from the date of this notice within which to file protest against her enrollment. If at the expiration of that time no protest has been filed, the name of Emma Lavers will be placed upon the final roll of citizens by blood of the Chickasaw Nation, to be submitted to the Secretary of the Interior for his approval.

Respectfully,
SIGNED

Tams Bixby
Commissioner.

Registered.
Incl. 9-NB-538.

9-NB-538

COPY
Muskogee, Indian Territory, January 10, 1907.

A. A. Chapman,
Ravia, Indian Territory.

Dear Sir:

You are hereby notified that the Commissioner to the Five Civilized Tribes, on January 10, 1907, rendered his decision granting the application for the enrollment of Emma Lavers as a citizen by blood of the Chickasaw Nation.

The attorneys for the Choctaw and Chickasaw Nations have been furnished a copy of this decision and have been allowed fifteen days from the date of this notice within which to file protest against her enrollment. If at the expiration of that time no protest has been filed, the name of Emma Lavers will be placed upon the final roll of citizens by blood of the Chickasaw Nation to be submitted to the Secretary of the Interior for his approval.

Respectfully,
SIGNED

Tams Bixby
Commissioner.

Registered.

9-NB-538

COPY

Muskogee, Indian Territory, January 10, 1907.

Mansfield, McMurray & Cornish,
  Attorneys for Choctaw and Chickasaw Nations,
    South McAlester, Indian Territory.

Gentlemen:

Inclosed herewith you will find a copy of the decision of the Commissioner to the Five Civilized Tribes, rendered January 10, 1907, granting the application for the enrollment of Emma Lavers as a citizen by blood of the Chickasaw Nation.

You are hereby advised that you will be allowed fifteen days from the date of this notice within which to file protest against her enrollment. If, at the expiration of that time no protest has been filed, the name of Emma Lavers will be placed upon the final roll of citizens by blood of the Chickasaw Nation, to be submitted to the Secretary of the Interior for his approval.

Respectfully,
SIGNED

Tams Bixby
Commissioner.

Registered.
Incl. 9-NB-538.

AP

REFER IN REPLY TO THE FOLLOWING:
538

DEPARTMENT OF THE INTERIOR,
COMMISSIONER TO THE FIVE CIVILIZED TRIBES.

Muskogee, Indian Territory, February 28, 1907.

Amanda Palmer,
  Sulphur, Indian Territory.

Dear Madam:

You are hereby advised that on February 21, 1907, the Secretary of the Interior approved the enrollment of your child, Emma Lavers as a New Born citizen of the Chickasaw Nation, under the Act of Congress approved March 3, 1905, and her name appears upon the roll of citizens enrolled under said Act, opposite No. 573.

Selection of allotment should now be made for said child at the land office in the Nation in which the land is located.

Applications for Enrollment of Chickasaw Newborn
Act of 1905   Volume VII

Respectfully,
Tams Bixby
Commissioner.

(Louise Thompson
Born September 10, 1904)

BIRTH AFFIDAVIT.

DEPARTMENT OF THE INTERIOR.
COMMISSION TO THE FIVE CIVILIZED TRIBES.

IN RE APPLICATION FOR ENROLLMENT, as a citizen of the   Chickasaw   Nation, of   Louise Thompson   , born on the   10   day of   Sept   , 1904

Name of Father: Greenwood Thompson   a citizen of the   Choctaw   Nation.
Name of Mother: Minnie B Thompson   a citizen of the   Chickasaw Nation.

Postoffice   Durant I.T.

AFFIDAVIT OF MOTHER.

UNITED STATES OF AMERICA, Indian Territory,⎫
    Central   DISTRICT.⎭

I,   Minnie B Thompson   , on oath state that I am   29   years of age and a citizen by   Blood   , of the   Chickasaw   Nation; that I am the lawful wife of Greenwood Thompson   , who is a citizen, by   Blood   of the   Choctaw Nation; that a   Female   child was born to me on   10   day of Sept   , 1904, that said child has been named   Louise Thompson   , and is now ~~living~~. Dead

Minnie B Thompson
Witnesses To Mark:

Subscribed and sworn to before me this   Sixteenth day of   March   , 1905.

Hugh L Cox
Notary Public.

161

Applications for Enrollment of Chickasaw Newborn
Act of 1905 Volume VII

AFFIDAVIT OF ATTENDING PHYSICIAN OR MID-WIFE.

UNITED STATES OF AMERICA, Indian Territory, ⎱
    Central   DISTRICT. ⎰

    I,   J. F. Park   , a   M.D.   , on oath state that I attended on Mrs. Minnie B Thompson   , wife of Greenwood Thompson   on the 10   day of Sept , 1904; that there was born to her on said date a   Female   child; that said child is now ~~living~~ and is said to have been named Louise Thompson
      Dead

                              J.F. Park, M.D.

Witnesses To Mark:
    {

Subscribed and sworn to before me this Sixteenth day of March   , 1905.

                      Hugh L Cox
                          Notary Public.

Department of the Interior,
COMMISSION TO THE FIVE CIVILIZED TRIBES.

    In the matter of the death of   Louise Thompson   a citizen of the Chickasaw   Nation, who formerly resided at or near   Durant   , Ind. Ter., and died on the 12 day of   September , 1904

AFFIDAVIT OF RELATIVE.

UNITED STATES OF AMERICA, ⎱
  INDIAN TERRITORY,
_____District. ⎰

    I,_____, on oath state that I am _____ years of age and a citizen by _____ , of the _____ Nation; that my postoffice address is _____ , Ind. Ter.; that I am_____ of _____ who was a citizen, by_____of the _____Nation and that said_____died on the _____day of _____, 190__

Witnesses To Mark:
    { _____
      _____

   Subscribed and sworn to before me this _____ *day of* _____, 190__

                    Notary Public.

Applications for Enrollment of Chickasaw Newborn
Act of 1905   Volume VII

AFFIDAVIT OF ACQUAINTANCE.

UNITED STATES OF AMERICA, ⎫
INDIAN TERRITORY,
  Central   District. ⎰

I,   Mrs. M. J. Graham   , on oath state that I am   59   years of age, and a citizen by Blood   of the   Chickasaw Nation; that my postoffice address is   Colbert   , Ind. Ter.; that I was personally acquainted with   Louise Thompson   who was a citizen, by   blood   , of the   Chickasaw Nation; and that said   Louise Thompson died on the   12   day of September   , 1904

Mrs. M. J. Graham

Witnesses To Mark:

{

Subscribed and sworn to before me this   7   *day of*   Oct   , 1905

T.J. Vaughan
Notary Public.

Affidavit.

United States of America,
  Indian Territory)
Central District)

I, Greenwood Thompson, of Durant, Indian Territory, do solemnly swear that I am the father of Louise Thompson, now deceased; that the said Louise Thompson was born on the Sept 10 - 1904, and died on the 12 day of Sept 1904. That the mother of the said Louise Thompson is Minnie B Thompson, my wife.

Witness my hand this the 2d, day of May, 1905.

Greenwood Thompson

Subscribed and sworn to before me this May 2d, 1905.

Claude C. *(Illegible)*
Notary Public.

Commission Expires on _____

163

9-1091.

Muskogee, Indian Territory, March 21, 1905.

Green Thompson,
    Durant, Indian Territory.

Dear Sir:

Receipt is hereby acknowledged of your letter of March 16, 1905, enclosing affidavits of Minnie B. Thompson and J. F. Parks to the birth of Louise Thompson, daughter of Greenwood and Minnie B. Thompson, September 10, 1904.

It is noted in the application that this child is now dead and you are advised that under the provisions of the act of Congress approved March 3, 1905, the Commission is authorized for a period of sixty days from that date to receive applications for the enrollment of children born to enrolled citizens by blood of the Choctaw and Chickasaw Nations between September 25, 1902, and March 4, 1905, and living on said latter date. You will therefore see that the Commission is without authority to enroll children born to citizens of the Choctaw and Chickasaw Nations subsequent to September 25, 1902, who were not living on March 4, 1905.

You are therefore requested to forward an affidavit giving the correct date of the death of Louise Thompson.

Respectfully,

Chairman.

9--1091.

Muskogee, Indian Territory, May 15, 1905.

Greenwood Thompson,
    Durant, Indian Territory.

Dear Sir:

Receipt is hereby acknowledged of your letter of May 6, enclosing your affidavit to the death of your daughter, Louise Thompson, which occurred September 10, 1904, and the same has been filed with our records.

Respectfully,

Chairman.

Applications for Enrollment of Chickasaw Newborn
Act of 1905   Volume VII

9-NB-539

Muskogee, Indian Territory, August 22, 1905.

Green Thompson,
Durant, Indian Territory.

Dear Sir:

It appears from your affidavits that your child Louise Thompson born September 10, 1904, died September 12, 1904.

For the purpose of completing the proof of the death of this child there is inclosed you herewith blank for the affidavit of an acquaintance which lease have executed and returned to this office as early as practicable.

Respectfully,

EB 1-22

Commissioner.

COPY

Muskogee, Indian Territory, October 31, 1905.

Green Thompson,
Durant, Indian Territory.

Dear Sir:

You are hereby advised that is appearing from the records of this office that your child, Louise Thompson, died prior to March 4, 1905, the Commissioner to the Five Civilized Tribes on October 31, 1905, dismissed the application for her enrollment as a citizen by blood of the Chickasaw Nation.

Respectfully,
SIGNED

Tams Bixby
Commissioner.

Chic. N.B - 540
(Ruby Lourinda Roark
Born May 19, 1904)

165

CHICKASAW   540

NEW BORN

ACT OF CONGRESS APPROVED MARCH 30, 1905.

Ruby Lourinda Roark
(Born May 19, 1904)

CANCELLED

Record transferred to
Chickasaw   New Born *(Illegible)*
ACT OF CONGRESS APPROVED APRIL 26, 1906.

JUL 13 1906

Chic. N.B - 541
(Vie Bacon
Born August 27, 1904)

C O P Y.

DEPARTMENT OF THE INTERIOR,
COMMISSION TO THE FIVE CIVILIZED TRIBES.

W.F.
DCL

In the matter of the application for the enrollment of William Henderson Bacon, et al., as citizens of the Chickasaw Nation consolidating the applications of

William Henderson Bacon, et al.,	9-1408
Sam J. Bacon, et al.,	9-1406
William J. Bacon, et al.,	9-1559
Mattie Davis, et al.,	9-1409

--: D E C I S I O N :--

It appears from the census card records in this case that on October 13, 1898, William Henderson Bacon appeared before the Commission and made personal application for the enrollment of himself and his children, Gertrude Bacon, Will Hubbard Bacon and Anna Bacon, as citizens of the Chickasaw Nation; that on November 27, 1898, Sam J. Bacon, a son of said William Henderson Bacon, appeared before the Commission and made personal application for the enrollment of himself and his children, Nellie Bacon and Bailey Bacon, as citizens of the Chickasaw Nation; that on October 10, 1899, William J. Bacon, a son of said William Henderson Bacon, appeared before the Commission and made personal application for the enrollment of himself as a citizen of the Chickasaw Nation; that on October 14, 1898, application was made for the enrollment of Henry Clinton Bacon, a son of said William J. Bacon, as a citizen of the Chickasaw Nation; that on October 13, 1898, Mattie Davis, a daughter of said William Henderson Bacon, appeared before the Commission and made personal application for the enrollment of herself as a citizen of the Chickasaw Nation; that written applications were subsequently made to this Commission for the enrollment as citizens of said nation, as follows, to-wit: on May 24, 1900, for Sammie Bacon, (born December 17, 1899), infant child of said Sam J. Bacon; on October 4, 1901, for Frances Belle Bacon, (born July 3, 1900), and on July 29, 1902, for Robert Bacon, (born February 11, 1902), infant children of said William J. Bacon; and on September 11, 1901, for Marian Jessie Davis, (born August 8, 1901), infant child of said Mattie Davis. Proceedings were had in the matter of these applications at Ardmore, Indian Territory, on November 25, 1898, and at Atoka, Indian Territory, on December 5, 1899.

The record in this case further shows that the principal applicant, William Henderson Bacon, is a son of Harvey Bacon, deceased, a white man and missionary to the Indians, who was adopted by the Chickasaw Indians in the State of Mississippi prior to their removal to what constitutes the present Chickasaw Nation in Indian Territory, as is evidenced by a certified copy of a patent to land, which is filed with and made a part of the record in this case, which land in the State of Mississippi was granted to said Harvey Bacon under the provisions of the Fifth Article of the Treaty between the United States and the Chickasaw Indians, concluded at Pontotoc Creek on May 24, 1834.

It further appears from the record herein that the applicants in this case are lineal descendants of said Harvey Bacon and claim their rights as citizens of the Chickasaw Nation by virtue of his said adoption by the Chickasaw Indians and of the subsequent recognition by the Chickasaw Nation of said Harvey Bacon and his descendants, the applicants herein, as citizens of said nation.

It further appears from an examination of the tribal rolls in the possession of the Commission that the principal applicant, William Henderson Bacon, is identified, (as the head of a family), upon the 1878 Chickasaw Annuity Roll, Panola County, number 1; that the applicants, William Henderson Bacon, Gertrude Bacon and Mattie Davis, are identified upon the 1893 Chickasaw Leased District Payment Roll, number 1, page 137; and that the applicant, Sam J. Bacon, is identified upon the 1893 Chickasaw Leased District Payment Roll, number 1, page 137; and that the applicant, William J. Bacon, is identified upon said 1893 Chickasaw Leased District Payment Roll, number 2, page 8. The applicants, Sammie Bacon, Frances Belle Bacon, Robert Bacon and Marian Jessie Davis, having been born subsequent to the date of the original application, made by their parents, are identified by proper birth certificates filed with and made a part of the record in this case.

It further appears that all the applicants herein who were then living, were on June 28, 1898, residents in good faith of Indian Territory, all applicants listed upon census cards in 1898 and 1899 having been first examined as to such fact, although their testimony was not reduced to writing.

It is, therefore, the opinion of this Commission that William Henderson Bacon, Gertrude Bacon, Will Hubbard Bacon, Anna Bacon, Sam J. Bacon, Nellie Bacon, Bailey

Applications for Enrollment of Chickasaw Newborn
Act of 1905   Volume VII

Bacon, Sammie Bacon, Robert Bacon, Mattie Davis and Marian Jessie Davis should be enrolled as citizens of the Chickasaw Nation, in accordance with the provisions of the acts of Congress approved June 28, 1898 (30 Stat., 495), and July 1, 1902 (32 Stat., 641)m and it is so ordered.

COMMISSION TO THE FIVE CIVILIZED TRIBES.

Tams Bixby	Chairman
T. B. Needles	Commissioner
C. R. Breckinridge	

Muskogee, Indian Territory,   Commissioner.

Jun 10 1904

9-N.B. 541.

DEPARTMENT OF THE INTERIOR,
COMMISSIONER TO THE FIVE CIVILIZED TRIBES.

In the matter of the application for the enrollment of Vie Bacon as a citizen of the Chickasaw Nation.

- - : D E C I S I O N : - -

It appears from the record herein that on March 28, 1905, there was filed with the Commission to the Five Civilized Tribes an application for the enrollment of Vie Bacon as a citizen of the Chickasaw Nation.

It further appears from the record herein, and from the records of this office, that the applicant who is a white child, was born August 27, 1904, and is a daughter of Sam J. Bacon, a recognized and enrolled citizen of the Chickasaw Nation, whose name appears as No. 4869 upon the final roll of citizens of said Nation approved by the Secretary of the Interior September 22, 1904, enrolled thereon as an adopted white, and Lucy Bacon, a non-citizen.

It further appears from the record herein, and from the records of this office, that Sam J. Bacon is a son of William Henderson Bacon who was a son of Harvey Bacon, deceased, a white man and missionary to the Indians, who was adopted by the Chickasaw Indians in the state of Mississippi prior to their removal to what constitutes the present Chickasaw Nation in the Indian Territory, and who received land in said state under the provisions of the Fifth Article of the Treaty between the United States and the Chickasaw Indians concluded at Pontotoc Creek on May 24, 1834, the said William Henderson Bacon having been born subsequent to the adoption of his father, Harvey Bacon.

It further appears from the record herein that the applicant, Vie Bacon, was living on March 4, 1905.

The Act of Congress approved March 3, 1905 (33 Stats., 1060), provides:

"That the Commission to the Five Civilized Tribes is authorized for sixty days after the date of the approval of this act to receive and consider applications for enrollment of children born subsequent to September twenty-fifth, nineteen hundred and two, and prior to March fourth, nineteen hundred

168

and five, and who were living on said latter date, to citizens by blood of the Choctaw and Chickasaw tribes of Indians whose enrollment has been approved by the Secretary of the Interior prior to the date of the approval of this act; and to enroll and make allotments to such children."

    I am therefore of the opinion that, in accordance with the opinion of the Assistant Attorney General for the Department of the Interior dated September 1, 1905 (I.T.D. 10622-1905), Vie Bacon should be enrolled as a citizen of the Chickasaw Nation under the provisions of law above quoted, and it is so ordered.

                                    Tams Bixby   Commissioner.

Muskogee, Indian Territory.
     NOV 11 1905

BIRTH AFFIDAVIT.

DEPARTMENT OF THE INTERIOR.
COMMISSION TO THE FIVE CIVILIZED TRIBES.

    IN RE APPLICATION FOR ENROLLMENT, as a citizen of the   Chickasaw   Nation, of   Vie Bacon   , born on the 27 day of   Aug , 1904

Name of Father: Sam J. Bacon   a citizen of the   Chickasaw Nation.
Name of Mother: Lucy Bacon   a citizen of the ——————— Nation.

                       Postoffice   Utica I.T.

AFFIDAVIT OF MOTHER.

UNITED STATES OF AMERICA, Indian Territory,
        Central   **DISTRICT.**

    I,   Lucy Bacon   , on oath state that I am 28   years of age and a citizen by ————, of the — — — Nation; that I am the lawful wife of Sam J Bacon   , who is a citizen, by Blood   of the   Chickasaw   Nation; that a   Female child was born to me on 27th   day of   August   , 1904; that said child has been named   Vie Bacon   , and was living March 4, 1905.

                                   Lucy Bacon

Witnesses To Mark:

    Subscribed and sworn to before me this 25th   day of March   , 1905

                            W.J. O'Donby
                                  Notary Public.

Applications for Enrollment of Chickasaw Newborn
Act of 1905   Volume VII

AFFIDAVIT OF ATTENDING PHYSICIAN OR MID-WIFE.

UNITED STATES OF AMERICA, Indian Territory, ⎫
   Central   DISTRICT. ⎰

    I, A.J. Wells   , a Physician   , on oath state that I attended on
Mrs. Lucy Bacon   , wife of Sam J Bacon   on the 27th day of August   ,
1904; that there was born to her on said date a   Female   child; that said child was
living March 4, 1905, and is said to have been named Vie Bacon

                                A.J. Wells M.D.

Witnesses To Mark:

   {

    Subscribed and sworn to before me this 25th   day of March   , 1905

                       W.J. O'Donby
                         Notary Public.

Mr   Sam Bacon

                AND

M iss Lucy Sims

Marriage Certificate

DEPARTMENT OF THE INTERIOR,
COMMISSIONER TO THE FIVE CIVILIZED TRIBES.
FILED

DEC 2 1905

Tams Bixby COMMISSIONER.

Issued   Nov 25   *190* 5

         Pat Henry   *Clerk*

By   *Deputy*

Marriage Certificate

STATE OF
TEXAS

COUNTY OF

This Instrument Witnesseth that on the **25**th day of **August** A.D. **1902** there was issued out of the office of the Clerk of the County Court of said County a License for the Marriage of

Mr **Sam Bacon**

and Miss **Lucy Sims**

and on the **25"** day of **August** A.D. **1902** said parties were legally united in Marriage by a properly authorized person, named in said License and due return thereof made to this office in the manner and form required by law, all of which is duly entered upon the Marriage Records of my office in Vol **N.** Page **294**

Witness my hand and official seal at my office in **Bonham** Texas on this the **25**th day of Nov. A.D. **1905**

Pat Henry
Clerk County Court Fannin County Texas
By _____
Deputy

171

Chickasaw 1406

Muskogee, Indian Territory, March 31, 1905.

Sam J. Bacon,
      Utica, Indian Territory.

Dear Sir:

Receipt is hereby acknowledged of the affidavits of Lucy Bacon and A. J. Wells to the birth of Vie Bacon, daughter of Sam J. and Lucy Bacon, August 27, 1904.

You are advised that the act of Congress of March 3, 1905, authorizes the Commission, for a period of sixty days, to receive applications for the enrollment of children born to enrolled citizens by blood of the Choctaw and Chickasaw Nations prior to March 4, 1905, and as it appears from our records that you are an adopted white person, and not a citizen by blood of the Chickasaw Nation, you will see that the Commission is without authority to enroll your child.

Respectfully,

Chairman.

––––––––––––

9-NB-541

COPY

Muskogee, Indian Territory, November 11, 1905.

Sam J. Bacon,
      Utica, Indian Territory.

Dear Sir:

Inclosed herewith you will find a copy of the decision of the Commissioner to the Five Civilized Tribes, rendered November 11, 1905, granting the application for the enrollment of your infant child, Vie Bacon as a citizen of the Chickasaw Nation.

The attorneys for the Choctaw and Chickasaw Nations have been furnished a copy of this decision and have been allowed fifteen days from the date of this notice within which to file protest against the enrollment of your said child. If at the expiration of that time no protest has been filed, her name will be placed upon the final roll of citizens of the Chickasaw Nation to be submitted to the Secretary of the Interior for his approval.

Respectfully,
SIGNED

Tams Bixby
Commissioner.

Registered.
Incl. 9-NB-541.

––––––––––––

172

9-NB-541

Muskogee, Indian Territory, November 11, 1905.

Mansfield, McMurray & Cornish,
 Attorneys for Choctaw and Chickasaw Nations,
  South McAlester, Indian Territory.

Gentlemen:

  Inclosed herewith you will find a copy of the decision of the Commissioner to the Five Civilized Tribes, rendered November 11, 1905, granting the application for the enrollment of Vie Bacon as a citizen of the Chickasaw Nation.

  You are hereby advised that you will be allowed fifteen days from the date of this notice within which to file protest against the enrollment of this applicant. If at the expiration of that time no protest has been filed, her name will be placed upon the final roll of citizens of the Chickasaw Nation to be submitted to the Secretary of the Interior for his approval.

       Respectfully,
        SIGNED

         Tams Bixby
         Chairman.

9-N.B. 541.

Muskogee, Indian Territory, November 17, 1905.

Sam J. Bacon,
 Utica, Indian Territory.

Dear Sir:

  You are hereby notified that before any further no further action can be taken relative to the enrollment of your minor child Vie Bacon, as a citizen of the Chickasaw Nation, it will be necessary that this office be furnished with either the original or a certified copy of your marriage certificate showing your marriage to Lucy Bacon. This matter should receive your immediate attention.

  An envelope which requires no postage is enclosed herewith for reply.

    Respectfully,

        Commissioner.

Env.

7[sic]-NB-541

Muskogee, Indian Territory, December 5, 1905.

Sam J. Bacon,
    Utica, Indian Territory.

Dear Sir:

Receipt is hereby acknowledged of your letter of December 1, 1905, transmitting a certified copy of marriage record between Sam Bacon and Lucy Sims of August 25, 1902, which you offer in support of the application for the enrollment of your child Vie Bacon as a citizen of the Chickasaw Nation and the same has been filed with the record in this case.

Respectfully,

Acting Commissioner.

———————

9-NB-541
Mem 186

Muskogee, Indian Territory, December 14, 1905.

Apple & Franklin,
    Attorneys at Law,
        Muskogee, Indian Territory.

Gentlemen:

Receipt is hereby acknowledged of your letter of December 8, 1905, stating that you have been retained by Sam J. Bacon in the matter of the application for the enrollment of his minor child Vie Bacon and you ask to be informed when the enrollment of this child is approved by the Secretary of the Interior and also you request to be informed of any action in the case of William Jesse Bacon whom you also represent.

In reply to your letter you are advised that you will be notified of such action as is taken in these cases.

Complying with your request there is inclosed herewith a copy of the testimony of Lucy Bacon of December 8, 1905, in the matter of the alleged application for her enrollment as an intermarried citizen of the Choctaw[sic] Nation together with receipt therefor which please sign and return to this office.

Respectfully,

EB 2-14.   Commissioner.

Mem 186
9-NB-541

Muskogee, Indian Territory, May 15, 1906.

Apple & Franklin,
    Attorneys at Law,
        Muskogee, Indian Territory.

Gentlemen:

    Receipt is hereby acknowledged of your letter of My 10, 1906, in which you transmit motion for consideration of the application of Lucy Bacon for enrollment as an intermarried citizen of the Chickasaw Nation under the act of Congress approved April 26, 1906, and the same has been filed in the matter of the alleged application for the enrollment of this person; you also ask the status of the application of Vi[sic] Bacon for enrollment as a new born citizen of the Chickasaw Nation, and you are advised that her name has been placed upon a schedule of citizens of said nation which has been forwarded the Secretary of the Interior. You will be notified when her enrollment is approved by him.

                Respectfully,

                    Acting Commissioner.

Chic. N.B - 542
      (Swill Nelson
      Born June 11, 1905)

CHICKASAW

542

NEW BORN

ACT OF CONGRESS APPROVED MARCH 30, 1905.

Swill Nelson
(Born June 11, 1905)

CANCELLED

(Illegible....)

ACT OF CONGRESS APPROVED APRIL 26, 1906.
JUL 13 1906

Chic. N.B - 543
> *(Vinie Underwood*
> *Born March 1, 1904)*

DEPARTMENT OF THE INTERIOR
Commissioner to the Five Civilized Tribes
Chickasaw Land Office
Ardmore, Ind. Ter., September 15, 1905.

Testimony of J. Ernest Williams in the matter of the alleged application for enrollment of Vinie Underwood as a New Born citizen by blood of the Chickasaw Nation.

J. Ernest Williams, being duly sworn by Fred T. Marr, notary public, testified as follows:

EXAMINATION BY THE COMMISSIONER

Q Please state your name and post office address.   A   J. Ernest Williams, Ardmore, Indian Territory.

Q You were formerly an employe[sic] of the Commission to the Five Civilized Tribes, were you? A Yes, sir.

Q In connection with your duties as an employe[sic] of the Commission you were detailed on several appointments at different places in the Chickasaw Nation during the months of April and May for the purpose of receiving proofs of birth of children of citizens by blood of the Choctaw and Chickasaw Nations entitled to enrollment under the Act of Congress approved March 3, 1905 (33--Stats. 1060), were you? A Yes, sir.

Q In connection with this work you were at Ada, Indian Territory were you, as one appointment? A Yes, sir.

Q Do you remember what time you were at Ada? A I was there from April 24 to May 2, inclusive, 1905.

Q I have here a communication signed by Mr. J. E. Grigsby, of Ada, I. T., dated September 7, 1905, in which he states that he submitted to an officer of the Commission at Ada a proof of birth of the infant child of George Underwood and wife, Susie Porter Underwood.   I would like you to state if you have any recollection of any such application and when it was received, under what circumstances and what disposition you made of it and what was the character of this application.   A   I don't remember Mr. Grigsby but I do remember that an application of that character was brought to me at the hotel some time in the night of May 2, 1905, and I received the application and told him that I would forward it to the Commission for proper disposition and on the next morning I was detailed by you to serve some summons in that part of the Nation and I started on the morning of the third to serve them, and the last thing I did before I started I went to the post office and mailed this application in connection with two others that I had received late that evening to the Commission at Muskogee.   There was no letter of transmittal with the applications because I had fixed my machine, boxed it up, fastened it up, before I left the office where I was receiving applications the day before, and I had no menas[sic], no immediate means, of writing a letter of transmittal so they were just sent in an envelope addressed to the Commission at Muskogee.

Q Do you remember whether this was an application for the enrollment of Vinie Underwood or not? A I don't think the name of the child was stated in the application. The Underwoods, as I understood it, were Snake Indians and wouldn't make application for the child and they didn't give any information to the man that brought it about the child. He was informed as to the date of the birth of the child and he saw and knew it was still living but he could not in the short time he had discover the given name of the child. He had been to see me at the office a day or two prior to the second, when he brought the application, and asked me what was necessary and I told him and gave him an application to have filled out. He came back with the affidavit; I don't remember who the affidavit was signed by, I think it was signed by some Indian living close to the Underwoods.

Q That was just the day before the expiration of the sixty days allowed within which to receive these applications? A The day the sixty days elapsed, the last day of the sixty days.

Q Did you discuss with him any defects in this affidavit, that of the name not having been filled in? A I told him I didn't know how much weight that would have with the Commission but told him I thought it would be filed, that it could be considered as an application made for the child and subsequently proof could be offered as to who the child was, and that it might possibly be enrolled.

Q You think that he was doing the best he could under the circumstances, that he didn't know the name of the child, that he was doing the best he could to protect the right of the child? A That was what he told me. I don't know what interest he had in the matter, if any. He didn't tell me but I presume he had some.

Q Inasmuch as the name of the child was not filled in in that birth affidavit, do you recollect any other names or any other name appearing on said affidavit by which it could be identified? A All I remember is it was stated in the affidavit that the child was some Underwood, I don't remember the name of the father or the mother.

Q That application was presented to you on May 2, 1905? A Yes, sir, about ten o'clock in the evening.

Cinda Yates, stenographer for the Commissioner to the Five Civilized Tribes, states on oath that she reported the above and foregoing proceedings on the 15th day of September, 1905, and that same is a true and correct transcript of her stenographic notes thereof.

Cinda Yates

Subscribed and sworn to before me this 16th day of September, 1905.

Fred T. Marr
NOTARY PUBLIC.

Applications for Enrollment of Chickasaw Newborn
Act of 1905   Volume VII

9-NB-543.

DEPARTMENT OF THE INTERIOR,
COMMISSIONER TO THE FIVE CIVILIZED TRIBES.

In the matter of the application for the enrollment of Vinie Underwood as a citizen by blood of the Chickasaw Nation.

D E C I S I O N.

It appears from the record in this case that on May 2, 1905, application was made to the Commission to the Five Civilized Tribes for the enrollment of Vinie Underwood as a citizen by blood of the Chickasaw Nation.

It further appears from the record herein and from the records of the Commission to the Five Civilized Tribes that the applicant was born on March 1, 1904, and is the daughter of George Underwood, a recognized and enrolled citizen by blood of the Chickasaw Nation, whose name appears as number 42 upon the final roll of citizens by blood of the Chickasaw Nation approved by the Secretary of the Interior December 12, 1902, and Susie Underwood, whose name (as Susie Porter) appears as number 2689 upon the final roll of citizens by blood of the Chickasaw Nation approved by the Secretary of the Interior December 12, 1902; and that said applicant was living on March 4, 1905.

The Act of Congress approved March 3, 1905 (33 Stats., 1070) provides:

"That the Commission to the Five Civilized Tribes is authorized for sixty days after the date of the approval of this act to receive and consider applications for enrollment of children born subsequent to September twenty-fifth, nineteen hundred and two, and prior to March fourth, nineteen hundred and five, and who were living on said latter date, to citizens by blood of the Choctaw and Chickasaw tribes of Indians whose enrollment has been approved by the Secretary of the Interior prior to the date of the approval of this act; and to enroll and make allotments to such children."

I am, therefore, of the opinion that Vinie Underwood should be enrolled as a citizen by blood of the Chickasaw Nation under the provisions of law above quoted, and it is so ordered.

Tams Bixby   Commissioner.

Muskogee, Indian Territory.
    APR 25 1906

Applications for Enrollment of Chickasaw Newborn
Act of 1905   Volume VII

(The below letter typed as given.)

Hon. Tmas Bixby,
      Commissioner.

Sir: As to the matter above inquired about, I desire to make a statement which perhap will explain why I have not yet succeeded in making the prof as required by your letter of Sept. 22, 1905. George Underwood the father of the said infant Vinie Underwood, is very anxious to complete the proof as to the birth of the child, but his wife susie (Porter) Underwood will not appear and make the affidavit as you require. I Understand that the reason of it is that her father Yashia or Joushia Porter, who is one the snakes of the chickasaw nation will not, permit her to make it; to perhaps make the statement more acurate she will not sign the affidavit because she is afraid of her father. I doubt that he knows that any thin has been done toward having the child enrolled. It was for this reason that she did not appear at the time your enrolling board was here last spring.
George Underwood has already made and filed his affidavit as to the birth and death of the child; I can obtain other evidence to the effect that she claimed this child as her own, that it was with the said George Underwod, and The said Susie Underwood his wife. During the summer of 1904, I was at their house several times, and she had this child, then at each time I was there. There is no possible doubt but that this is her child and born to her and her husband. I know of no way to secure her affidavit unless you desire to send a man to go and get it. As I have already stated in another communication, that the midwife, one Sippy Brown has gone crazy, and hence her affidavit cannot be obtained. If affidavits of the above character will be sufficient to establish the paternity I can secure them at once. Trusting that I may hear from you at an early date.

I am yours truly,

(Signed) J. E. Grigsby.

(The five affidavits below typed as given.)

United States of America

Southern District of the

Indian Territory.   Before me the undersigned authority personally

appeared S E Hawkins, who after being duly sworn deposes and says that he knows that George Underwood and Susie Porter were husband and wife. That they had one child last year. When I first saw it was a very little child. I saw it in the summer of 1904. I saw them have it at church at High Hill church about one mile from the residence of the Said George and Susie Underwood. I have not interest in the matter of the enrolment of the said child. I am No kin to the said Susie (Porter) Underwood or to George Underwood. Know that the child is dead, it died in the month of August of 1905. It was buried at the grave yard close to the home of said George Underwood.

SE Hawkins

Sworn to and subscribed before me this the 9th day of Dec 1905.

JB Tolbert

Notary Public of the Southern District of the INdian Territory?

My Com Ex. 10/3/1909

United States of America

Southern District of the

Indian Territory.   BEFORE ME THE UNDERSIGNED authority

personally appeared George Colbert, who after being duly sworn to tell the truth the whole truth and nothing but the truth, deposess and says that he is a citizen by blood of the chickasaw nation, that I am Interpreter for the chickasaw legislature, and that I am a minister of the gospel. that I am 52 years of Age. Further stating says that he know that Susie Porter and George Underwod were married about three years ago but the exact day of the marriage he does not now remember. I know that they are Husband & wife. I know that they had a child and I saw it two or three months after it was born. They told me that it was their child. I do not know the date of its birth but it was a very small child when I first saw it, last year. I have no interest in the matter of the enrollment of the child. And I am not any Kin to them. I do not know the name, of the child. I heard this summer that it had died. I do not know the exact time it died. I think that id died since the fourth of March 1905.

George Colbert

Sworn to and subscribed before me this the 9th day of Dec 1905.

JB Tolbert

Notary Public of the Souther District of the Indian Territory?

My Com Ex - 10/3/1909

United States of America

Southern District of the

Indian Territory.   Before me the undersigned authority, personally

appeared J F Jackson, who after being sworn by me to tell the truth, the whole truth and nothing but the truth, deposes and says that he has resided and engaged in business in the town of Ada for 5 Years.

That in the summer of 1904, I was engaged in the furniture and undertaking business in the town of Ada I T. That George Underwood and his wife Susie came into my place of business in the early part of the summer of 1904, and that while there I noticed that they had a very young baby, and I engaged in a conversation with them in reference thereto, and among other things they stated to me that the child was their that Susie was the mother of the child. At this time the baby was a month or two of age judging from appearances. That after wards they came to my store to buy a baby buggy for it. I have known them 3 Years and this is the only child I have ever known them to have. I have heard that this child died three or four months ago. I am no kin to these parties, and have no interest in the enrollment of the said child nor do I have any interest in its allotment.

J F Jackson

Sworn to and subscribed before me this the 11 day of Dec 1905.

J B Tolbert

Notary Public in and for tye southern District of the Indian Territoy

---

United States of America

Southern District of the

Indian Territory,

AFFIDAVIT

On this the 31st day of August 1905, personally, appeared before me George Underwood Who after being duly sworn upon oath deposes and says that he a chickasaw India, residing in the chickasaw nation of the Indian Territory, near Ada; That on the ____ day of _____ 19 oI, at the residence George Colbert, in the Chichasaw nation I T, he and Susie Porter, were married, by George Colbert performing the marriage ceremony.

That there was born to the said George Underwood and His wife Susie porter Underwood, a female child on the 1st day of March 1904. Further swearing the said George Underwood says that at the time the said child was born, there were present the said George Underwood, and Walton Harris, and Sippy Brown, who acted as the midwife at the time the child was born. That this time, and for a long time prior thereto the said Sippy Brown has been out of her mind and that she is incapable of making the the affidavit as the attending midwife. That Said child was named Vinie Underwood. That she was living on the four day of March 1905, but has since died, dying on the 18th day of August 1905. Affiant further says that he has in possession at his home the certificate of the marrriage as herein set out. Witness   his

WG Currie   George x Underwood
JE Grigsby   mark

Sworn to and subscribed before me this the 31st day of August 1905.

W.G. Currie

Notary Public in and for the Southern District of the Indian Territory.

_____

United State of America
southern District of the
Indian Territory.

BEFORE ME the undersigned authority, personally appeared Sid Reidel, who after being duly sworn by me to tell the truth, the whole truth and nothing but the truth, deposes and says that he a resident of the town of Ada I T. That he has resided therein for about 2 years and that he a white man and that he is of the age of 29 Years.

That in the month of September 1904, I has an occasion to go to the house of George Underwood, an Indian living about three mile from the town of Ada, I T. and while there I was unterduced to George Underwood and his wife Susie. I went there for the purpose of witnessing the signature of the said Susie Underwood to an instrument in writing, and while I was there George Underwood and the said Susie represented themselves as husband and wife. I saw an infant in a hammock, and both George Underwood and His wife Susie Underwood, stated that the baby was their's and they further stated that it was sick. The child was very small and it appeared to be about ten or twenlve months old. After that I saw the said Susie Underwood have the child with her in the Town of Ada.

Sid Riedel

Sworn to and subscribed before me this the 9th day of Dec 1905

Robt Winnbush
Notary Public

_____

Applications for Enrollment of Chickasaw Newborn
Act of 1905   Volume VII

(The letter below typed as given.)

TO THE COMMISSION FOR THE FIVE CIVILIZED TRIBES
MUSKOGEE INDINA TERRITORY,

gentlemen: in the matter of enrolling infant children I desire to make this statement;

George Underwood a citizen of the Chickasaw nation call upon me this day in a professional way and consulted me concernig the filing of an application for the enrollment of his infant child, he being the father and Susie Underwood his wife (but whose enrooled name with the commission is Susie Porter) being the mother. He told me that he had colled on the commission at Ada and that he had been informed that he would have to have the affidavit of the attending physcian or the midwife attending at the birth of the child; but he told me that he had found out the the physcian was crazy and that eh could not get the physcian to make the affidavit. He told me that he was Present himself at the birth of the child and that he could make the affidavit that the child was born to his wife. I advised him to go home about three miled from Ada and bring his wife into town and have her make the birth affidavit and that eh should also make affidavit to the birth.
He then left my office and said that eh would go and bring his wife in to town to go before the commission sitting at Ada at this time. But he failed to come and so I desiring that the childs right to enrollment might not be prejudiced employed a notary public to go to his house and get the affidavits of the parents and we called at the house of the parents and when we got there George underwood told us that his wife did not want the child enrolled, and hence no affidavits were made. I will further state that while I do not Know the childs name I have seen it with its mother and it appears to be at the last time I saw it about one year and a half old.

Trusting that the commission will look into this matter, and enroll this child.

I am Respectfully Yours.

This Ada I T May 2nd 1905.   JE Grigsby

Rec'd May 2 1905
(Illegible)

(The above letter given again.)

Muskogee, Indian Territory, May 9, 1905.

A. A. Chapman,
    Ravia, Indian Territory.

Dear Sir:

Referring to your affidavit of May 2, 1905; also your letter of recent date, relative to making application for the enrollment of an infant child of George Underwood as a citizen of the Choctaw[sic] Nation, you are advised that it appears from our records that on April 9, 1903, the Secretary of the Interior approved the Commission's decision of October 29, 1902, refusing the application of David F. Underwood, et al. for identification as Mississippi Choctaws, of which departmental action the applicants were notified on April 23, 1903.

You are further advised that it does not appear from our records that any application has ever been made to this Commission by or on behalf of any person by the name of George Underwood for identification as a Mississippi Choctaw or for enrollment as a citizen of the Choctaw Nation.

Respectfully,

Commissioner in Charge.

9-NB-543.   (Copy).

Muskogee, Indian Territory, September 22, 1905.

J. E. Grigsby,
    Attorney at Law,
        Ada, Indian Territory.

Dear Sir:

Receipt is hereby acknowledged of your letter of September 7, 1905, relative to the application made by you for the infant child of George Underwood and his wife Susie Porter Underwood. You state therein that you filed this application with the officer in charge of the enrollment party at Ada, Indian Territory on May 2, 1905.

You are advised that from the information contained in your letter this office has been able to find and identify said application made by you at that time. You are further advised that the child, Vinie Underwood, has been listed for enrollment as a citizen by blood of the Chickasaw Nation.

It will be necessary, however, before the rights of said child as a citizen by blood of the Chickasaw Nation can be finally determined, for you to supply this office with proper proof of her birth and a blank for that purpose is inclosed herewith. You will notice that there is a blank for the affidavit of the mother of said child and the attending midwife. It is stated in the affidavit of George Underwood now on file that the midwife in attendance at the birth of said child is now non compos mentis.

It will, therefore, be necessary for you to furnish in lieu of the affidavit of said midwife the affodavits[sic] of two disinterested persons relative to the birth of said child. Said affidavits must set forth said child's name, the date of her birth, the names of her parents and whether or not she was living on March 4, 1905.

It also appears that the said Vinie Underwood is now dead. For the purpose of making her death a matter of record there is inclosed herewith blank for proof of death which you are requested to have properly filled out, executed and return to this office.

Respectfully,

SIGNED

Wm. O. Beall
Acting Commissioner.

B C
D C
Env.

9-NB-542[sic]

Muskogee, Indian Territory, November 28, 1905.

J. E. Grigsby,
        Attorney at Law,
                Ada, Indian Territory.

Dear Sir:

In the matter of the application for the enrollment of Vinie Underwood your attention is invited to office letter of September 22, 1905, and you are requested to have the proof requested therein forwarded this office at the earliest date practicable in order that disposition may be made of the application for the enrollment of said child.

Respectfully,

Acting Commissioner.

9-NB-543

Muskogee, Indian Territory, December 8, 1905.

J. E. Grigsby,
    Attorney at Law,
        Ada, Indian Territory.

Dear Sir:

Receipt is hereby acknowledged of your letter without date referring to the application for the enrollment of Vinie Underwood in which you state that it is impracticable to secure the affidavit of the mother for the reason that her father is a Snake Indian and will not permit her to sign the same; you state that you can obtain other affidavits to the effect that Vinie Underwood is the child of George and Susie Underwood and if that will be sufficient you will secure them at once.

In reply to your letter you are advised that if you will forward the affidavits of three or four disinterested persons who know that Vinie Underwood is the child of George and Susie Underwood, the date of her birth and also the date of her death, the same will receive consideration in the matter of the enrollment of said child.

Respectfully,

Acting Commissioner.

Ada, I. T. Dec. 11th 1905.

To the Commission to the Five Tribes,
        Muskogee, I. T.

Gentlemen: I have yours of recent date directing me to secure the affidavits of three or four disinterested persons, that know the Vinie Underwood was the child of George and Susie Underwood. I herewith send to you the affidavits of four persons two of whom are white me and all of them uninterested in the matter. Trusting that there will be no necessity of further affidavits, but if this is not sufficient, I can obtain many other of like character but to find any person who knows that this child is the child of these parties except, that they had the care and custody of the same and held the same out to all persons that it was their[sic], perhaps cannot be done. Trusting that this will be sufficient, and I shall hear from you at an early date as to your action in the premises I,

Am your[sic] truly,
    J. E. Grigsby,
    Attorney for George Underwood.

9-NB-543

Muskogee, Indian Territory, December 14, 1905.

J. E. Grigsby,
      Attorney at Law,
          Ada, Indian Territory.

Dear Sir:

    Receipt is hereby acknowledged of your letter of December 11, 1905, inclosing the affidavits of J. F. Jackson, Sid Riedel, George Colbert and S. E. Hawkins to the birth of Vinie Underwood and the same have been filed with the record in the matter of the enrollment of said child.

    If further evidence is necessary to determine the right to enrollment of this child you will be duly advised.

                Respectfully,

                          Commissioner.

9-NB-543

COPY

Muskogee, Indian Territory, April 25, 1906.

George Underwood,
      Ada, Indian Territory.

Dear Sir:

    Inclosed herewith you will find a copy of the decision of the Commissioner to the Five Civilized Tribes, rendered April 25, 1906, granting the application for the enrollment of your minor child Vinie Underwood as a citizen by blood of the Chickasaw Nation.

    The attorneys for the Choctaw and Chickasaw Nations have been furnished a copy of the decision and have been allowed fifteen days from the date of this notice within which to file protest against her enrollment. If at the expiration of that time no protest has been filed, the name of Vinie Underwood will be placed upon the final roll of citizens by blood of the Chickasaw Nation to be submitted to the Secretary of the Interior for his approval.

                Respectfully,

                SIGNED   *Tams Bixby*

Registered.
                          Commissioner.
Incl. 9-NB-543.

187

9-NB-543

COPY

Muskogee, Indian Territory, April 25, 1906.

J. E. Grigsby,
    Attorney at Law,
        Ada, Indian Territory.

Dear Sir:

You are hereby notified that the Commissioner to the Five Civilized Tribes, on April 25, 1906, rendered his decision granting the application for the enrollment of Vinie Underwood as a citizen by blood of the Chickasaw Nation.

The attorneys for the Choctaw and Chickasaw Nations have been furnished a copy of this decision and have been allowed fifteen days from the date of this notice within which to file protest against her enrollment. If at the expiration of that time no protest has been filed, the name of Vinie Underwood will be placed upon the final roll of citizens by blood of the Chickasaw Nation to be submitted to the Secretary of the Interior for his approval.

Respectfully,

SIGNED   *Tams Bixby*

Registered.   Commissioner.

9-NB-543

Muskogee, Indian Territory, April 25, 1906.

Mansfield, McMurray & Cornish,   **COPY**
    Attorneys for Choctaw and Chickasaw Nations,
        South McAlester, Indian Territory.

Gentlemen:

Inclosed herewith you will find a copy of the decision of the Commissioner to the Five Civilized Tribes, rendered April 25, 1906, granting the application for the enrollment of Vinie Underwood as a citizen by blood of the Chickasaw Nation.

You are hereby advised that you will be allowed fifteen days from the date of this notice within which to file protest against her enrollment. If at the expiration of that time no protest has been filed, the name of Vinie Underwood will be placed upon the final roll of citizens by blood of the Chickasaw Nation to be submitted to the Secretary of the Interior for his approval.

Respectfully,

SIGNED   *Tams Bixby*

Commissioner.

Registered.

Incl. 9-NB-543.

7-2319

9-NB-543

Muskogee, Indian Territory, January 12, 1906.

J. E. Grigsby,

    Ada, Indian Territory.

Dear Sir:

Receipt is hereby acknowledged of your letter of January 9, 1906, asking where you can obtain a copy of the Choctaw laws and treaties; you also ask what the rulings of the Commission to the Five Civilized Tribes have been where a white person marries a Choctaw woman in the State of Arkansas in 1875 or 1875 and moves to and resides in the Choctaw Nation for twenty or thirty years, and is permitted to serve on the Choctaw juries, vote in their elections and is otherwise recognized as a Choctaw citizen.

In reply to your letter you are advised that it is possible you can procure a copy of the Choctaw laws by addressing inquiry to the National Secretary of the Choctaw Nation at Tuskahoma, Indian Territory.

As to the question submitted for opinion, you are advised that this office does not render opinions upon hypothetical cases of citizenship for enrollment.

In compliance with your request There is inclosed herewith for execution application for the enrollment of your infant child your information, copy of Departmental letter of December 13, 1905, transmitting opinion of the Assistant Attorney General of December 8, 1905, in the Choctaw enrollment case of Loula West et al.

Further replying to your letter you are advised that it does not appear from the records of this office that application has been made by or on behalf of C. T. Wilburn for enrollment as a citizen of the Choctaw Nation. It does appear that Martha Wilburn, wife of Charles Wilburn, and her nine children have been enrolled as citizens by blood of the Choctaw Nation and their enrollment as such approved by the Secretary of the Interior.

Referring to the application for the enrollment of Vinie Underwood, you are advised that no further action has been taken in the matter of her enrollment, but you will be notified of such action as is taken therein.

189

Respectfully,

LM 7/12   Commissioner.

_____

9-NB-543

Muskogee, Indian Territory, March 7, 1906.

James E. Griggsby[sic],
    Attorney at Law,
        Ada, Indian Territory.

Dear Sir:

Receipt is hereby acknowledged of your letter of March 1, 1906, asking the condition of the application for the enrollment of Vinie Underwood, child of George and Susie Underwood.

In reply you are advised that this application is now receiving consideration and when a decision is reached you will be notified of the action taken therein.

Respectfully,

Acting Commissioner.

_____

9-NB-543

Muskogee, Indian Territory, April 2, 1906.

James E. Grigsby,
    Attorney at Law,
        Ada, Indian Territory.

Dear Sir:

Receipt is hereby acknowledged of your letter without date asking to be notified when a decision is reached in the matter of the application of Vinie Underwood for enrollment as a citizen of the Chickasaw Nation.

In reply to your letter you are advised that you will be notified of such action as is taken in this case.

Respectfully,

Acting Commissioner.

_____

9-NB-543

Muskogee, Indian Territory, May 15, 1906.

J. E. Grigsby,
> Attorney at Law,
>> Ada, Indian Territory.

Dear Sir:

Receipt is hereby acknowledged of your letter of May 11, 1906, in which you ask if the attorneys for the Chickasaw Nation filed protest to the decision of the Commissioner to the Five Civilized Tribes enrolling Vinie Underwood as a new born citizen of the Chickasaw Nation.

In reply to your letter you are advised that no protest has been filed by the attorneys for the Choctaw and Chickasaw Nations for the enrollment of Vinie Underwood as a new born citizen of the Chickasaw Nation and her name will be placed upon the next schedule of new born citizens of said nation to be prepared for forwarding to the Secretary of the Interior.

> Respectfully,

> Acting Commissioner.

9-NB-543

Muskogee, Indian Territory, September 7, 1906.

James E. Grigsby,
> Attorney at Law,
>> Ada, Indian Territory.

Dear Sir:

Replying to your letter of August 24, 1906, relative to the application for the enrollment of Vinie Underwood, infant daughter of George and Susie Underwood, as a citizen by blood of the Chickasaw Nation, you are advised that said applicant has been finally enrolled by the Secretary of the Interior, said enrollment being approved August 22, 1906.

> Respectfully,

> Acting Commissioner.

9-NB-543

Muskogee, Indian Territory, June 30, 1906.

J. E. Grigsby,
         Attorney at Law,
                  Ada, Indian Territory.

Dear Sir:

Receipt is hereby acknowledged of your letter of June 20, 1906, in which you ask if the enrollment of Vinie Underwood, daughter of George and Susie Underwood has yet been approved by the Department.

In reply to your letter you are advised that the name of Vinie Underwood will be placed upon the next schedule of new born citizens of the Chickasaw Nation under the act of Congress approved March 3, 1905, which is prepared for forwarding the Secretary of the Interior and you will be advised when her enrollment is approved by him.

Respectfully,

Commissioner.

Chic. N.B - 544
         (Joseph Lenn Ruddell
         Born September 26, 1905)

CHICKASAW 544

NEW BORN

ACT OF CONGRESS APPROVED MARCH 30, 1905.

Joseph Lenn Ruddell
(Born Sept 26, 1905)

CANCELLED

Record transferred to
CHICKASAW   NEW BORN   No 218

ACT OF CONGRESS APPROVED APRIL 26, 1906.
AUG 8- 1906

Chic. N.B - 545
>*(Henry Charles Preston Hays*
>*Born February 16, 1905)*

CHICKASAW   545

NEW BORN

ACT OF CONGRESS APPROVED MARCH 30, 1905.

Henry Charles Preston Hays
(Born Feb. 16, 1905)

CANCELLED

Record transferred to Chick
asaw   New born   258

ACT OF CONGRESS APPROVED APRIL 26, 1906.

JUL 23 1906

Chic. N.B - 546
>*(Jesse Thompson*
>*Born March 25, 1904)*

DEPARTMENT OF THE INTERIOR,
COMMISSIONER TO THE FIVE CIVILIZED TRIBES.
MUSKOGEE, IND. TER.   September 14, 1905.

In the matter of the application for the enrollment of Jesse Thompson as a citizen by blood of the Chickasaw Nation.

Culberson Thompson being first duly sworn testifies as follows:

Examination by the Commissioner:

Q What is your name? A Culberson Thompson.
Q How old are you? A About thirty-six or thirty-seven.
Q What is your post office address? A Gowan.
Q Are you a citizen by blood of the Chickasaw Nation? A Yes, sir.
Q What is the name of your wife? A Lucy Thompson.
Q Are you lawfully married to her? A Been married to her about thirteen years.
Q Are you the father of Jesse Thompson? A Yes, sir.

Q And Lucy Thompson is the mother of that child? A Yes, sir.

Q When was Jesse Thompson born? A 1904, March 25th.

Q Is Jesse Thompson still living? A Died.

Q When did he die? A April 20, 1904.

Q In case this office should decide that Jesse Thompson is entitled to enrollment in either the Choctaw or Chickasaw Nation in which nation do you elect to have him enrolled - as a Choctaw or as a Chickasaw? A Chickasaw.

Q In case Jesse Thompson is finally enrolled as a citizen by blood of the Chickasaw Nation do you relinquish all his right, title and interest in and to the tribal property of the Choctaw Nation? A Yes, sir.

Q Have you got any evidence of your marriage to Lucy Thompson? A No, sir.

Q By whom were you married - married by preacher or judge? A Preacher.

Q What was his name? A Joe James.

It will be necessary for you, in the matter of the enrollment of your son, Jesse Thompson, to file with this office evidence of your marriage to Lucy Thompson.

Witness excused.

Chas. T. Difendafer being first duly sworn states that the above and foregoing is a full, true and correct transcript of his stenographic notes taken in said cause on said date.

Chas.T. Difendafer

Subscribed and sworn to before me this 14th day of September, 1905.

Myron White
Notary Public.

BIRTH AFFIDAVIT.

DEPARTMENT OF THE INTERIOR.
COMMISSION TO THE FIVE CIVILIZED TRIBES.

IN RE APPLICATION FOR ENROLLMENT, as a citizen of the   Choc   Nation, of   Jesse Thompson   , born on the 25 day of   March , 1904

Name of Father: Culberson Thompson   a citizen of the Choc[sic]   Nation.
Name of Mother: Lucy Thompson   a citizen of the Choc   Nation.

Postoffice   Gowen, I.T.

Applications for Enrollment of Chickasaw Newborn
Act of 1905   Volume VII

UNITED STATES OF AMERICA, Indian Territory, ⎤
    Central   DISTRICT. ⎦

      I, Lucy Thompson   , on oath state that I am 28   years of age and a citizen by   blood   , of the   Choctaw   Nation; that I am the lawful wife of Culberson Thompson   , who is a citizen, by blood   of the   Choctaw[sic]   Nation; that a   male   child was born to me on 25 day of March   , 1904; that said child has been named Jesse Thompson   , and was living March 4, 1905.

                                her
                     Lucy x Thompson

Witnesses To Mark: mark
    ⎰ Chas.T. Difendafer
    ⎱ OL Johnson

      Subscribed and sworn to before me this 25 day of   April   , 1905

                              OL Johnson
                                Notary Public.

UNITED STATES OF AMERICA, Indian Territory, ⎤
    Central   DISTRICT. ⎦

      I, Wynie Bonaparte   , a midwife   , on oath state that I attended on Mrs. Lucy Thompson   , wife of Culberson Thompson   on the 25 day of March   , 1904; that there was born to her on said date a   male   child; that said child was living March 4, 1905, and is said to have been named Jesse Thompson

                               her
                     Wynie x Bonaparte

Witnesses To Mark: mark
    ⎰ Chas.T. Difendafer
    ⎱ OL Johnson

      Subscribed and sworn to before me this 25 day of   April   , 1905

                              OL Johnson
                                Notary Public.

BIRTH AFFIDAVIT.

DEPARTMENT OF THE INTERIOR.
COMMISSION TO THE FIVE CIVILIZED TRIBES.

IN RE APPLICATION FOR ENROLLMENT, as a citizen of the   Choctaw[sic]   Nation,
of   Jesse Thompson   , born on the ....day of ...., 1........

Name of Father: Culberson Thompson   a citizen of the   Chickasaw Nation.
Name of Mother: Lucy Thompson   a citizen of the   Choctaw   Nation.

Postoffice   Gowen I.T.

AFFIDAVIT OF MOTHER.

UNITED STATES OF AMERICA, Indian Territory, ⎫
    Central   **DISTRICT.**⎰

  I, Lucy Thompson   , on oath state that I am 23   years of age and a citizen
by   blood   , of the   Choctaw   Nation; that I am the lawful wife of Culberson
Thompson   , who is a citizen, by blood   of the   Chickasaw   Nation; that
a   male   child was born to me on   25   day of   March   , 1904; that said child
has been named   Jesse Thompson   , and was living March 4, 1905.

her
Lucy x Thompson
mark

Witnesses To Mark:
  ⎧ Lee Silman
  ⎩ Culberson Thompson

  Subscribed and sworn to before me this 29 day of   April   , 1905

J Anderson
Notary Public.

Attendant
AFFIDAVIT OF ~~ATTENDING PHYSICIAN OR MID-WIFE~~.

UNITED STATES OF AMERICA, Indian Territory, ⎫
    Central   **DISTRICT.**⎰

was present

  I,   Culberson Thompson   , a..........................., on oath state that I ~~attended on~~
Mrs.   Lucy Thompson   , wife of Culberson Thompson   on the 25   day of
March   , 1904; that there was born to her on said date a   male   child; that said
child was living March 4, 1905, and is said to have been named Jesse Thompson

Culberson Thompson

Witnesses To Mark:

$\left\{ \vphantom{\begin{array}{c}a\\b\end{array}} \right.$

Subscribed and sworn to before me this   29 day of   April   , 1905

J Anderson
Notary Public.

NEW-BORN AFFIDAVIT.

Number.................

...CHOCTAW ENROLLING COMMISSION...

IN THE MATTER OF THE APPLICATION FOR ENROLLMENT, as a citizen of the
Choctaw   Nation, of   Jesse Thompson

born on the   25th   day of ____March____190 4

Name of father Culberson Thompson   a citizen of   Chickasaw
Nation final enrollment No. 3424
Name of mother Lucy Thompson   a citizen of   Choctaw
Nation final enrollment No. 723

Postoffice   Gowen I.T.

AFFIDAVIT OF MOTHER.

UNITED STATES OF AMERICA
INDIAN TERRITORY
  Central   DISTRICT

I   Lucy Thompson   , on oath state that I
am   27   years of age and a citizen by   blood   of the   Choctaw   Nation,
and as such have been placed upon the final roll of the   Choctaw   Nation, by the Honorable
Secretary of the Interior my final enrollment number being   723 ; that I am the lawful wife
of   Culberson Thompson   , who is a citizen of the   Chickasaw   Nation, and as
such has been placed upon the final roll of said Nation by the Honorable Secretary of the
Interior, his final enrollment number being   3424   and that a   Male   child was born
to me on the   25th   day of   March   190 4; that said child has been named   Jesse
Thompson   , and is now living.   Witness   her
                    Jno.T. Hyde   Lucy x Thompson
Witnesseth.   mark
   Must be two ⎤   Sampson Winship
   Witnesses who ⎰
   are Citizens.   Eastman Wade

197

Subscribed and sworn to before me this   28   day of   Jany   190 5

E.F. Lester

Notary Public.

My commission expires:
2/6/1906

AFFIDAVIT OF ATTENDING PHYSICIAN OR MIDWIFE

UNITED STATES OF AMERICA
INDIAN TERRITORY
Central   DISTRICT

I,   Winnie Bonaparte   a   midwife
on oath state that I attended on Mrs.   Lucy Thompson   , wife
of   Culberson Thompson   on the   25th   day of   March   , 190 4 , that there
was born to her on said date a   male   child, that said child is now living, and is said to have
been named   Jessie[sic] Thompson
Attest E.F. Lester   her
                                   Winnie x Bonaparte   *M.D.*
Subscribed and sworn to before me this, the mark   28   day of
Jany   190 5

WITNESSETH: E.F. Lester   Notary Public.
Must be two witnesses ⎧   Sampson Winship
who are citizens   ⎨
                       ⎩   Eastman Wade

We hereby certify that we are well acquainted with   Winnie Bonaparte
a   midwife   and know   her   to be reputable and of good standing in the
community.

Sampson Winship   Gowan, I.T.

Eastman Wade   Gowan, I.T.

198

Applications for Enrollment of Chickasaw Newborn
Act of 1905   Volume VII

November 20th 1893
Gaines County

Culberson Thompson and Lucy York

Certificate of Marriage————

This is to certify that I united Mr Culberson Thompson and Miss Lucy York in Holy Matrimony according to the laws of the Choctaw Nation

Gaines County this 20th day of November, 1893.

Joseph James

United States of America,)
Indian Territory   )
Central District   )

    I, Lucy Thompson, on oath state that I am twenty-eight years of age and a citizen by blood of the Choctaw Nation; that I am the lawful wife of Culberson Thompson who is a citizen by blood of the Chickasaw Nation, that a male child was born to us on March 25, 1904; that said child was living March 4, 1905 and died April 20, 1905 and I hereby elect for said child to be finally enrolled as a citizen by blood of the Chickasaw Nation, under the provisions of Section 21 of the Act of Congress approved June 28, 1898.

her

Witnesses to mark   Lucy x Thompson
Max Coffman   mark
John F Rucker

Subscribed and sworn to before me this 18 day of Sept 1906

(Name Illegible)
Notary Public.

Applications for Enrollment of Chickasaw Newborn
Act of 1905   Volume VII

Ardmore, Indian Territory, May 2, 1905.

Commission to the Five Civilized Tribes,
Muskogee, Indian Territory.

Gentlemen:

There are herewith transmitted, for proper disposition birth affidavits of the following named persons: Davidson Carney, Albert Carney, Lindsey Cann and Jesse Thompson.

Your attention is respectfully directed to the signature of the Notary Public before whom the affidavits in these cases were executed and to his seal thereto, as the signature is that of J. Anderson, while the seal bears the name of J. W. Anderson.

In the connection it is suggested that it might be well to ascertain whether or not there is such a person as J. ANderson[sic], who is a Notary Public, for the Central District of the Indian Territory and if so whether or not the enclosed affidavits were executed before him.

Respectfully,
Fred T. Marr,

HC 110 Chief Clerk.

7-NB-1243.

Muskogee, Indian Territory, June 12, 1905.

Culberson Thompson,
Garvin[sic], Indian Territory.

Dear Sir:

Referring to the application for the enrollment of your infant child, Jessie[sic] Thompson, it appears that you are a citizen by blood of the Chickasaw Nation and that your wife, Lucy Thompson, is a citizen by blood of the Choctaw Nation.

Your attention is called to the provision of the act of Congress approved June 28, 1898, as follows:

The several tribes may, by agreement, determine the right of persons who for any reason may claim citizenship in two or more tribes, and to allotment of lands and distribution of moneys belonging to each tribe; but if no such agreement be made, then such claimant shall be entitled to such rights in one tribe only, and may elect in which tribe he will take such right; but if he fail or refuse to make such selection in due time, he shall be enrolled in the tribe with whom he has resided, and there be given such allotment and distributions, and not elsewhere.

200

It will therefore be necessary for you and your wife to appear before a Notary Public or other officer authorized to administer oaths and by affidavit elect in which nation you desire to have said child enrolled, forwarding same, when properly executed, to the Commission.

Respectfully,

Chairman.

7-NB-1243

Muskogee, Indian Territory, July 28, 1905.

Culberson Thompson,
Gowen, Indian Territory,

Dear Sir:

Referring to the application for the enrollment of your infant child, Jessie[sic] Thompson, it appears that you are a citizen by blood of the Chickasaw Nation and that your wife, Lucy Thompson, is a citizen by blood of the Choctaw Nation.

Your attention is called to the provision of the act of Congress approved June 28, 1898, as follows:

"The several tribes may, by agreement, determine the right of persons who for any reason may claim citizenship in two or more tribes, and to allotment of lands and distribution of moneys belonging to each tribe; but if no such agreement be made, then such claimant shall be entitled to such rights in one tribe only, and may elect in which tribe he will take such right; but if he fail or refuse to make such selection in due time, he shall be enrolled in the tribe with whom he has resided, and there be given such allotment and distributions, and not elsewhere."

It will therefore be necessary for you and your wife to appear before a Notary Public or other officer authorized to administer oaths and by affidavit elect in which nation you desire to have said child enrolled, forwarding same, when properly executed, to this office.

Respectfully,

Commissioner.

7- NB 1243

Muskogee, Indian Territory, September 1, 1905.

J. Poe,
  Wilburton, Indian Territory.

Dear Sir:

  I am in receipt of your letter of August 27th in reference to the enrollment of Jesse Thompson, infant child of Culberson and Lucy Thompson, as a citizen by blood of the Choctaw Nation.

  In reply to your letter you are advised that an application for the enrollment of Jesse Thompson, born March 25, 1904, was filed with the Commission to the Five Civilized Tribes on April 25, 1905.

  It appears from the record in this case that Culberson Thompson, the father of the child, is a citizen by blood of the Chickasaw Nation, and the mother, Lucy Thompson, is a citizen by blood of the Choctaw Nation. Culberson Thompson has been repeatedly requested to forward to this office the joint affidavit of himself and his wife, electing whether they desire to have child finally enrolled as a citizen of the Choctaw or Chickasaw Nation. Final determination upon this application is suspended until the affidavits of election are forwarded to this office. The child not having been enrolled as a citizen of the Choctaw Nation, no allotment has consequently been made in his name.

Respectfully,

Commissioner.

---

7)NB-1243

Muskogee, Indian Territory, September 8, 1905.

J. Poe,
  Wilburton, Indian Territory.

Dear Sir:

  Receipt is hereby acknowledged of your letter of the 4th instant, in which you state that Culberson Thompson informed you that he has forwarded an affidavit of election in the matter of the enrollment of his minor child, Jesse Thompson. You request if such affidavit has not been received, that you be supplied with the necessary blanks and that the matter will be attended to at once.

Applications for Enrollment of Chickasaw Newborn
Act of 1905   Volume VII

It is not necessary that any blanks be prepared for this purpose as the affidavit required is merely the joint affidavit of the mother and father of the child, electing whether they desire to have Jesse finally enrolled as a citizen of the Choctaw or Chickasaw Nation.

When this joint affidavit has been supplied disposition will be made of the application for the enrollment of Jesse Thompson.

Respectfully,

Acting Commissioner.

7-NB-1243

Muskogee, Indian Territory, December 4, 1905.

Culberson Thompson,
Wilburton, Indian Territory.

Dear Sir:

Receipt is hereby acknowledged of your letter of November 28, 1905, asking the status of the enrollment of your son Jesse Thompson.

In reply to your letter you are advised that the name of your son Jesse Thompson has not yet been placed upon a schedule of new born citizens of the Chickasaw Nation but it is probably that his name will be placed upon the next schedule of such citizens prepared for that purpose. You will be notified when his enrollment is approved by the Department.

Respectfully,

Acting Commissioner.

9-NB-546

Muskogee, Indian Territory, January 8, 1906.

C. A. Thompson,
Thurston, Indian Territory.

Dear Sir:

Receipt is hereby acknowledged of your letter of January 4, 1906, asking if your child Jesse Thompson has been enrolled.

In reply to your letter you are advised that the name of Jesse Thompson, child of Culberson and Lucy Thompson has not yet been placed upon a schedule of new born citizens of the Chickasaw Nation prepared for forwarding to the Secretary of the Interior, but in event further evidence is necessary to determine the right of this child to enrollment you will be duly notified.

Respectfully,

Commissioner.

9-NB-546

Muskogee, Indian Territory, March 9, 1906.

Culberson Thompson,
>> Thurston, Indian Territory.

Dear Sir:

Receipt is hereby acknowledged of your letter of March 4, 1906, asking if the application for the enrollment of your child Jesse Thompson has been approved.

In reply to your letter you are advised that the name of your child Jesse Thompson will be placed upon the next schedule of new born citizens of the Chickasaw Nation to be prepared for forwarding to the Secretary of the Interior and you will be notified when his enrollment is approved.

Respectfully,

Acting Commissioner.

9-NB-546

Muskogee, Indian Territory, June 14, 1906.

J. S. Mullen,
>> Attorney at Law,
>>> Ardmore, Indian Territory.

Dear Sir:

Receipt is hereby acknowledged of your letter of May 27, 1906, in which you ask if further evidence is necessary in the matter of the application for the enrollment of Jesse Thompson as a new born citizen of the Chickasaw Nation under the act of Congress approved March 3, 1905.

In reply to your letter you are advised that the name of Jesse Thompson, child of Culberson and Lucy Thompson, has been placed upon a schedule of new born citizens of the Chickasaw Nation which has been forwarded the Secretary of the Interior and you will be notified when his enrollment is approved by the Department.

Respectfully,

Commissioner.

Chic. N.B - 547
    (Emma Courtney
    Born September 29, 1902)

BIRTH AFFIDAVIT.

DEPARTMENT OF THE INTERIOR.
COMMISSION TO THE FIVE CIVILIZED TRIBES.

IN RE APPLICATION FOR ENROLLMENT, as a citizen of the   Chickasaw   Nation, of   Emma Courtney   , born on the 29th day of   September , 1902

Name of Father: Tyson Courtney   a citizen of the   Chickasaw Nation.
Name of Mother: Sophia Courtney   a citizen of the   Chickasaw Nation.

        Postoffice   Norton, Indian Territory.

AFFIDAVIT OF MOTHER.

UNITED STATES OF AMERICA, Indian Territory, ⎫
    Southern   **DISTRICT.** ⎭

    I, Sophia Courtney   , on oath state that I am 34   years of age and a citizen by   blood   , of the   Chickasaw   Nation; that I am the lawful wife of   Tyson Courtney   , who is a citizen, by blood   of the   Chickasaw   Nation; that a female   child was born to me on 29th day of   September   , 1902; that said child has been named   Emma Courtney   , and was living March 4, 1905.

                                   her
                       Sophia x Courtney
Witnesses To Mark: mark
    ⎰ C.W. Rowland
    ⎱ Sam Courtney

Subscribed and sworn to before me this 2nd day of   February   , 1906

C.H. *(Illegible)*
Notary Public.

AFFIDAVIT OF ATTENDING PHYSICIAN OR MID-WIFE.

UNITED STATES OF AMERICA, **Indian Territory,** ⎞
  Southern   **DISTRICT.** ⎠

I,   Betsie Courtney   , a ...., on oath state that I attended on
Mrs.   Sophia Courtney   , wife of   Tyson Courtney   on the   29th day of
September   , 1902; that there was born to her on said date a   female   child; that
said child was living March 4, 1905, and is said to have been named   Emma Courtney

her
Betsie x Courtney
mark

Witnesses To Mark:
  ⎧ C.W. Rowland
  ⎩ Sam Courtney

Subscribed and sworn to before me this 2nd day of   February   , 1906

C.H. *(Illegible)*
Notary Public.

BIRTH AFFIDAVIT.

Department of the Interior,
COMMISSION TO THE FIVE CIVILIZED TRIBES.

IN RE APPLICATION FOR ENROLLMENT, as a citizen of the   Chickasaw   Nation,
of   Emma Courtney   , born on the   15[sic]   day of   September   , 190 2

Name of Father: Tyson Courtney   a citizen of the   Chickasaw   Nation.
Name of Mother: Sophia Courtney   a citizen of the   Chickasaw   Nation.

Post-Office: Norton, I. T.

AFFIDAVIT OF MOTHER.

UNITED STATES OF AMERICA, ⎞
    INDIAN TERRITORY,   ⎟
Southern   District. ⎠

I,   Sophia Courtney   , on oath state that I am   34   years of age and a
citizen by   blood , of the   Chickasaw   Nation; that I am the lawful wife of

Applications for Enrollment of Chickasaw Newborn
Act of 1905   Volume VII

Tyson Courtney   , who is a citizen, by blood   of the   Chickasaw   Nation; that a   female   child was born to me on   15   day of   September   , 190 2, that said child has been named   Emma Courtney   , and is now living.

her
Sophia x Courtney
mark

WITNESSES TO MARK:

   ⎧ G.D. Rodgers
   ⎩ TW Leoby

Subscribed and sworn to before me this 6 *day of* November , 190 2

C.S. Stephens
Notary Public.

AFFIDAVIT OF ATTENDING PHYSICIAN OR MID-WIFE.

UNITED STATES OF AMERICA, ⎫
   INDIAN TERRITORY,   ⎬
Southern   District. ⎭

   I,   Betsie Courtney   , a   ————   , on oath state that I attended on Mrs.   Sophia Courtney   , wife of   Tyson Courtney   on the   15   day of September , 190 2; that there was born to her on said date a   female   child; that said child is now living and is said to have been named   Emma Courtney

her
Betsie x Courtney
mark

WITNESSES TO MARK:

   ⎧ G.D. Rodgers
   ⎩ TW Leoby

Subscribed and sworn to before me this 6 *day of* November , 190 2

C.S. Stephens
Notary Public.

9-NB-547.

DEPARTMENT OF THE INTERIOR,
COMMISSIONER TO THE FIVE CIVILIZED TRIBES.

In the matter of the application for the enrollment of Emma Courtney as a citizen by blood of the Chickasaw Nation.

D E C I S I O N.

It appears from the record herein that on March 4, 1905, there was filed with the Commissioner to the Five Civilized Tribes an application for the enrollment of Emma Courtney as a citizen by blood of the Chickasaw Nation.

It further appears from the record herein, and from the records of the Commission to the Five Civilized Tribes, that the applicant was born on September 29, 1902, and is the daughter of Tyson Courtney and Sophia Courtney, both of whom are recognized and enrolled citizens by blood of the Chickasaw Nation, their names appearing as numbers 2576 and 2577, respectively, upon the final roll of citizens by blood of the Chickasaw Nation, approved by the Secretary of the Interior, December 12, 1902; and that said applicant was living on March 4, 1905.

The Act of Congress approved March 3, 1905 (33 Stats., 1070), provides:

"That the Commission to the Five Civilized Tribes is authorized for sixty days after the date of the approval of this act to receive and consider applications for enrollment of children born subsequent to September twenty-fifth, nineteen hundred and two, and prior to March fourth, nineteen hundred and five, and who were living on said latter date, to citizens by blood of the Choctaw and Chickasaw tribes of Indians whose enrollment has been approved by the Secretary of the Interior prior to the date of the approval of this act; and to enroll and make allotments to such children."

I am, therefore, of the opinion that Emma Courtney should be enrolled as a citizen by blood of the Chickasaw Nation, under the provisions of law above quoted, and it is so ordered.

Tams Bixby   Commissioner.

Muskogee, Indian Territory.
JUN 13 1906

(The affidavit below typed as given.)

Southern District
Indian Territory

    Before me personally appeared Tyson Courtney a full blood Chickasaw Indian and to me well known and being informed by interpreter Sam Courtney states in regard to the different dates it was a of some one unknown to him and that the right date is September 29th 1902 sworn to and subscribed to this Feb 2nd 1906.

his
Tyson x Courtney

Witness to mark   mark
C.W. Rowland   C.H. *(Illegible)*
Sam Courtney   Notary Public

P.O. Willis I T

C O P Y

9-870.

Muskogee, Indian Territory, October 22, 1902.

O'Dus L. Collins,
      Troy, Indian Territory.

Dear Sir:

    Receipt is hereby acknowledged of your letter of the 20th inst., enclosing the application for enrollment as a citizen of the Chickasaw Nation of Emma Courtney, infant daughter of Tison[sic] and Sophia Courtney, born September 29, 1902.

    The same is returned to you herewith, and you are informed that the Commission cannot receive or consider the application for enrollment of this child as a citizen of the Chickasaw Nation, it appearing that said child was born September 29, 1902, subsequent to the ratification by the citizens of the Choctaw and Chickasaw Nations on September 25, 1902, of an agreement recently entered into between the United States and the citizens of these two Nations.

    Section twenty-eight of the agreement above referred to provides as follows:

    "The names of all persons living on the date of the final ratification of this agreement entitled to be enrolled as provided in section 27 hereof shall be placed upon the rolls made by said Commission; and no child born thereafter to a citizen or freedman and no person intermarried thereafter to a citizen shall be entitled to

209

enrollment or to participate in the distribution of the tribal property of the Choctaws and Chickasaws."

Respectfully,

Signed   Tams Bixby
Acting Chairman.

Enc B 1 67.

C O P Y.

Muskogee, Indian Territory, November 10, 1902.

Mansfield, McMurray & Cornish,
Attorneys for Choctaw and Chickasaw Nations,
South McAlester, Indian Territory.

Gentlemen:

On October 20, 1902, there was received at this office, an application for the enrollment as a citizen of the Chickasaw Nation, of Emma Courtney, the infant daughter of Tyson and Sophia Courtney, born September 29, 1902.

Accompanying this application was the affidavit of the mother, Sophia Courtney to the birth of her child, Emma Courtney on the 29th of September, 1902.

The application and the accompanying affidavits were on October 20, 1902, returned to Odus L. Collins of Troy, Indian Territory, by whom they were submitted, with the information that the Commission could not receive or consider the application for the enrollment of the child, Emma Courtney, as she was born subsequent to September 25, 1902, in accordance with the following provision of the act of Congress of July 1, 1902 (32 Stats., 641):

"The names of all persons living on the date of the final ratification of this agreement entitled to be enrolled as provided in section 27 hereof shall be placed upon the rolls made by said Commission; and no child born thereafter to a citizen or freedman and no person intermarried thereafter to a citizen shall be entitled to enrollment or to participate in the distribution of the tribal property of the Choctaws and Chickasaws."

At the appointment of the Commission at Tishomingo, Indian Territory, the week of November 3, 1902, Sophia Courtney and Betsie Courtney personally appeared before the representatives of the Commission at that place and there renewed the application for the enrollment of the child, Emma Courtney, as a citizen of the Chickasaw Nation and made affidavits to the date of the birth of this child as September 15, 1902.

This matter is brought to your attention in order that you may for the protection of the interests of the Chickasaw Nation introduce evidence showing the exact date of the birth of this child in order that she may not be enrolled if born subsequent to September 25, 1902.

Respectfully,

SIGNED Tams Bixby
Acting Chairman.

COPY   9-870.

Muskogee, Indian Territory, November 21, 1902.

Tyson Courtney,
Norton, Indian Territory.

Dear Sir:

Receipt is hereby acknowledged of the application for enrollment as a citizen of the Chickasaw Nation of Emma Courtney, infant daughter of Tyson and Sophia Courtney, born September 15, 1902.

It appears from our records that on October 22, 1902, a letter was received at this office from O'Dus L. Collins, dated October 20, 1902, enclosing an application for enrollment as a citizen of the Chickasaw Nation of Emma Courtney, infant daughter of Tyson and Sophia Courtney.

In her affidavit to the birth of the child, the mother stated that Emma Courtney was born September 29, 1902. The affidavit of the attending midwife also stated that the child was born September 29, 1902.

You are informed that before any action will be taken by the Commission in the matter of enrolling the child, Emma Courtney, that it will be necessary for you and your wife to appear in person before the Commission at its office at Muskogee, Indian Territory, with at least two disinterested witnesses and explain under oath the reasons why the mother and the attending midwife made oath on or about October 20, 1902, that Emma Courtney was born September 29, 1902; and subsequently thereto, and on November 6, 1902, the mother and her daughter, Betsie Courtney, made oath that the child, Emma Courtney, was born September 15, 1902. It is important that this matter be explained with as little delay as possible.

Respectfully,

SIGNED   *Tams Bixby*
Acting Chairman.

211

9-870.

Muskogee, Indian Territory, July 26, 1905.

Chief Clerk,
      Chickasaw Land Office,
            Ardmore, Indian Territory.

Dear Sir:

    Referring to Chickasaw roll card No. <u>870</u> Tyson Courtney, et al., there is inclosed herewith copy of name and information this pay placed at No. 7 on said card, Emma Courtney.

    You are therefore directed to make duplicate Chickasaw care No. 870 in the possession of your office conform to the information thereon and add the name of this applicant to the list of undetermined applicants for enrollment in the Chickasaw Nation.

                    Respectfully,

Incl. K-23.   Commissioner.

9-870

Muskogee, Indian Territory, October 30, 1905.

Tyson Courtney,
      Norton, Indian Territory.

Dear Sir:

    In the matter of the application for the enrollment of your child Emma Courtney as a citizen of the Chickasaw Nation, you are advised that it will be necessary for Sophia and Betsy Courtney to appear at this office accompanied by persons who know of the correct date of the birth of your child Emma Courtney.

    It appears from the records now in this office that in the affidavits of Sophia and Betsy Courtney received October 22, 1902, the date of the birth of said child was given as September 29, 1902, while the affidavits executed November 6, 1902, gave the date of the birth of said child as September 15, 1902.

    This matter should receive immediate attention.

                    Respectfully,

                              Commissioner.

REFER IN REPLY TO THE FOLLOWING:

9-870.

DEPARTMENT OF THE INTERIOR,
COMMISSIONER TO THE FIVE CIVILIZED TRIBES.

Muskogee, Indian Territory, January 24, 1906.

Tyson Courtney,
    Norton, Indian Territory.

Dear Sir:

    Referring to the application for the enrollment of your child, Emma Courtney, you are advised that it appears from the affidavits heretofore filed that there is a discrepancy as to the date of the birth of this child.

    There in inclosed herewith an application for her enrollment partially filled out in which the date of birth is left blank, which you are requested to have executed, inserting the correct date of the birth of said child and attaching to this application a statement as to why the date of her birth was given in one application as September 29, 1902, and in the other application, September 15, 1902. This matter should receive your immediate attention.

                   Respectfully,

                      Wm. O. Beall

LBA 1/24.

                   Acting Commissioner.

9-NB-547

COPY

Muskogee, Indian Territory, June 13, 1906.

Mansfield, McMurray & Cornish,
    Attorneys for Choctaw and Chickasaw Nations,
        South McAlester, Indian Territory.

Gentlemen:

    Inclosed herewith you will find a copy of the decision of the Commissioner to the Five Civilized Tribes, rendered June 13, 1906, granting the application for the enrollment of Emma Courtney as a citizen by blood of the Chickasaw Nation, under act of March 3, 1905.

    You are hereby advised that you will have fifteen days from the date of this notice within which to file protest against her enrollment. If at the expiration of that time no protest has been filed, the name of Emma Courtney will be placed upon the final roll of citizens by blood of the Chickasaw Nation to be submitted to the Secretary of the Interior for his approval.

Respectfully,
SIGNED

Tams Bixby
Commissioner.

Registered.
Incl. 9-NB-547

9-NB-547

Muskogee, Indian Territory, June 13, 1906.
COPY

Tyson Courtney,
Norton, Indian Territory.

Dear Sir:

Inclosed herewith you will find a copy of the decision of the Commissioner to the Five Civilized Tribes, rendered June 13, 1906, granting the application for the enrollment of your minor child, Emma Courtney, as a citizen by blood of the Chickasaw Nation, under act of March 3, 1905.

The attorneys for the Choctaw and Chickasaw Nations have been furnished a copy of this decision and have been allowed fifteen days from the date of this notice within which to file protest against her enrollment. If at the expiration of that time no protest has been filed, the name of Emma Courtney will be placed upon the final roll of citizens by blood of the Chickasaw Nation to be submitted to the Secretary of the Interior for his approval.

Respectfully,
SIGNED

Tams Bixby
Commissioner.

Registered.
Incl. 9-NB-547

Chic. N.B - 548
*(Bowden Weightman
Born October 6, 1905)*

Applications for Enrollment of Chickasaw Newborn
Act of 1905   Volume VII

BIRTH AFFIDAVIT.

DEPARTMENT OF THE INTERIOR.
COMMISSION TO THE FIVE CIVILIZED TRIBES.

IN RE APPLICATION FOR ENROLLMENT, as a citizen of the   Chickasaw   Nation, of   Bowden Weightman   , born on the 6   day of   October   , 1905

Name of Father: Vern H Weightman   a citizen of the   US   ~~Nation.~~
Name of Mother: Willie Weightman nee Pound a citizen of the   Chickasaw   Nation.

Postoffice   Kiowa Ind Ter

AFFIDAVIT OF MOTHER.

UNITED STATES OF AMERICA, Indian Territory, ⎱
      Central   DISTRICT. ⎰

I,   Willie Weightman nee Pound   , on oath state that I am   17   years of age and a citizen by   blood   , of the   Chickasaw   Nation; that I am the lawful wife of   Vern H Weightman   , who is a citizen, ~~by~~ .... of the   US   Nation; that a   male   child was born to me on   6   day of   October   , 1905; that said child has been named   Bowden Weightman   , and was living ~~March 4~~, Feb. 12 1906.

Willie Weightman nee Pound
Witnesses To Mark:

⎰

Subscribed and sworn to before me this 12   day of   February   , 1906

HB Rowley
Notary Public.

AFFIDAVIT OF ATTENDING PHYSICIAN OR MID-WIFE.

UNITED STATES OF AMERICA, Indian Territory, ⎱
      Central   DISTRICT. ⎰

I,   J M Vanderpool   , a Physician   , on oath state that I attended on Mrs.   Willie Weightman   , wife of   Vern H Weightman   on the 6   day of October   , 1905; that there was born to her on said date a   male   child; that said child was living March 4, 1905, and is said to have been named Bowden Weightman

J.M. Vanderpool M.D.
Witnesses To Mark:

⎰

215

Applications for Enrollment of Chickasaw Newborn
Act of 1905   Volume VII

Subscribed and sworn to before me this 12   day of   February   , 1906

HB Rowley
Notary Public.

Chic. N.B - 549
*(John Lewis
Born March 1, 1905)*

BIRTH AFFIDAVIT.

DEPARTMENT OF THE INTERIOR.
COMMISSION TO THE FIVE CIVILIZED TRIBES.

IN RE APPLICATION FOR ENROLLMENT, as a citizen of the   Chickasaw   Nation, of   John Lewis   , born on the 1st day of   March   , 1905

Name of Father: Benjamin Byington   a citizen of the   Choctaw   Nation.
Name of Mother: Eliza Lewis, nee Byington   a citizen of the   Chickasaw   Nation.

Postoffice   Caney, I. T.

AFFIDAVIT OF MOTHER.

UNITED STATES OF AMERICA, Indian Territory, ⎤
   Central   DISTRICT. ⎦

I,   Eliza Lewis   , on oath state that I am   17   years of age and a citizen by blood   , of the   Chickasaw   Nation; that ~~I am the lawful wife of~~   by Benjamin Byington   , who is a citizen, by blood   of the   Choctaw   Nation; that a male   child was born to me on   1st day of   March   , 1905; that said child has been named   John Lewis   , and was living March 4, 1905.

Eliza Lewis

Witnesses To Mark:
⎧
⎩

Subscribed and sworn to before me this 28th day of   April   , 1905

W.H. Angell
Notary Public.

216

AFFIDAVIT OF ATTENDING PHYSICIAN OR MID-WIFE.

UNITED STATES OF AMERICA, Indian Territory, }
     Central   DISTRICT. }

I, Ada Dana , a midwife , on oath state that I attended on Mrs. Eliza Lewis , ~~wife of~~ on the 1st day of March , 1905; that there was born to her on said date a male child; that said child was living March 4, 1905, and is said to have been named John Lewis

Ada Dana

Witnesses To Mark:

{

Subscribed and sworn to before me this 28th day of April , 1905

W.H. Angell
Notary Public.

Department of the Interior,
COMMISSION TO THE FIVE CIVILIZED TRIBES.

In the matter of the death of John Lewis a citizen of the Chickasaw Nation, who formerly resided at or near Caney , Ind. Ter., and died on the 19th day of March , 1905

AFFIDAVIT OF RELATIVE.

UNITED STATES OF AMERICA, }
    INDIAN TERRITORY,
   Central   District. }

I, Eliza Lewis , on oath state that I am 17 years of age and a citizen by blood , of the Chickasaw Nation; that my postoffice address is Caney , Ind. Ter.; that I am the mother of John Lewis who was a citizen, by blood , of the Chickasaw Nation and that said John Lewis died on the 19th day of March , 1905

Eliza Lewis

Witnesses To Mark:

{

Applications for Enrollment of Chickasaw Newborn
Act of 1905   Volume VII

Subscribed and sworn to before me this   28th   *day of*   April   *, 190* 5

W.H. Angell
Notary Public.

AFFIDAVIT OF ACQUAINTANCE.

UNITED STATES OF AMERICA, ⎫
   INDIAN TERRITORY,   ⎬
Central   District. ⎭

    I,   Ada Dana   , on oath state that I am   21   years of age, and a citizen by blood   of the   Choctaw   Nation; that my postoffice address is   Caney   , Ind. Ter.; that I was personally acquainted with   John Lewis   who was a citizen, by   blood , of the   Chickasaw   Nation; and that said   John Lewis   died on the   19th   day of   March   , 190 5

                    Ada Dana

Witnesses To Mark:

{

Subscribed and sworn to before me this   28th   *day of*   April   *, 190* 5

W.H. Angell
Notary Public.

Department of the Interior,
COMMISSION TO THE FIVE CIVILIZED TRIBES.

    In the matter of the death of   John Lewis   a citizen of the   Chickasaw Nation, who formerly resided at or near   Caney   , Ind. Ter., and died on the   19th day of   March   , 1905

AFFIDAVIT OF RELATIVE.

UNITED STATES OF AMERICA, ⎫
   INDIAN TERRITORY,   ⎬
Central   District. ⎭

    I,   Eliza Lewis   , on oath state that I am   18   years of age and a citizen by blood   , of the   Chickasaw   Nation; that my postoffice address is   Lewis   , Ind. Ter.; that I am   Mother   of   John Lewis   who was a citizen, by   blood   , of the Chickasaw   Nation and that said   John Lewis   died on the   19th   day of   March , 1905

                Eliza Lewis

Applications for Enrollment of Chickasaw Newborn
Act of 1905 Volume VII

Witnesses To Mark:

{

Subscribed and sworn to before me this 27th *day of* December , 190 5

E.A. Newman
Notary Public.

AFFIDAVIT OF ACQUAINTANCE.

UNITED STATES OF AMERICA,
INDIAN TERRITORY,
Central   District.

I, Etta Dana , on oath state that I am 22 years of age, and a citizen by blood of the Choctaw Nation; that my postoffice address is Lewis , Ind. Ter.; that I was personally acquainted with John Lewis who was a citizen, by blood , of the Chickasaw Nation; and that said John Lewis died on the 19th day of March , 190 5

Etta Dana

Witnesses To Mark:

{

Subscribed and sworn to before me this 27th *day of* December , 190 5

E.A. Newman
Notary Public.

IN THE MATTER OF THE ENROLLMENT
OF JOHN LEWIS, AS A CHICKASAW BY
BLOOD.

Comes now Eliza Lewis, who first being duly sworn deposes and says that she is 18 of age, that she resides at Lewis I T, and that she is a citizen of the Chickasaw Nation by blood and that she is the mother of John Lewis, and that she wishes to have his name enrolled as a citizen of the Chickasaw Nation.

Eliza Lewis

Subscribed in my presence and sworn to before me this the i7th[sic] day of Feb 1906.

E.A. Newman
Notary Public.

219

(The affidavit below typed as given.)

DEPARTMENT OF THE INTERIOR,
COMMISSION TO THE FIVE CIVILIZED TRIBES

IN The matter of the enrollment of John Lewis, as a citizen by blood of the Chickasaw Nation Indian Territory.

COMES now Ramsey Roberts and Etta Dana, being first duly sworn depose and say that they are 3(?) and 22 of age respectfuly, and reside at Lewis I T.

Affiant say that they are acquainted with Eliza Lewis and John Lewis who was a citizen by blood of the Chickasaw Nation Affiants say that the mother of John Lewis, is Eliza Lewis, and that the putative father of John Lewis is Ben Byington, and that said child was born out of wedlock.

Affiants further say that Eliza Lewis maiden name was Eliza Robinson, that her name appears upon the Chickasaw Roll as a Chickasaw by blood as number, 2,i38.

Affiants further say that they are not related to Eliza Lewis, and that they are disinterested persons, but are near neighbors of said Eliza Lewis; That they were present on the first day of march 1905, when a male child was born to Eliza Lewis, and that said child was living on the 4th day of march 19o5; and is said to have been named John Lewis, and further affiants sayeth not.

Ramsey Roberts

Etta Dana

Subscribed in my presense in my presense and sworn to before me this the 27th day of Dec, i905.

EA Newman

7-NB-1449.

Muskogee, Indian Territory, June 19, 1905.

Eliza Lewis,
Caney, Indian Territory.

Dear Madam:

Referring to the application for the enrollment of your infant child, John Lewis, born March 1, 1905, it is noted in the affidavits heretofore filed in this office that you give your name as Eliza Lewis, nee Byington, and state that you are a citizen by blood of the Chickasaw Nation. It also appears that the applicant died on April 28, 1905.

Applications for Enrollment of Chickasaw Newborn
Act of 1905 Volume VII

In order that you may be properly identified you are requested to state when, where and under what name you were listed for enrollment, the names of your parents and other members of your family for whom application was made at the same time, if you have selected an allotment, give your roll number as the same appears upon your allotment certificate, and if you are now married, or have been married, please give the name of your present, or former husband.

In this connection you are also requested to furnish the affidavits of two persons who are disinterested and not related to the applicant, who have actual knowledge of the facts; that the child was born, the date of his birth, that he was living on March 4, 1905, that you were his mother and that he died on March 19, 1905.

Please give this matter your prompt attention.

Respectfully,

Chairman.

7-NB-1449.

Muskogee, Indian Territory, August 21, 1905.

Eliza Lewis,
Caney, Indian Territory.

Dear Madam:

On June 19, 1905, the Commission to the Five Civilized Tribes addressed a letter to you in reference to the application for the enrollment of your infant child John Lewis as a citizen by blood of the Chickasaw Nation in which letter you were requested to state when, where and under what name you were listed for enrollment, the names of your parents and other members of your family for whom application was made at the same time, and if you have selected your allotment to give your roll number as the same appears upon your allotment certificate and if you are now married, or have been married, to give the name of your present or former husband or husbands. You were also requested to furnish the affidavits of two disinterested persons, who are not related to your said son John Lewis, said affidavits to set forth said child's name, the date of his birth, the names of his parents and the date of his death. To this letter no response has been received.

You are therefore again requested to furnish such information and affidavits and are advised that until the same are supplied the right of your said son as a citizen by blood of the Chickasaw Nation can not be finally determined.

Respectfully,

Commissioner.

221

7-NB-1449

Muskogee, Indian Territory, January 2, 1906.

Eliza Lewis,
    Caney, Indian Territory.

Dear Madam:

Receipt is hereby acknowledged of the joint affidavit of Ramsey Roberts and Etta Dana to the birth of John Lewis a citizen by blood of the Chickasaw Nation on March 1, 1905; also your affidavit and the affidavits of Etta Dana to the death of John Lewis on March 19, 1905, and the same have been filed with the record in this case.

It appearing that the father of this child is an enrolled citizen by blood of the Choctaw Nation you are requested to forward your affidavit stating in which nation you desire to have your child John Lewis enrolled.

Respectfully,

Commissioner.

7-NB 1449

Muskogee, Indian Territory, February 23, 1906.

E. A. Newman,
    Atoka, Indian Territory.

Dear Sir:

Receipt is hereby acknowledged of your letter of February 17, 1906, enclosing affidavit of Eliza Lewis electing to have her son John Lewis enrolled as a citizen by blood of the Chickasaw Nation and the same has been filed with the record on the matter of the enrollment of said child.

Replying to that portion of your letter in which you state authority from Eliza Lewis to act as her attorney in this matter you are advised that the petition enclosed with your letter appears to authorize one C. B. Weeks to act as attorney of record for Eliza Lewis and the same is returned you herewith.

Respectfully,

EB 1-23.

Acting Commissioner.

(The above letter given again except with date of February 24, 1906.)

7-1449

Muskogee, Indian Territory, March 22, 1906.

Chief Clerk,
     Chickasaw Land Office,
          Ardmore, Indian Territory.

Dear Sir:

     There is inclosed herewith copy of Choctaw new born card 1449, John Lewis, and you are directed to make duplicate card of this number in your possession conform to the information thereon.

                    Respectfully,

                                    Acting Commissioner.

EB 2-22.

Chic. N.B - 550
         (Wesley Lee Parker
         Born June 27, 1899)
         (Homer J. Parker
         Born December 17, 1900)
         (Leonard Overton Parker
         Born December 31, 1902)
         (Lota May Parker
         Born December 14, 1904)

9-D-454.

DEPARTMENT OF THE INTERIOR,
COMMISSION TO THE FIVE CIVILIZED TRIBES.
Muskogee, Ind. Ter., November 17, 1905.

     In the matter of the application for the enrollment of Wesley Lee Parker et al., et al, as citizens by blood of the Chickasaw Nation.

     Robert E. Lee, attorney at law, Ardmore, Indian Territory, appearing as attorney for the applicants.

Applications for Enrollment of Chickasaw Newborn
Act of 1905   Volume VII

       Wilson Parker being first duly sworn testified as follows:
By the Commissioner:
Q What is your name? A Wilson Parker.
Q How old are you? A Forty-four.
Q Your postoffice address? A Cornish, Indian Territory.
Q Are you acquainted with Wesley Lee Parker, Homer J. Parker, Leonard Overton parker and Lota May Parker? A Yes sir.
Q What is the name of the mother of these children? A Emma Smith.
Q Is she a citizen of the Chickasaw Nation? A No sir.
Q White woman? A Yes sr.
Q Citizen of the United States? A Yes sir.
Q Who is the father of these children? A I am their father.
Q Were you ever married to Emma Smith? A No sir.
Q When was Wesley Lee born? A I don't know exactly when he was born; he was six years old lat[sic] June.
Q When was Homer J. born? A He was born December 17, I think.
Q What year? A I don't remember what year; he is four now.
Q When was Leonard Overton born? A He was born two years ago?[sic] Born in December; he is two years old.
Q Is he a twin to Home J. A No, he is two years younger.
Q When was Lota May born? A The 17th day of last December.
Q 1904? [sic] Yes, she is one year old this coming December.
Q You state that you have never been married to Emma Smith, the mother of these children? A No.
Q Had you been living with her as husband and wife? A I have taken care of the children.
Q Well, answer the question, have you been living in the same house with her? A I have not lived with her but I have provided for her.
Q Where does Emma Smith live? A She lives close to home, three miles and a half south.
Q How far from your home does she live? A Three miles and a half.
Q You say you have never lived with Emma Smith at all? A No.
Q Are you certain that you are the father of these children? A Yes, I claim to be; I recognize them the same as my own children.
Q How long have you known Emma Smith? A I have known her 23 or 24 years I guess.
Q Since you have been going to see Emma Smith, do you [sic] of any other man going to see her? A No.
Q Under what name have these children gone? A They have gone by the name of Parker.
Q Under your name? A Yes sir.
Q Have they been recognized in the community in which you live as your children?
A Yes sir.
Q Have you so held them out? A Yes sir.
Q Always recognized them as your children? A Yes sir.
Q Have you provided for them in any way since their birth? A Yes sir.
Q What way? A Fed them and clothed them and supported them in every way a man could support a child.

Applications for Enrollment of Chickasaw Newborn
Act of 1905   Volume VII

Q Did you pay her regularly so much a month? A Yes

Q Have you provided for them entirely? A Yes sir.

Q Who has charge of these children at the present time? A They are at home with their mother now.

Q Are you married? A Yes sir.

Q How long have you been married? A I have been married twenty-four years this coming August.

Q These children have never resided with you in your own family? A Yes, they go back and forth; I take them home every now and then and when they want to go home again I take them back again. They go back when they want to.

Q Is your wife Mary C. Parker living? A Yes sir.

Witness is identified as Wilson Parker on Chickasaw Field Card No. 504o[sic], opposite No. 1604 upon the lists approved by the Secretary of the Interior December 12, 1902.

Q Are all these children living? A Yes sir.

Examination by the Commission by Mr. Lee.

Q I believe you stated that you had recognized these children as your own ever since the borth[sic] of each? A Yes sir.

Q I will ask you if you procured a physician to wait upon the mother of these children at their birth, and paid the bill A Yes sir.

Q You also procured a home for these children and paid the bills and expense; house rental and groceries and bills since the birth of each? A Yes sir.

Q Are you still providing for those four children mentioned in this application? A Yes, I sent them a bill of groceries the other day before I left home.

Q What provision have you recently made relative to providing them with a home and everything? These four children? A I gave them a home on one of my places up there.

Q Gave them a home on your place? A Yes sir.

Q You have at all times since the birth of each of the four children for which application is here made, provided for them and cared for them the same as you did for the children of your own household by your legally wedded wife? A Yes sir.

By the Commissioner.

Q So that your two families are living on the same place now? A No, on one of my places.

Witness excused.

Mary C. Parker being first duly sworn testified as follows:

Examination by the Commissioner:

Q What is your name? A Mary C. Parker.

Q How old are you? A Forty-two years old.

Q What is your postoffice address? A Cornish.

Q Are you the wife of Wilson Parker who has just testified relative to these children? A Yes, I am his wife.

Q Do you know anything about the parentage of these four children your husband has just testified about? A Yes, I know all the children.

225

Applications for Enrollment of Chickasaw Newborn
Act of 1905   Volume VII

Q Who is the mother is them? A Emma Smith.

Q Who is the father of these children? A Mr. Parker claims to be. I guess he is.

Q That is all the knowledge you is[sic] that he claims to be the father? A Yes, I know that he has supported them and cared for them as far as that is concerned, all the time.

Q Since their birth? A Yes, and I have taken care of the two oldest ones. I have kept them in my house for as much as a year at a time.

Q You have recognized them, have you, as the children of your husband? A Yes, I have taken care of them just the ame[sic] as I did my own.

Q Has Emma Smith ever been married? A Not that I know of.

Q She lives close to your house? A Three miles and a half.

Q Does she ever visit your house? A No.

Q But the children come over do they? A Yes, the children comes[sic].

Q Under what name have these children gone since their birth? A Went by the name of Parker.

Q That is your husband's name? A Yes sir.

Q Never was known by the name of Smith? A No sir.

Q Outside of the recognition of these children by your husband, Wilson Parker and their support, you have no further knowledge relative to the parentage of these children? A No.

Witness excused.

B. O. Tucker being first duly sworn testified as follows:

By the Commissioner:

Q What is your name? A B. O. Tucker.

Q How old are you? A Twenty-five.

Q What is your postoffice address? A Ardmore.

Q Are you acquainted with Wesley Lee Parker, Homer J. Parker, Leonard Overton Parker and Lota May Parker? A Yes sir.

Q These children relative to whom Wilson Parker has just testified? A Yes sir.--Claim to be.

Q Who is the mother of these children? A Emma Smith.

Q Who is the father of them? A Wilson Parker.

Q Upon what do you base your knowledge? A Well, he has supported them and taken care of them ever since I have known him.

Q You know that of your own personal knowledge? A Yes sir. I have seen them at his house; he used to keep one or two of them a good deal of the time; I have been there all times of the year when the children were there.

Q You live at Ardmorre[sic] and Wilson Parker lives at Cornish? A I live at Ardmore now; my place is near Cornish though.

Q You used to live in the same country? A Yes sir.

Q Then you don't know anything about the birth of this last child Lota May? A No, I have heard Mr. Parker speak of the child.

Q And acknowledge her as his own? A Yes, he is at my house very often.

Q Do you know under what names these children have gone since their birth? A Well, supposed to be; everybody know[sic] them to be his children.

Q Have they taken the name of Smith or Parker? A Parker, I suppose.

Q What do you know about it? You lived in that community. Were those children known as Smith or Parker? A Parker. They were known as Wilson Parker's children.

q Do you know of your own personal knowledge that Parker has supported these children since their birth? A Yes sir.

Q Is Emma Smith living? A Yes, she was a little while ago. I haven't seen her for three or four months.

Q Is she a non-citizen of the Chickasaw Nation? A Yes.

Examination by the Commission by Mr. Lee.

Q Do you know when Emma Smith lived there in Ardmore? A Yes sir.

Q I will ask you, to refresh your recollcetion[sic], if that last child was not born in the city of Ardmore? A Yes, I believe so. I belive[sic] one of Mr. Parker's boys Guy was at my house at the time and told me so.

Q Wilson Parker has always recognized all four of these children to his friends and made a statements[sic] to his friends that they were his children and took the Parker name?
A Yes.

By the Commissioner.

Q Do you know whether or not Emma Smith has been keeping company with anyone else during the last six or eight years? A I don't know a thing about it. I havn't[sic] known her more than four years.

Q What has she been doing while she was at Ardmore? A She kept house I expect. Mr. parker had her there, residing there with the children; he bought the furniture.

Witness excused.

Wilson Parker being recalled, testified as follows:

By the Commissioner.

Q How long have you know Emma Smith? A I have known her since she was a child pretty near; about twenty-five years.

Q Where has she lived during that time? A She lived there on my farm.

Q From then until the present date? A Yes; well, she lived at Ardmore last year.

Q When did she go to Ardmore? A She went to Ard last-- I believe it was in October a year ago; she staid[sic] in Ardmore one year.

Q What do you mean? She lived there from last October to this October? A No, I moved her up to Ardmore in February or March last--

Q This year? A Yes.

Q While she was living at Ardmore did you go down to see her[sic] A Yes, I went around to see her.

Q With the exception of this residence in Ardmore for a year had she, always previous to that time, lived near your home? A Yes sir.

Q You have ever[sic] reason to think, have you, that these children are your children? A Yes sir.

Q You have never questioned it at any time? A No sir.

By Mr?[sic] Lee:

Q You moved Emma Smith to Ardmore yourself, and then moved her away from there did you not? A Yes sir.

Applications for Enrollment of Chickasaw Newborn
Act of 1905   Volume VII

Q You visited her while she was at Ardmore and saw that these children were properly cared for and fed? A Yes sir.

Q Prior to that time where did you live? A I lived at home?[sic]

Q While you were at Cornish prior to your removal of Emma Smith to Ardmore, where did Emma Smith live? A She lived at Cornish, Indian Territory within three miles.

Q You visited Emma Smith at regular intervals during this time did you? A Yes sir.

Q You provided for these children while she was at Cornish? A Yes sir.

Q Prior to your removal to Cornish where did you live? A I lived close to Cornish, Indian Territory three miles southwest of Cornish

Q Where did Emma Smith live at that time? A She lived at that time she lived on the old ranch place about three miles from Cornish. I lived southwest of Cornish.

Q Prior to the time of the removal of yourself and Emma Smith up to the Cornish country where did you live? A Lived in the city of cornish[sic]; right in town.

Q I will ask you if you ever lived near Burneyville and where Emma Smith lived when you lived in that community, if you so live there.[sic] A I lived at old Cheek at that time.

By the Commissioner:

Q How far is Burneyville from Cornish? A Twelve miles.

By Mr?[sic] Lee.

Q Where did Emma Smith Live during that time that you lived at Cheek? A She lived at Cheek; had a farm there.

Q I will ask you if, all the time prior to the borth[sic] of the oldest, and up to the borth of the last child, if she has not always lived near your residence? A Yes sir.

Q So far as you know no other man has visited Emma Smith other than yourself, for the purpose of begetting children? A No sir.

Q Or for any sexual purpose? A No sir.

Q You have ever[sic] reason to believe that these children are yours and not any other mans'? A Yes, that's all.

Witness excused.

Mary C. Parker being recalled, testified as follows:

By the Commisioner[sic]:

Q Were you present at the birth of Wesley Lee Parker and Homer J?[sic] Parker? A Yes sir.

Q In what capacity did you act? A Well, I dressed them.

Q Did you act as midwife? A No, but I dressed the children, both of them.

Q How is it that you made an affidavit that you acted as midwife at the birth of these two children (No answer.)

Q Did the doctor attend Emma Smith at the birth of Wesley Lee and Homer J. Parker? A Yes, there was a doctor there both times.

Q What was his name? A Hallard.

Q Where does he live? A I don't know where he lives now; her did live at Cornish.

Q Has he moved away from there? A Yes, he moved away about two years ago.

Q You were present yourself were you, when these two children were born? A Yes, I was present; I washed and dressed both of them.

228

Applications for Enrollment of Chickasaw Newborn
Act of 1905   Volume VII

Frances R. Lane upon oath states that as stenographer to the Commissioner to the Five Civilized Tribes she correctly reported the testimony in the above entitled cause and that the foregoing is an accurate transcript of her stenographic notes thereof.

Frances R Lane

Subscribed and sworn to before me this November 18, 1905.

Myron White
Notary Public.

DEPARTMENT OF THE INTERIOR
Commissioner to the Five Civilized Tribes
Chickasaw Land Office
Ardmore, Ind. Ter., January 19, 1906.

In the matter of the application for the enrollment of Wesley Lee Parker, Homer J. Parker, Leonard Parker and Lotie[sic] May Parker, applicants represented by Robert E. Lee, attorney at law, Ardmore, Indian Territory, no appearance on behalf of attorneys for the Choctaw and Chickasaw Nations, no notice to attorneys for the Choctaw and Chickasaw Nations of the submission of this testimony.

Laura Emma Smith, being first duly sworn by Fred T. Marr, notary public, testified as follows:

Examination by Mr. Beall:

Q What is your name? A Laura Emma Smith.
Q How old are you? A Twenty six years old.
Q Where do you live? A Near Cornish.
Q In the Chickasaw Nation? A Yes, sir.
Q You are a white woman? A Yes, sir.
Q You say your name is Smith at present? A Yes, sir.
Q What is your husband's name? A I haven't got any husband.
Q Smith is your maiden name? A Yes, sir.
Q You have never been married? A No, sir.
Q Application has been made to the Commissioner to the Five Civilized Tribes for the enrollment of four children, Wesley Lee Parker, Homer J. Parker, Leonard Parker and Lotie May Parker, as citizens by blood of the Chickasaw Nation. Do you know these children? A Yes, sir.
Q Whose children are they? A Wilson Parker's.
Q Wilson Parker is the father of them? A Yes, sir.
Q Wilson Parker is a Chickasaw Indian? A Yes, sir.
Q Who is the mother of these four children? A I am.

Applications for Enrollment of Chickasaw Newborn
Act of 1905   Volume VII

Q Were you ever married to Wilson Parker? A No, I have never been married to him but I lived with him as his second wife.

Q Has Wilson Parker a wife? A Yes, sir.

Q What is her name? A Her name is Smith same as my name.

Q What relation is Wilson Parker's wife to you? A She is a sister to me.

Q When was Wilson Parker married to her? A I don't remember.

Q How long have they been married? A Twenty five years I believe, as well as I remember it is twenty five years.

Q How old a man is Wilson Parker? A He says he is forty years old.

Q How old is your sister? A She is thirty eight.

Q How old are you? A I am twenty six.

Q Has you sister any children by Wilson Parker? A Yes, sir, she has five children.

Q Those children were born to her in lawful wedlock with Wilson Parker? A Yes, sir.

Q You say you are the mother of these four children, Wesley Lee Parker, Homer J. Parker, Leonard Parker and Lotie May Parker? A Yes, sir.

Q When was Wesley Lee Parker born? A He is six years old, he will be seven in June, the twenty seventh of June.

Q How old is Homer J. Parker? A Five years old.

Q How old is Leonard Parker? A He is three.

Q When was he born? A In 1902.

Q What time in 1902? A The last day of December, the thirty first.

Q How old is Lotie May Parker? A She is a year old the fourteenth of December.

Q You state these four children are named Parker? A Yes, sir.

Q You say your name is Smith and that you have never been married? A Yes, sir.

Q How did these children come to have the name Parker? A Because that is their father's name, they take the name of their father.

Q Is Wilson Parker's lawful wife living? A Yes, sir.

Q She is your sister? A Yrs, sir.

Q Where do your live? A In the Chickasaw Nation near Cornish.

Q How do you live in reference to your sister, the lawful wife of Wilson Parker, do you live in the same house? A No, I live alone.

Q How far do you live from Wilson Parker? A Four miles and a half.

Q You have a home of your own? A Yes, sir.

Q You live there with these four children by yourself? A My nephew, Thomas Parker, lives with me.

Q How old is he? A Twenty one years old.

Q What are you doing living with Thomas Parker? A Him and his wife, he is a married man, live there.

Q Thomas Parker and his wife live with you? A Yes, sir.

Q Did you ever live with any other man besides Wilson Parker? A No, sir.

Q You mean to say that you actually lived with this man, Wilson Parker, when he was married to your sister? A Yes, sir, I have.

Q And these four children were born to you at the time your sister was his lawful wife, is that correct? A Yes, sir.

Q You are willing to swear that you have never lived with any other man? A Yes, sir, I will swear that.

Q The oldest one of these children is now about six or seven years old, isn't he? A Yes, sir, he will be seven in June.

Q Where was that child born? A He was born close to Cornish.

Q In whose house? A Wilson Parker's house.

Q You were living with Wilson Parker in his house at the time your oldest child was born? A Yes, he brought me there.

Q Where had you been living before that? A At Marlow.

Q Who had you been living with there? A I boarded at a hotel.

Q Who did you board with? A Summers was the name.

Q How old were you when your first child was born? A Nineteen years old.

Q What were you doing in Marlow? A I just went there to board.

Q Who paid your board? A Parker.

Q When did your mother die? A She died when I was thirteen years old.

Q Is your father living? A No, sir.

Q How long has he been dead? A Four years.

Q Your father was living then when your two oldest children were born? A Yes, sir.

Q What is his name? A W. D. Smith.

Q Did you live with your father? A No, sir.

Q Where was he living when your oldest child was born? A With his oldest son, John Smith.

Q Is John Smith your brother? A Yes, sir.

Q Where does he live? A He lives at Cheek.

Q How old is he? A Forty two years old.

Q Have you any means of livelihood now? A No, sir.

Q How do you live? A Wilson Parker has been supporting me until now he is convicted.

Q Where is Wilson Parker now? A He is in jail.

Q In jail here in Ardmore? A Yes, sir.

Q On what charge? A He said something about forging a check.

Q Has he ever been convicted before of any crime? A No.

Q Has he ever been indicted? A I think he has, he has had a right smart of trouble in the court.

Q You state you never lived with any other man prior to the birth of your oldest son, Wesley Lee Parker? A No, sir.

Q Have you ever lived with any other man since then? A No, sir.

Q And you now under oath solemnly swear that the only man you ever had intercourse with and the father of these four children is this man, Wilson Parker? A Yes, sir.

George Byram, being first duly sworn by Fred T. Marr, notary public, testified as follows:

Examination by Mr. Beall:

Q What is your name? A George Bryam.

Q What is your age and post office address? A Age thirty two, Cornish is my post office.

Q Are you a citizen of either the Choctaw or Chickasaw Nation? A No, sir.

Q You are a white man? A Yes, sir.

Q How long have you lived in the Chickasaw Nation? A Eighteen years, about eighteen years.

Q Do you know this woman, Laura Emma Smith? A Yes, sir.

Q How long have you known her? A Four years.

Q What is the general reputation of this woman in the neighborhood where she lives?

A Outside of living with Wilson Parker I never heard aught against her.

Q Do you know Wilson Parker's wife? A Yes, sir.

Q What is her name? A I don't know her given name, I always knew her as Mrs. Parker.

Q Is she living? A Yes, sir.

Q She lives with Wilson Parker at Cornish? A Yes, sir.

Q And this woman, who has these illegitimate children, lives out in the country about four miles? A Yes, sir.

Q You have no way of knowing who the father of these children is? A No, sir.

Examination by Robert E. Lee:

Q How are these children know in that community? A As Wilson Parker's children.

Q Generally known as Wilson Parker's children? A Yes, sir.

Q What name has Mrs. Parker here relative to Wilson Parker? A As Wilson Parker's second wife.

Q Do you know whether or not Wilson Parker on one or two occasions has been arrested on the charge of adultery for living with this woman? A I have heard he has.

Q Wilson Parker spends part of his time with wife number one and part with number two? A Yes, sir.

Q It is not current report that this woman lives with any one except Wilson Parker?

A No, sir.

Q You have known them for four years? A Yes, sir.

Cinda Yates, stenographer for the Commissioner to the Five Civilized Tribes, states on oath that she reported the above and foregoing proceedings on the 19th day of January, 1906, and that same is a true and correct transcript of her stenographic notes thereof.

Cinda Yates

Subscribed and sworn to before me this 22d day of January, 1906.

Fred T. Marr
Notary Public.

9-D-454.
O.L.J.

DEPARTMENT OF THE INTERIOR.
COMMISSIONER TO THE FIVE CIVILIZED TRIBES.

In the matter of the application for the enrollment of Wesley Lee Parker, et al., as citizens by blood of the Chickasaw Nation.

D E C I S I O N .

It appears from the records herein that on April 28, 1905, application was made to the Commission to the Five Civilized Tribes for the enrollment of Wesley Lee Parker, Homer J. Parker, Leonard Overton Parker and Lota May Parker as citizens by blood of the Chickasaw Nation.

It further appears from the record herein and the records of the Commission to the Five Civilized Tribes that Wesley Lee Parker was born June 27, 1899; that Homer J. Parker was born December 17, 1900; that Leonard Overton Parker was born December 31, 1902; that Lota May Parker was born December 14, 1904; and that all of said applicants are the illegitimate children of Wilson Parker, a recognized and enrolled citizen by blood of the Chickasaw Nation, whose name appears as No. 1603 upon the final roll of citizens by blood of the Chickasaw Nation approved by the Secretary of the Interior December 12, 1902, and Laura Emma Smith, a non-citizen white woman; and that all of said applicants were living on March 4, 1905.

I am therefore of the opinion that Wesley Lee Parker, Homer J. Parker, Leonard Overton Parker and Lota May Parker should be enrolled as citizens by blood of the Chickasaw Nation under the provisions of the Act of Congress approved March 3, 1905 (33 Stats., 1070), and it is so ordered.

Tams Bixby Commissioner.

Muskogee, Indian Territory.
JUL 28 1906

BIRTH AFFIDAVIT.
DEPARTMENT OF THE INTERIOR.
COMMISSION TO THE FIVE CIVILIZED TRIBES.

IN RE APPLICATION FOR ENROLLMENT, as a citizen of the   Chickasaw   Nation, of   Leonard Overton Parker   , born on the 31st day of   December   , 1902

Name of Father: Wilson Parker   a citizen of the   Chickasaw Nation.
Name of Mother: Laura Emma Parker   a citizen of the   Chickasaw Nation.

Applications for Enrollment of Chickasaw Newborn
Act of 1905   Volume VII

Postoffice   Ardmore I.T.

AFFIDAVIT OF MOTHER.

UNITED STATES OF AMERICA, Indian Territory, ⎱
Ardmore   DISTRICT. ⎰

I,   Laura Emma Parker   , on oath state that I am   twenty six   years of age and a citizen by ...., of the   United States   Nation; that I am the ~~lawful~~ *common law* wife of   Wilson Parker   , who is a citizen, by blood   of the   Chickasaw Nation; that a   male   child was born to me on   Thirty first day of December   , 1902; that said child has been named   Leonard Overton Parker   , and was living March 4, 1905.

(Seal)   Laura Emma Parker

Witnesses To Mark:
⎰ Robt E Lee
⎱ Ola Halloway

Subscribed and sworn to before me this 23rd   day of   March   , 1905

Ola Halloway
Notary Public.

AFFIDAVIT OF ATTENDING PHYSICIAN OR MID-WIFE.

UNITED STATES OF AMERICA, Indian Territory, ⎱
Wetumka I.T.   DISTRICT. ⎰

I,   Dr J.A. Hemphill   , a   physician   , on oath state that I attended on Mrs.   Laura Emma Parker   , wife of   Wilson Parker   on the   31st   day of December   , 1902; that there was born to her on said date a   male   child; that said child was living March 4, 1905, and is said to have been named Leonard Overton Parker

Dr J.A. Hemphill

Witnesses To Mark:
⎰
⎱ (Seal)

Subscribed and sworn to before me this 20 day of   April   , 1905

H. H. Holman
Notary Public.

234

Applications for Enrollment of Chickasaw Newborn
Act of 1905   Volume VII

DEPARTMENT OF THE INTERIOR.
COMMISSION TO THE FIVE CIVILIZED TRIBES.

IN RE APPLICATION FOR ENROLLMENT, as a citizen of the   Chickasaw   Nation, of   Leonard Overton Parker   , born on the 31st   day of   December   , 1902

Name of Father: Wilson Parker   a citizen of the   Chickasaw   Nation.
Name of Mother: Laura Emma Parker   a citizen of the   Chickasaw   Nation.

Postoffice   Ardmore I.T.

AFFIDAVIT OF MOTHER.

UNITED STATES OF AMERICA, Indian Territory,
      Ardmore   **DISTRICT.**

I,   Laura Emma Parker   , on oath state that I am   twenty six   years of age and a citizen by ...., of the   United States   Nation; that I am the ~~lawful~~ common law wife of   Wilson Parker   , who is a citizen, by   blood   of the   Chickasaw Nation; that a   male   child was born to me on   Thirty first   day of   December   , 1902; that said child has been named   Leonard Overton Parker   , and was living March 4, 1905.
(Seal)   Laura Emma Parker
Witnesses To Mark:
      Robt E Lee
      Ola Halloway

Subscribed and sworn to before me this 23rd   day of   March   , 1905.

Ola Halloway
Notary Public.

AFFIDAVIT OF ATTENDING PHYSICIAN OR MID-WIFE.

UNITED STATES OF AMERICA, Indian Territory,
      Wetumka I.T.   **DISTRICT.**

I,   Dr J.A. Hemphill   , a   physician   , on oath state that I attended on Mrs.   Laura Emma Parker   , wife of   Wilson Parker   on the   31st   day of December   , 1902; that there was born to her on said date a   male   child; that said child was living March 4, 1905, and is said to have been named Leonard Overton Parker

Dr J.A. Hemphill

Applications for Enrollment of Chickasaw Newborn
Act of 1905   Volume VII

Witnesses To Mark:

    {
      (Seal)

Subscribed and sworn to before me this 20   day of   April   , 1905

H. H. Holman

Notary Public.

BIRTH AFFIDAVIT.

DEPARTMENT OF THE INTERIOR.
COMMISSION TO THE FIVE CIVILIZED TRIBES.

IN RE APPLICATION FOR ENROLLMENT, as a citizen of the   Chickasaw   Nation, of   Lota May Parker   , born on the 14th day of December   , 1904

Name of Father: Wilson Parker   a citizen of the   Chickasaw   Nation.
Name of Mother: Laura Emma Parker   a citizen of the   Chickasaw   Nation.

Postoffice   Ardmore I.T.

AFFIDAVIT OF MOTHER.

UNITED STATES OF AMERICA, Indian Territory, ⎫
   Ardmore   **DISTRICT.** ⎬

    I,   Laura Emma Parker   , on oath state that I am   twenty six   years of age and a citizen by _____, of the   United States   Nation; that I am the ~~lawful~~ *common law* wife of   Wilson L. Parker   , who is a citizen, by blood   of the   Chickasaw Nation; that a   female   child was born to me on   Fourteenth day of December   , 1904; that said child has been named   Lota May Parker   , and was living March 4, 1905.

Laura Emma Parker

Witnesses To Mark:
   { Robt E Lee
    Ola Halloway
(Seal)

Subscribed and sworn to before me this 23   day of   March   , 1905

Ola Halloway

Notary Public.

236

Applications for Enrollment of Chickasaw Newborn
Act of 1905   Volume VII

AFFIDAVIT OF ATTENDING PHYSICIAN OR MID-WIFE.

UNITED STATES OF AMERICA, Indian Territory, }
   Ardmore   DISTRICT. }

     I,   Dr J.F. Son   , a   physician   , on oath state that I attended on Mrs.   Laura Emma Parker   , wife of   Wilson L. Parker   on the   14th day of December   , 1904; that there was born to her on said date a   female   child; that said child was living March 4, 1905, and is said to have been named Lota May Parker

J.F. Son M.D.

Witnesses To Mark:

   {
   { (Seal)
     Subscribed and sworn to before me this 15 day of   April   , 1905

Ola Halloway
Notary Public.

C O P Y .

Ardmore, Indian Territory,
Southern District.

In re application for enrollment of Lota May Parker, born on the 14th day of December, 1904.
     I, William[sic] Parker, state on oath that I am a citizen of the Chickasaw Nation, that I am the father of Lota May Parker whose mother's name is Laura Emma Parker.
     I further state that Laura Emma Parker is my common law wife, that I have lived with her as such for a number of years, that I have provided for her and supported her and four children among the number of children being the above named applicant. That the applicant, Lota May Parker, was living on March 4th, 1905, and is yet living with her mother in the Southern District of the Indian Territory.
           (Signed) W. L. Parker.

Subscribed and sworn to before me this sworn to before me, Ola Holloway, a notary public within and for the Southern District of the Indian Territory, on this the 26th day of April, 1905.
           (Signed) Ola Holloway.
               Notary Public.

(SEAL)
My commission expires Jan. 17th 1909.

C O P Y .

Ardmore, Indian Territory,
Southern District.
In re application for enrollment of Homer J. Parker as a citizen of the Chickasaw Nation.

I, Wilson L. Parker state on oath that Homer J. Parker was born on the 17th day of December, 1900, that he was living on the 5th day of March, 1905, that said child is a Chickasaw Indian by blood and is a son of Wilson Parker, affiant herein, by Laura Emma Parker, his common law wife, that affiant Wilson L. Parker has lived with and cohabited with Laura Emma Parker for a number of years and that Homer J. Parker is one of four children born as the fruits of the union above mentioned, and that said child has always lived within the Southern District of Indian Territory.
(Signed) W. L. Parker.

Subscribed and sworn to before me on this the 26th day of April, 1905.
(Signed) Ola Holloway.
Notary Public.

(SEAL)
My commission expires Jan. 17th, 1909.

———————

C O P Y .

Ardmore, Indian Territory,
Southern District.

In re application for enrollment of Wesley Lee Parker as a citizen of the Chickasaw Nation.

I, Wilson L. Parker, state on oath that I am the father of Wesley Lee Parker, born on the 27th day of June, 1899, that the applicant Wesley Lee Parker is a citizen of the Chickasaw Nation by blood, that Wesley Lee Parker is the son of Lara[sic] Emma Parker, my common law wife, that I have lived with and cohabited with Laura Emma Parker since the year 1898, and that said child is the fruit of said union between myself, a Chickasaw Indian by blood, and Laura Emma Parker. That said child was living on the 25th day of September, 1902, and also on the 5th day of March, 1905, and is yet living and has always resided within the Southern District of the Indian Territory.
(Signed) W. L. Parker

Subscribed and sworn to before me this the 26th day of April, 1905.

(Signed) Ola Halloway
Notary Public.

(SEAL)
My commission expires Jan. 17th, 1909.

———————

C O P Y .

Ardmore, Indian Territory,
Southern District.

In re application for enrollment of Leonard Overton Parker as a citizen of the Chickasaw Nation.

I, Wilson L. Parker, state on oath that I am the father of Leonard Overton Parker born on the 31st day of December, 1902, that the applicant Leonard Overton Parker is a citizen of the Chickasaw Nation by blood, that Leonard Overton Parker id[sic] the son of Laura Emma Parker, my common law wife, that I Have[sic] lived with and cohabited with Laura Emma Parker for many years, and that child is the fruit of said union between me, a Chickasaw Indian by blood, and Laura Emma Parker. That said child was living on the 5th day of March, 1905, and is yet living, and has always resided within the Southern District of the Indian Territory.

(Signed) W. L. Parker

Subscribed and sworn to before me this the 26th day of April, 1905.

(Signed) Ola Halloway
Notary Public.

(SEAL)
My commission expires Jan. 17th, 1909.

9-D-454

Muskogee, Indian Territory, July 28, 1906.

Laura Emma Smith,   **COPY**
    Cornish, Indian Territory.

Dear Madam:

Inclosed herewith you will find a copy of the decision of the Commissioner to the Five Civilized Tribes, rendered July 28, 1906, granting the application for the enrollment of your children, Wesley Lee Parker, Homer J. Parker, Leonard Overton Parker and Lota May Parker as citizens by blood of the Chickasaw Nation.

The attorneys for the Choctaw and Chickasaw Nations have been furnished a copy of this decision and have been allowed fifteen days from the date of this notice within which to file protest against their enrollment. If at the expiration of that time no protest has been filed, the names of Wesley Lee Parker, Homer J. Parker, Leonard Overton Parker and Lota May Parker will be placed upon the final roll of citizens by blood of the Chickasaw Nation to be submitted to the Secretary of the Interior for his approval.

Respectfully

SIGNED   *Tams Bixby*

Registered.   Commissioner.

Incl. 9-D-454

9-D-454

Muskogee, Indian Territory, July 28, 1906.

Robert E. Lee,
      Attorney at Law,
            Ardmore, Indian Territory.

Dear Sir:

You are hereby notified that the Commissioner to the Five Civilized Tribes, on July 28, 1906, rendered his decision granting the application for the enrollment of Wesley Lee Parker, Homer J. Parker, Leonard Overton Parker and Lota May Parker as citizens by blood of the Chickasaw Nation.

The attorneys for the Choctaw and Chickasaw Nations have been furnished a copy of this decision and have been allowed fifteen days from the date of this notice within which to file protest against their enrollment. If at the expiration of that time no protest has been filed, the names of Wesley Lee Parker, Homer J. Parker, Leonard Overton Parker and Lota May Parker will be placed upon the final roll of citizens by blood of the Chickasaw Nation to be submitted to the Secretary of the Interior for his approval.

Respectfully,

Registered.   Commissioner.

9-D-454

Muskogee, Indian Territory, July 28, 1906.

Wilson Parker,   **COPY**
      Cornish, Indian Territory.

Dear Sir:

Inclosed herewith you will find a copy of the decision of the Commissioner to the Five Civilized Tribes, rendered July 28, 1906, granting the application for the enrollment of your children, Wesley Lee Parker, Homer J. Parker, Leonard Overton Parker and Lota May Parker as citizens by blood of the Chickasaw Nation.

The attorneys for the Choctaw and Chickasaw Nations have been furnished a copy of this decision and have been allowed fifteen days from the date of this notice within which to file protest against their enrollment. If at the expiration of that time no protest has been filed, the names of Wesley Lee Parker, Homer J. Parker, Leonard Overton Parker and Lota May Parker will be placed upon the final roll of citizens by blood of the Chickasaw Nation to be submitted to the Secretary of the Interior for his approval.

Respectfully

SIGNED   *Tams Bixby*

Registered.   Commissioner.

9-D-454

Muskogee, Indian Territory, July 28, 1906.

Mansfield, McMurray & Cornish,   **COPY**
    Attorneys for Choctaw and Chickasaw Nations,
        South McAlester, Indian Territory.

Gentlemen:

Inclosed herewith you will find a copy of the decision of the Commissioner to the Five Civilized Tribes, rendered July 28, 1906, granting the application for the enrollment of your children, Wesley Lee Parker, Homer J. Parker, Leonard Overton Parker and Lota May Parker as citizens by blood of the Chickasaw Nation.

You are hereby advised that you will be allowed fifteen days from the date of this notice within which to file protest against their enrollment. If at the expiration of that time no protest has been filed, the names of Wesley Lee Parker, Homer J. Parker, Leonard Overton Parker and Lota May Parker will be placed upon the final roll of citizens by blood of the Chickasaw Nation to be submitted to the Secretary of the Interior for his approval.

Respectfully

SIGNED   *Tams Bixby*

Registered.   Commissioner.
Incl. 9-D-454

9-NB-550

Muskogee, Indian Territory, August 29, 1906.

Ledbetter & Bledsoe,
    Attorneys at Law,
       Ardmore, Indian Territory.

Centlemen[sic]:

    Receipt is hereby acknowledged of your letter of August 22, 1906, asking if protest has been filed by the attorneys for the Choctaw and Chickasaw Nations against the enrollment as citizens of the Chickasaw Nation the Chickasaw Nation of Wesley, Homer J., Leonard Overton and Lota May Parker.

    You are advised that no protest has been filed by the attorneys for the Choctaw and Chickasaw Nations against the enrollment of these children and their names have been placed upon a schedule of citizens by blood of the Chickasaw Nation which has been forwarded the Secretary of the Interior and you will be notified when their enrollment is approved by him.

                Respectfully,

                        Acting Commissioner.

(The above letter given again except with date of August 30, 1906.)

9-1840
9-NB-550

Muskogee, Indian Territory, November 9, 1906.

Robert E. Lee,
    Attorney at Law,
       Ardmore, Indian Territory.

Dear Sir:

    Receipt is hereby acknowledged of your letter of October 31, 1906, in which you refer to office letter of October 26, 1906, advising that on October 15, 1906, the Secretary of the Interior approved the enrollment of Lenord[sic] Overton and Lota May Parker as citizens by blood of the Chickasaw Nation and ask what action has been taken relative to the other two children Wesley Lee and Homer J. Parker.

On reply you are advised that on September 24, 1906, the Secretary of the Interior approved the enrollment of Wesley Lee and Homer J. Parker as citizens by blood of the Chickasaw Nation.

Respectfully,

Commissioner.

Chic. N.B - 551

*(Susie Ayakatubby
Born February 6, 1905)*

DEPARTMENT OF THE INTERIOR,
COMMISSIONER TO THE FIVE CIVILIZED TRIBES.

In the matter of the application for the enrollment as a citizen by blood of the Chickasaw Nation . . . . . .

SUSIE AYAKATUBBY........9-NB-551.

9-NB-551,
O.L.J.

DEPARTMENT OF THE INTERIOR,
COMMISSIONER TO THE FIVE CIVILIZED TRIBES.

In the matter of the application for the enrollment of Susie Ayakatubby as a citizen by blood of the Chickasaw Nation.

D E C I S I O N.

It appears from the record herein that on May 3, 1905, there was received at the office of the Commission to the Five Civilized Tribes an application for the enrollment of Susie Ayakatubby as a citizen by blood of the Chickasaw Nation.   The envelope containing said application was post marked "Muskogee, Ind. T., May 2, 1905, 4 P. M."

It appears from the record herein that said applicant was born on February 6, 1905, and is the illegitimate daughter of Agnes Ayakatubby, whose name appears as number 23 upon the final roll of citizens by blood of the Chickasaw Nation approved by the Secretary of the Interior December 12, 1902; and that said child was living on March 4, 1905.

The Act of Congress approved March 3, 1905 (33 Stats., 1070), provides:

243

Applications for Enrollment of Chickasaw Newborn
Act of 1905   Volume VII

"That the Commission to the Five Civilized Tribes is authorized for sixty days after the date of the approval of this act to receive and consider applications for enrollment of children born subsequent to September twenty-fifth, nineteen hundred and two, and prior to March fourth, nineteen hundred and five, and who were living on said latter date, to citizens by blood of the Choctaw and Chickasaw tribes of Indians whose enrollment has been approved by the Secretary of the Interior prior to the date of the approval of this act; and to enroll and make allotments to such children."

I am of the opinion that following the ruling of the Department in the case of Byington Wade (I.T.D. 11786-1904), said application for the enrollment of Susie Ayakatubby was made within the time provided by the Act of Congress above qouted[sic], and that said applicant should be enrolled as a citizen by blood of the Chickasaw Nation, under the provisions of said act, and it is so ordered.

Tams Bixby   Commissioner.

Muskogee, Indian Territory.
DEC 18 1906

BIRTH AFFIDAVIT.

DEPARTMENT OF THE INTERIOR.
COMMISSION TO THE FIVE CIVILIZED TRIBES.

IN RE APPLICATION FOR ENROLLMENT, as a citizen of the   Chickasaw   Nation, of   Susie Iyakatubby[sic]   , born on the   6th day of   February   , 1905

Name of Father: Not Married   a citizen of the   ~~Chickasaw~~ Nation.
Name of Mother: Agness[sic] Iyakatubby   a citizen of the   Chickasaw   Nation.

Postoffice   Jesse, I.T.

AFFIDAVIT OF MOTHER.

UNITED STATES OF AMERICA, Indian Territory, ⎫
   Southern   DISTRICT. ⎭

I, Agness Iyakatubby   , on oath state that I am   25   years of age and a citizen by   Blood   , of the   Chickasaw   Nation; that I am the lawful wife of Not Married   , who is a citizen, by ———   of the   ———   Nation; that a Female   child was born to me on   6th day of   February   , 1905; that said child has been named   Susie Iyakatubby   , and was living March 4, 1905.

her
Agness x Iyakatubby
mark

244

Applications for Enrollment of Chickasaw Newborn
Act of 1905   Volume VII

Witnesses To Mark:
    { Marvin J Burris
    { J.O. Crawford

     Subscribed and sworn to before me this 1st day of May , 1905

            W.F. Harrison
               Notary Public.

AFFIDAVIT OF ATTENDING PHYSICIAN OR MID-WIFE.

UNITED STATES OF AMERICA, Indian Territory, }
    Southern   **DISTRICT.** }

     I, Minie Iyakatubby , a Midwife , on oath state that I attended on Mrs. Agness Ayakatubby , wife of ———— on the 6th day of February , 1905; that there was born to her on said date a Female child; that said child was living March 4, 1905, and is said to have been named Susie Iyakatubby

                       her
                Minie x Iyakatubby
Witnesses To Mark: mark
    { Marvin J Burris
    { J.O. Crawford

     Subscribed and sworn to before me this 1st day of May , 1905

            W.F. Harrison
               Notary Public.

9-9

         Muskogee, Indian Territory, March 23, 1906.

Agnes Iyakutubby[sic]
    Jesse, Indian Territory.

Dear Madam:

     Receipt is hereby acknowledged of your letter of March 13, 1906, asking if the enrollment of your child Susie Iyakutubby has been approved.

     In reply to your letter you are advised that the question as to whether or not the application for the enrollment of your child Susie Iyakutubby was received within the time provided by the act of Congress approved March 3, 1905 has not yet been determined, but in the event additional legislation is enacted providing for the enrollment of children of citizens of the Choctaw and Chickasaw Nations, the matter of the enrollment of this child will receive further consideration.

Respectfully,

Acting Commissioner.

I made application for the enrollment of my child about the latter part of Feb. 1905.

Yours truly

Could not find letter from her
from Feb till May 15, 1906

Agnes Iyakatubby

9-9

Muskogee, Indian Territory, April 3, 1906.

Agnes Iyakatubby,
    Jesse, Indian Territory.

Dear Madam:

Receipt is hereby acknowledged of your letter without date stating that you made application for the enrollment of your child Susie Iyakatubby in the latter part of February 1905.

In reply to your letter you are advised that it does not appear from the records of this office that application was made for the enrollment of said child prior to the one received at this office May 3, 1905.

Respectfully,

Acting Commissioner.

9-NB-551.

Muskogee, Indian Territory, December 18, 1906.

Agnes Ayakatubby,
    Jesse, Indian Territory.

Dear Madam:

Inclosed herewith you will find a copy of the decision of the Commissioner to the Five Civilized Tribes, rendered December 18, 1906, granting the application for the enrollment of your child, Susie Ayakatubby, as a citizen by blood of the Chickasaw Nation.

The attorneys for the Choctaw and Chickasaw Nations have been furnished a copy of this decision and have been allowed fifteen days from the date of this notice within which to file protest against the enrollment of your child. If at the expiration of that time no protest has been filed, the name of Susie Ayakatubby will be placed upon the final roll of citizens by blood of the Chickasaw Nation to be submitted to the Secretary of the Interior for his approval.

Respectfully,

SIGNED   *Tams Bixby*
Commissioner.

Registered
Incl. 9-NB-551.

9-NB-551.

Muskogee, Indian Territory, December 18, 1906.

Mansfield, McMurray & Cornish,
    Attorneys for Choctaw and Chickasaw Nations,
        South McAlester, Indian Territory.

Gentlemen:

Inclosed herewith you will find a copy of the decision of the Commissioner to the Five Civilized Tribes, rendered December 18, 1906, granting the application for the enrollment of Susie Ayakatubby as a citizen by blood of the Chickasaw Nation.

You are hereby advised that you will be allowed fifteen days from the date of this notice within which to file protest against her enrollment. If at the expiration of that time no protest has been filed, the name of Susie Ayakatubby will be placed upon the final roll of citizens by blood of the Chickasaw Nation to be submitted to the Secretary of the Interior for his approval.

Respectfully,

SIGNED   *Tams Bixby*
Commissioner.

Registered
Incl. 9-NB-551.

9-NB-551.

Muskogee, Indian Territory, December 18, 1906.

Agnes Ayakatubby,
    Jesse, Indian Territory.

Dear Madam:

    Inclosed herewith you will find a copy of the decision of the Commissioner to the Five Civilized Tribes, rendered December 18, 1906, granting the application for the enrollment of your child, Susie Ayakatubby, as a citizen by blood of the Chickasaw Nation.

    The attorneys for the Choctaw and Chickasaw Nations have been furnished a copy of this decision and have been allowed fifteen days from the date of this notice within which to file protest against the enrollment of your child. If at the expiration of that time no protest has been filed, the name of Susie Ayakatubby will be placed upon the final roll of citizens by blood of the Chickasaw Nation to be submitted to the Secretary of the Interior for his approval.

Respectfully,

SIGNED   *Tams Bixby*
Commissioner.

Registered
Incl. 9-NB-551.

––––––––––

9-NB-551.

Muskogee, Indian Territory, December 18, 1906.

Mansfield, McMurray & Cornish,
    Attorneys for Choctaw and Chickasaw Nations,
        South McAlester, Indian Territory.

Gentlemen:

    Inclosed herewith you will find a copy of the decision of the Commissioner to the Five Civilized Tribes, rendered December 18, 1906, granting the application for the enrollment of Susie Ayakatubby as a citizen by blood of the Chickasaw Nation.

    You are hereby advised that you will be allowed fifteen days from the date of this notice within which to file protest against her enrollment. If at the expiration of that time no protest has been filed, the name of Susie Ayakatubby will be placed upon the final roll of citizens by blood of the Chickasaw Nation to be submitted to the Secretary of the Interior for his approval.

Respectfully,

SIGNED   *Tams Bixby*

Commissioner.

Registered
Incl. 9-NB-551.

Chic. N.B - 552
    (Almina Dana
    Born October 15, 1903)

BIRTH AFFIDAVIT.   *No 67*

DEPARTMENT OF THE INTERIOR.
COMMISSION TO THE FIVE CIVILIZED TRIBES.

IN RE APPLICATION FOR ENROLLMENT, as a citizen of the   Chickasaw   Nation,
of   Elmina Dennie   , born on the 15 day of Oct , 1903

Name of Father: Peter Dennie   a citizen of the Chickasaw Nation.
Name of Mother: Mandy Dennie   a citizen of the Chickasaw Nation.

Postoffice   Ada I.T.

AFFIDAVIT OF MOTHER.

UNITED STATES OF AMERICA, Indian Territory, ⎫
    Southern   **DISTRICT.** ⎭

    I,   Mandy Dennie   , on oath state that I am 30   years of age and a citizen
by   blood   , of the   Chickasaw   Nation; that I am the lawful wife of Peter
Dennie   , who is a citizen, by   blood   of the   Chickasaw   Nation; that a
female   child was born to me on 15 day of October   , 1903, that said child has
been named Elmina   , and is now living.

                    her
               Mandy x Dennie
Witnesses To Mark: mark
    ⎰ Jno. P. Crawford
    ⎱ *(Name Illegible)*

Subscribed and sworn to before me this 19" day of   January   , 1905.

Jno. P Crawford
Notary Public.

AFFIDAVIT OF ATTENDING PHYSICIAN OR MID-WIFE.

UNITED STATES OF AMERICA, Indian Territory, ⎫
   Southern   **DISTRICT.** ⎰

    I,   Rena Orphan   , a midwife   , on oath state that I attended on
Mrs. Mandy Dennie   , wife of   Peter Dennie   on the 15 day of Oct , 1903;
that there was born to her on said date a   female   child; that said child is now living
and is said to have been named   Elmina

Rena Orphan

Witnesses To Mark:

{

    Subscribed and sworn to before me this 19" day of   January   , 1905.

Jno. P Crawford
Notary Public.

BIRTH AFFIDAVIT.

DEPARTMENT OF THE INTERIOR.
COMMISSION TO THE FIVE CIVILIZED TRIBES.

    IN RE APPLICATION FOR ENROLLMENT, as a citizen of the   Chickasaw   Nation,
of   Almina Denny   , born on the 15 day of Oct , 1903

Name of Father: Peter Denny   a citizen of the Chickasaw Nation.
Name of Mother: Mandy Denny   a citizen of the Chickasaw Nation.

Postoffice   Ada Ind. Ty.

AFFIDAVIT OF MOTHER.

UNITED STATES OF AMERICA, Indian Territory, ⎫
   Central   **DISTRICT.** ⎰

    I,   Mandy Denny   , on oath state that I am   27   years of age and a citizen
by   Blood   , of the   Chickasaw   Nation; that I am the lawful wife of
Petter[sic] Denny   , who is a citizen, by Blood   of the   Chickasaw   Nation;

250

that a   Female   child was born to me on   15   day of   Oct   , 1903; that said
child has been named   Almina Denny   , and was living March 4, 1905.

her
Mandy x Denny

Witnesses To Mark: mark
    { Judas Durant
    { Levi Orphan

       Subscribed and sworn to before me this 4   day of   May   , 1905

Edward D Sittel
Notary Public.

AFFIDAVIT OF ATTENDING PHYSICIAN OR MID-WIFE.

UNITED STATES OF AMERICA, Indian Territory, }
   Central   **DISTRICT.** }

    I,   Rena Orphan   , a mid-wife   , on oath state that I attended on
Mrs.   Mandy Denny   , wife of   Peter Denny   on the 15 day of   October   ,
1903; that there was born to her on said date a   female   child; that said child was
living March 4, 1905, and is said to have been named   Almina Denny

Rena Orphan

Witnesses To Mark:
    {

       Subscribed and sworn to before me this 4   day of   May   , 1905

Edward D Sittel
Notary Public.

BIRTH AFFIDAVIT.

DEPARTMENT OF THE INTERIOR.
COMMISSION TO THE FIVE CIVILIZED TRIBES.

    IN RE APPLICATION FOR ENROLLMENT, as a citizen of the   Chickasaw   Nation,
of   Almina Denny   , born on the 15   day of Oct   , 1903

Name of Father: Peter Denny   a citizen of the   Chickasaw   Nation.
Name of Mother: Mandy Denny   a citizen of the   Chickasaw   Nation.

Postoffice   Ada I.T.

Applications for Enrollment of Chickasaw Newborn
Act of 1905 Volume VII

AFFIDAVIT OF MOTHER.

I,   Mandy Denny   , on oath state that I am   27   years of age and a citizen by   blood   , of the   Chickasaw   Nation; that I am the lawful wife of   Peter Denny   , who is a citizen, by   blood   of the   Chickasaw   Nation; that a female   child was born to me on   the 15   day of   October   , 1903; that said child has been named   Almina Denny   , and was living March 4, 1905.

                                        Mandy Denny
Witnesses To Mark:

Subscribed and sworn to before me this 28   day of   April   , 1905

                              JE Williams
                                        Notary Public.

___

BIRTH AFFIDAVIT.
DEPARTMENT OF THE INTERIOR,
COMMISSIONER TO THE FIVE CIVILIZED TRIBES.

ENROLLMENT OF MINORS.   ACT OF CONGRESS, APPROVED APRIL 26, 1906.

IN RE APPLICATION FOR ENROLLMENT, as a citizen of the   Chickasaw   Nation, of   Almina Denney   , born on the   15   day of   Oct , 1903

Name of Father: Peter Denney   a citizen of the   Chickasaw   Nation.
Name of Mother: Amanda Hayes   a citizen of the   Chickasaw   Nation.

Tribal enrollment of father Chickasaw   Tribal enrollment of mother Chickasaw

                Postoffice   Cabaness Ind Ter

___

AFFIDAVIT OF MOTHER.

I,   Amanda Hayes   , on oath state that I am   29   years of age and a citizen by   blood   , of the   Chickasaw   Nation; that I was the lawful wife of   Peter Denney now deceased   , who is a citizen, by   blood   of the   Chickasaw   Nation; that a   female   child was born to me on   15   day of

252

Applications for Enrollment of Chickasaw Newborn
Act of 1905   Volume VII

Oct   , 1903 , that said child has been named Almina Denney   , and was living March 4, 1906.

Amanda Hayes

WITNESSES TO MARK:
- J R Runyan
- S R Talbert

Subscribed and sworn to before me this 9th day of   July   , 1906.

D.W. Swaffor[sic]
Notary Public.

AFFIDAVIT OF ATTENDING PHYSICIAN OR MID-WIFE.

UNITED STATES OF AMERICA, Indian Territory,
Central   **District.**

I,   Raner Orphan   , a   Midwife   , on oath state that I attended on   Amanda Hayes   , wife of Peter Denney   on the   15   day of   Oct , 1903 ; that there was born to her on said date a   female   child; that said child was living March 4, 1906, and is said to have been named   Almina Denney

WITNESSES TO MARK:

Subscribed and sworn to before me this .... day of ...., 1906.

Notary Public.

AFFIDAVIT OF MOTHER.

UNITED STATES OF AMERICA, Indian Territory,
Central   **District.**

I,   Mandy Jackson   , on oath state that I am   29   years of age and a citizen by   blood   , of the   Chickasaw   Nation; that I am the lawful wife of   Elam Jackson   , who is a citizen, by   Blood   of the   Choctaw   Nation; that a   Girl   child was born to me on 15th   day of   Oct , 1903 , that said child has been named Almina Denney   , and was living March 4, 1906.

Mandy Jackson

WITNESSES TO MARK:

253

Applications for Enrollment of Chickasaw Newborn
Act of 1905 Volume VII

Subscribed and sworn to before me this 15th day of   November   , 1906.

JP Boyd

Notary Public.

AFFIDAVIT OF ATTENDING PHYSICIAN OR MID-WIFE.

UNITED STATES OF AMERICA, **Indian Territory,** }
Central   **District.** }

I,   Rena Orphan   , a   Midwife   , on oath state that I
attended on   Mandy Denney   then   , wife of   Peter Denney   on the   15th   day of
October , 1903 ; that there was born to her on said date a   Female   child; that said child
was living March 4, 1906, and is said to have been named   Almina Denney

Rena Orphan

WITNESSES TO MARK:

Subscribed and sworn to before me this 15th day of   November   , 1906.

JP Boyd

Notary Public.

BIRTH AFFIDAVIT.

DEPARTMENT OF THE INTERIOR,
COMMISSIONER TO THE FIVE CIVILIZED TRIBES.

ENROLLMENT OF MINORS.   ACT OF CONGRESS, APPROVED APRIL 26, 1906.

IN RE APPLICATION FOR ENROLLMENT, as a citizen of the   Chickasaw   Nation,
of   Almina Dana   , born on the   15   day of   Oct   , 1903

Name of Father: Peter Dana   a citizen of the   Chickasaw   Nation.
Name of Mother: Amanda Dana   a citizen of the   Chickasaw   Nation.

Tribal enrollment of father   230   Tribal enrollment of mother   338

Postoffice   Cabaniss, I.T.

254

AFFIDAVIT OF MOTHER.

UNITED STATES OF AMERICA, **Indian Territory,**
    Southern   **District.**

I,   Amanda Dana   , on oath state that I am 29 years of age and a citizen by blood , of the Chickasaw Nation; that I ~~was~~ the lawful wife of Peter Dana (deceased) , who is a citizen, by blood of the Chickasaw Nation; that a female child was born to me on 15 day of October, 1903 , that said child has been named Almina Dana , and was living March 4, 1906.

WITNESSES TO MARK:

Subscribed and sworn to before me this .... day of ...., 1906.

....
                                     Notary Public.

AFFIDAVIT OF ATTENDING PHYSICIAN OR MID-WIFE.

UNITED STATES OF AMERICA, **Indian Territory,**
....**District.**

I,   Rena Orphan   , a midwife , on oath state that I attended on Amanda Dana , wife of Peter Dana on the 15" day of October , 1903 ; that there was born to her on said date a female child; that said child was living March 4, 1906, and is said to have been named Almina Dana

WITNESSES TO MARK:

Subscribed and sworn to before me this .... day of ...., 1906.

....
                                       Notary Public.

Muskogee, Indian Territory, May 2, 1905.

Peter Denny,
    Ada, Indian Territory.

Dear Sir:

Receipt is hereby acknowledged of the affidavits of Mandy Denny to the birth of Almina Denny, daughter of Peter and Manly[sic] Denny, October 15, 1903.

It is stated in the affidavit of the mother that she is a citizen by blood of the Chickasaw Nation. If this is correct, you are requested to state the name under which she was enrolled, the names of her parents, and if she has selected an allotment of the lands of the Choctaw or Chickasaw Nation please give her roll number as it appears upon her allotment certificate.

Respectfully,

Chairman.

Muskogee, Indian Territory, May 16, 1905.

Peter Denny,
    Ada, Indian Territory.

Dear Sir:

Receipt is hereby acknowledged of the affidavits of Mandy Denny to the birth of Almina Denny, daughter of Peter and Mandy Denny, October 15, 1903.

It is stated in the affidavit of the mother that she is a citizen by blood of the Chickasaw Nation. If this is correct, you are requested to state the name under which she was enrolled, the names of her parents, and if she has selected an allotment of the lands of the Choctaw or Chickasaw Nation please give her roll number as it appears upon her allotment certificate.

Respectfully,

Chairman.

9-78
9-111

Muskogee, Indian Territory, July 24, 1906.

S. B. Tobert,
    Ada, Indian Territory.

Dear Sir:

Receipt is hereby acknowledged of your letter of July 17, 1906, transmitting the affidavit of Amanda Hayes to the birth of Almina Denny, child of Peter Denny and Amanda Hayes, October 15, 1903, and the same has been filed with the record of this office as an application for the enrollment of said child.

It appears from the records of this office that the father of this child is enrolled as Peter Dana, and as Amanda Hayes was the lawful wife of Peter Dana, she should sign the affidavits in her present name, and for this purpose there is inclosed herewith a blank application which please have executed and return to this office as early as practicable, exercising care to see that all spaces are properly filled out.

Respectfully,

B C

Commissioner.

———————

AP

REFER IN REPLY TO THE FOLLOWING:
———————
9-NB-552

DEPARTMENT OF THE INTERIOR,
COMMISSIONER TO THE FIVE CIVILIZED TRIBES.

Muskogee, Indian Territory, September 14, 1906.

Peter Dana,
    Cabaniss, Indian Territory,

Dear Sir:

Referring to the application for the enrollment of your minor child, Almina Dana, you are advised that in the affidavits heretofore forwarded the surname is spelled "Denny", while on the final roll of citizens by blood of the Chickasaw Nation your name appears as "Dana", it will therefore be necessary that you have the inclosed blank executed, exercising care to see that the names are signed as they appear in the body of the affidavit, and that the Notary Public affixes his seal and signature to each separate affidavit.

This matter should receive your immediate attention.

Respectfully,

LM 1/14

Tams Bixby   Commissioner.

<table>
<tr><td>REFER IN REPLY TO THE FOLLOWING:
———————
552</td><td>**DEPARTMENT OF THE INTERIOR,**
COMMISSIONER TO THE FIVE CIVILIZED TRIBES.</td></tr>
</table>

Muskogee, Indian Territory, February 28, 1907.

Mandy Hayes, nee Jackson,
    Cabaniss, Indian Territory.

Dear Madam:

You are hereby advised that on February 21, 1907, the Secretary of the Interior approved the enrollment of your child, Almina Denny as a New Born citizen of the Chickasaw Nation, under the Act of Congress approved March 3, 1905, and her name appears upon the roll of citizens enrolled under said Act, opposite No. 575.

Selection of allotment should now be made for said child at the land office in the Nation in which said land is located.

Respectfully,
Tams Bixby
Commissioner.

Chic. N.B - 553
    (Karena Kaney
    Born January 7, 1905)

9-N.B.-553.
O.L.J.

DEPARTMENT OF THE INTERIOR,
COMMISSIONER TO THE FIVE CIVILIZED TRIBES.

----ooOOoo----

In the matter of the alleged application for the enrollment of Karena Kaney as a citizen by blood of the Chickasaw Nation.

Applications for Enrollment of Chickasaw Newborn
Act of 1905 Volume VII

It appears from the record herein that on May 3, 1905, there was received by the Commission to the Five Civilized Tribes written application for the enrollment of Karena Kaney as a citizen by blood of the Chickasaw Nation under the provisions of the Act of Congress approved March 3, 1905 (33 Stats., 1070).

It further appears from the record herein that the envelope containing said application shows that the same was mailed at Tishomingo, Indian Territory, May 1, 1905, at twelve o'clock, P. M. and was received at the Registry Division of the Muskogee, Indian Territory Post Office, May 2, 1905.

I am, therefore, of the opinion that following the ruling of the Department in the case of Byington Wade (I.T.D. 3936-1905), application was made for the enrollment of Karena Kaney as a citizen by blood of the Chickasaw Nation within the time limited by the provisions of the Act of Congress approved March 3, 1905 (33 Stats., 1070), and the same should now be determined upon its merits and it is so ordered.

Tams Bixby   Commissioner.

Muskogee, Indian Territory,
November 12th 1906.

9-N.B.-553.
O.L.J.

DEPARTMENT OF THE INTERIOR,
COMMISSIONER TO THE FIVE CIVILIZED TRIBES.

----ooOOoo----

In the matter of the alleged application for the enrollment of Karena Kaney as a citizen by blood of the Chickasaw Nation.

D E C I S I O N.

It appears from the record herein that application was duly made for the enrollment of Karena Kaney as a citizen by blood of the Chickasaw Nation within the time limited by the provisions of the Act of Congress approved March 3, 1905 (33 Stats., 1070).

It further appears from the record herein and from the records in the possession of this office that the applicant, Karena Kaney, was born January 7, 1905 and is the daughter of Mary Kaney and Harmon Kaney, both of whom are recognized and enrolled citizens by blood of the Chickasaw Nation, their names appearing as numbers 1489 and 3881, respectively, upon the final roll of citizens by blood of the Chickasaw Nation approved by the Secretary of the Interior December 12, 1902.

I am, therefore, of the opinion that Karena Kaney, should be enrolled as a citizen by blood of the Chickasaw Nation under the provisions of the Act of Congress approved March 3, 1905 (33 Stats., 1070), and it is so ordered.

Tams Bixby   Commissioner.

Muskogee, Indian Territory.
NOV 20 1906

———————

BIRTH AFFIDAVIT.

DEPARTMENT OF THE INTERIOR.
COMMISSION TO THE FIVE CIVILIZED TRIBES.

———————

IN RE APPLICATION FOR ENROLLMENT, as a citizen of the   Chickasaw Nation   Nation,
of   Karena Kaney   , born on the 7th   day of   January   , 1905

Name of Father: Marmon[sic] Kaney   a citizen of the   Chickasaw   Nation.
Name of Mother: Mary Kaney   a citizen of the   Chickasaw   Nation.

Postoffice   Woodville, Ind. Ter.

———————

AFFIDAVIT OF MOTHER.

UNITED STATES OF AMERICA, Indian Territory, }
    Southern   **DISTRICT.** }

    I,   Mary Kaney   , on oath state that I am   23   years of age and a citizen by
blood   , of the   Chickasaw   Nation; that I am the lawful wife of   Marmon Kaney,
who is a citizen, by blood   of the   Chickasaw   Nation; that a   female
child was born to me on   7th   day of   January   , 1905; that said child has been
named   Karena Kaney   , and was living March 4, 1905.

Mary Kaney

Witnesses To Mark:
  { J. L. Smith
  { D. D. Young.

Subscribed and sworn to before me this   30 day of   March   , 1905

M. D. Belt
Notary Public.

(SEAL)

———————

Applications for Enrollment of Chickasaw Newborn
Act of 1905   Volume VII

AFFIDAVIT OF ATTENDING PHYSICIAN OR MID-WIFE.

UNITED STATES OF AMERICA, Indian Territory,
   Southern   **DISTRICT.**

I,   Annie North   , a   midwife   , on oath state that I attended on
Mrs.   Mary Kaney   , wife of   Harmon Kaney   on the 7th day of   January ,
1905; that there was born to her on said date a   female   child; that said child was
living March 4, 1905, and is said to have been named   Karena Kaney

her

Annie X North

mark

Witnesses To Mark:
   { J. L. Smith
   { D. D. Young.

Subscribed and sworn to before me this   30 day of   March   , 1905

M. D. Belt

(SEAL)   Notary Public.

DEPARTMENT OF THE INTERIOR.
COMMISSION TO THE FIVE CIVILIZED TRIBES.

In the matter of the death of   Kerena[sic] Kaney
a citizen of the   Chickasaw   Nation, who formerly resided at or near   Woodville   ,
Ind. Ter., and died on the   8th day of   March   , 1905

AFFIDAVIT OF RELATIVE.

UNITED STATES OF AMERICA, Indian Territory,
   Southern   **DISTRICT.**

I,   Harmon Kaney   , on oath state that I am   44   years of age and a citizen
by blood , of the Chickasaw Nation; that my postoffice address is   Woodville   , Ind.
Ter.; that I am   father   of Karena Kaney   who was a citizen, by blood   , of the
Chickasaw   Nation and that said   Karena Kaney   died on the   8   day of   March
1905   , 1...........

Harmon Kaney.

Witnesses To Mark:
{

Subscribed and sworn to before me this   27   day of   March   , 1905.

Harry L. Person

(SEAL)   Notary Public.

AFFIDAVIT OF ACQUAINTANCE.

UNITED STATES OF AMERICA, Indian Territory,
    Southern   DISTRICT.

I, Joe Brown   , on oath state that I am 29   years of age, and a citizen by blood of the Chickasaw Nation; that my postoffice address is Ipsom Springs   , Ind. Ter.; that I was personally acquainted with Karena Kaney   who was a citizen, by blood , of the Chickasaw Nation; and that said Karena Kaney   died on the 8 day of March 1905   , 1............

Joe Brown

Witnesses To Mark:

{

        Subscribed and sworn to before me this 27   day of   March , 1905.

Harry L. Person

(SEAL)
Notary Public.

Department of the Interior,
COMMISSION TO THE FIVE CIVILIZED TRIBES.

In the matter of the death of   Kerena[sic] Kaney   a citizen of the Chickasaw Nation, who formerly resided at or near   Woodville   , Ind. Ter., and died on the 8th day of March , 1905

AFFIDAVIT OF RELATIVE.

UNITED STATES OF AMERICA,
    INDIAN TERRITORY,
    Southern   District.

I, Harmon Kaney   , on oath state that I am 44   years of age and a citizen by Blood , of the Chickasaw Nation; that my postoffice address is Woodville , Ind. Ter.; that I am father of Karena Kaney who was a citizen, by Blood , of the Chickasaw Nation and that said Karena Kaney died on the 8 day of March , 1905

Harmon Kaney

Witnesses To Mark:

{

Applications for Enrollment of Chickasaw Newborn
Act of 1905 Volume VII

Subscribed and sworn to before me this 27th *day of* March , 1905

Harry L Person
Notary Public.

_____

UNITED STATES OF AMERICA, ⎤
    INDIAN TERRITORY,   ⎬
Southern   District. ⎦

    I,   Joe Brown   , on oath state that I am 29   years of age, and a citizen by Blood   of the   Chickasaw Nation; that my postoffice address is   Isom Springs   , Ind. Ter.; that I was personally acquainted with   Karena Kaney   who was a citizen, by   Blood , of the   Chickasaw Nation; and that said   Karena Kaney   died on the 8th   day of   March   , 190 5

Joe Brown

Witnesses To Mark:

    ⎧
    ⎩

    Subscribed and sworn to before me this 27th   *day of*   March   , 1905

Harry L Person
Notary Public.

_____

(The Birth Affidavit of March 30, 1905, above, given again.)

_____

Muskogee, Indian Territory, July 6, 1905.

Harry L. Person,
    Tishomingo, Indian Territory.

Dear Sir:

    Receipt is hereby acknowledged of your letter of June 29, 1905, asking the status of the application of Karena Kaney for enrollment as a citizen by blood of the Chickasaw Nation under the act of Congress approved March 4, 1905.

    In reply to your letter you are advised that on May 3, 1905, there were received at the office of the Commission to the Five Civilized Tribes affidavits to the birth and death of Karena Kaney, daughter of Harmon and Mary Kaney, January 7, 1905, and March 8, 1905, respectively.   The envelope containing these affidavits was post marked at Tishomingo, Indian Territory, May 1, 1905, and was received at the Muskogee, post office May 2, 1905.   The question as to whether or not this application was received by the Commission to the Five Civilized Tribes within the time provided by the act of Congress approved March 3, 1905, and has not yet been determine but you will be notified of such action as is taken in this case.

Respectfully,

Commissioner.

Muskogee, Indian Territory, August 5, 1905.

Hanson King,
    Box 44,
        Woodville, Indian Territory.

Dear Sir:

Receipt is hereby acknowledged of your letter of August 3, 1905, in reference to the enrollment of your child Karena Kaney born January 7, 1905; you state that you was[sic] at Tishomingo, Indian Territory, when the enrolling clerk was there and made out your papers and left them with Mr. Harry Persons who was to forward them to the Commission to the Five Civilized Tribes, and you have received no notice of the enrollment of your child.

In reply to your letter you are advised that the application for the enrollment of your child Karena Kaney was not received by the Commission to the Five Civilized Tribes until May 3, 1905, and no action has yet been taken in the matter of the application for the enrollment of said child.

Respectfully,

Commissioner.

Muskogee, Indian Territory, October 28, 1905.

H. Kaney,
    Box 44,
        Woodville, Indian Territory.

Dear Sir:

Receipt is hereby acknowledged of your letter of October 24, 1905, in which you ask relative to the right of your child Karana[sic] Kaney.

264

In reply to your letter you are advised that no action has yet been taken in the matter of the enrollment as a citizen of the Chickasaw Nation of your child Karena Kaney.

Respectfully,

Commissioner.

————————

Muskogee, Indian Territory, March 21, 1906.

H. Kaney,
Woodville, Indian Territory.

Dear Sir:

Receipt is hereby acknowledged of your letter of February 28, 1906, in which you ask why the name of your child Karena Kaney has not been put upon the roll.

In reply to your letter you are advised that this office has not yet passed upon the question as to whether or not application for the enrollment of your child Karena Kaney was received within the time provided by the act of Congress approved March 3, 1905, and you will be notified of such action as is taken in this case.

Respectfully,

Acting Commissioner.

————————

9-N.B.-553.

COPY

Muskogee, Indian Territory, November 20, 1906.

Harmon Kaney,
Woodville, Indian Territory.

Dear Sir:

Inclosed herewith you will find a copy of the decision of the Commissioner to the Five Civilized Tribes, rendered November 20, 1906, granting the application for the enrollment of Karena Kaney as a citizen by blood of the Chickasaw Nation.

The attorneys for the Choctaw and Chickasaw Nations have been furnished a copy of this decision and have been allowed fifteen days from the date of this notice within which to file protest against her enrollment. If at the expiration of that time no protest has been filed, the name of Karena Kaney will be placed upon the final roll of citizens by blood of the Chickasaw Nation to be submitted to the Secretary of the Interior for his approval.

Respectfully,

SIGNED   *Tams Bixby*

Registered.   Commissioner.

Incl. 9 N.B. 553.

———————

9-N.B. 553.

COPY

Muskogee, Indian Territory, November 20, 1906.

Harry L. Person,
        Attorney at Law,
                Denison, Texas.

Dear Sir:

You are hereby notified that the Commissioner to the Five Civilized Tribes, on November 20, 1906, rendered his decision granting the application for the enrollment of Karena Kaney as a citizen by blood of the Chickasaw Nation.

The attorneys of the Choctaw and Chickasaw Nations have been furnished a copy of the decision and have been allowed fifteen days from the date of this notice within which to file protest against her enrollment. If at the expiration of that time no protest has been filed, the name of Karena Kaney will be placed upon the final roll of citizens by blood of the Chickasaw Nation to be submitted to the Secretary of the Interior for his approval.

Respectfully,

SIGNED   *Tams Bixby*

Registered.   Commissioner.

———————

9-N.B.-553.

COPY

Muskogee, Indian Territory, November 20, 1906.

Mansfield, McMurray & Cornish,
        Attorneys for Choctaw and Chickasaw Nations,
                South McAlester, Indian Territory.

Gentlemen:

Inclosed herewith you will find a copy of the decision of the Commissioner to the Five Civilized Tribes, rendered November 20, 1906, granting the application for the enrollment of Karena Kaney as a citizen by blood of the Chickasaw Nation.

Applications for Enrollment of Chickasaw Newborn
Act of 1905   Volume VII

You are hereby advised that you will be allowed fifteen days from the date of this notice within which to file protest against his enrollment. If at the expiration of that time no protest has been filed, the name of Karena Kaney will be placed upon the final roll of citizens by blood of the Chickasaw Nation to be submitted to the Secretary of the Interior for his approval.

Respectfully,

SIGNED   *Tams Bixby*

Commissioner.

Registered.

Incl. 9-N.B.-553.

9-NB-553

Muskogee, Indian Territory, May 2, 1907.

H. Kaney,
   Box 44,
      Woodville, Indian Territory.

Dear Sir:

Your letter of April 20, 1907, addressed to the United States Indian Agent has been by him referred to this office for consideration and appropriate action. Therein you state that Karena Kaney is a Chickasaw by blood; that she is enrolled at No. 1489 and has filed on an allotment.

It is not known for what purpose you forwarded this information, but you are advised that Mary Kaney, mother of Karena Kaney, appears at No. 1489 upon the roll of citizens by blood of the Chickasaw Nation.

You are further advised that the enrollment of Karena Kaney was approved by the Secretary of the Interior February 21, 1907, as a minor citizen of the Chickasaw Nation under the Act of Congress approved March 3, 1905, and her name appears at No. 576 upon said roll.

Respectfully,

Acting Commissioner.

www.ingramcontent.com/pod-product-compliance
Lightning Source LLC
Chambersburg PA
CBHW020248030426
42336CB00010B/662